89 - 2269

STUDIES IN INTERNATIONAL
POLITICAL ECONOMY
Stephen D. Krasner, Editor
Ernst B. Haas, Consulting Editor

Banker to the Third World

BANKER TO THE THIRD WORLD

U.S. Portfolio Investment
in Latin America, 1900–1986

BARBARA STALLINGS

UNIVERSITY OF CALIFORNIA PRESS
Berkeley · Los Angeles · London

University of California Press
Berkeley and Los Angeles, California

University of California Press, Ltd.
London, England

© 1987 by
The Regents of the University of California

Library of Congress Cataloging-in-Publication Data

Stallings, Barbara.
  Banker to the Third World.

  (Studies in international political economy)
  Bibliography: p.
  Includes index.
    1. Investments, American–Latin America–
History. 2. Loans, American–Latin America–
History. I. Title.
II. Title: Banker to the 3rd World. III. Series.
HG5160.5.A3S73 1987 332.6'7373'08 86-24988
ISBN 0-520-05726-0 (alk. paper)
ISBN 0-520-06164-0 (pbk.)

Printed in the United States of America

1 2 3 4 5 6 7 8 9

CONTENTS

LIST OF TABLES

LIST OF FIGURES

ACKNOWLEDGMENTS

This book has been in process longer than I care to remember. It began a decade ago as a dissertation in the Faculty of Economics at Cambridge University. Although it is hard to believe now, few people at that time knew about or were interested in private bank lending to the Third World. I became intrigued by the topic in part through an article by Emma Rothschild in the *New York Review of Books* and a later discussion at Stanford in the summer of 1976 between Rothschild and Wells Fargo vice president Robert Bee. Rothschild thought that the banks were in trouble even then; Bee painted a more comforting picture.

As usual over such a period of time, I have incurred a large number of debts. Although not all can be acknowledged here, I want to thank the people and institutions that have helped me the most. I have received financial support from a variety of sources. The two years I spent at Cambridge were financed by a Research Training Fellowship from the Social Science Research Council and a postdoctoral fellowship from the National Science Foundation. Later research time and facilities were provided by the Graduate School and the Nave Bequest of the University of Wisconsin; the Economics Faculty of Cambridge University; the Ibero-American Institute of Columbia University; and a second grant from the Social Science Research Council. In addition, although I never formally took it up, I was awarded an International Affairs Fellowship by the Council on Foreign Relations and that contact opened many doors in the banking community. Graphs for the book were financed and produced by the Cartographic Laboratory at the University of Wisconsin.

In the substantive preparation of the book, I was fortunate to have the research assistance of George Crane, Gastón Fernández, and Judith Thimke. Crucial assistance in data collection came from the staff of Morgan Guaranty's *World Financial Markets* and the Financial Studies Division of the World Bank's Program and Budgeting Department. The dozens of bankers, policymakers, and economists who answered my questions on borrowing and lending have also been essential to the final product, although few will agree with all its conclusions.

Finally, and most important, I have received the help and support of a number of colleagues and friends. When I first went to Cambridge as a graduate student, I was lucky to be assigned John Eatwell as a tutor. His clear grasp of economic theory was the basis of whatever I learned about economics. Moreover, he agreed to supervise my dissertation even though it lay outside his main field of interest. For both reasons I will always be grateful to him. Also at Cambridge, Agit Singh taught me about economic development and offered his considerable methodological skills to resolve some difficult problems in the dissertation itself. Back in the United States, I was able to draw on the generous advice of Michael Edelstein of Queens College, whose knowledge of "overseas investment in the age of high imperialism" goes far beyond his book of that title.

In addition to Messrs. Eatwell, Singh, and Edelstein, a number of other people also read drafts of the manuscript and provided suggestions that improved the book in significant ways. As usual, not all of the suggestions were followed so those who offered them cannot be held accountable. I would especially like to thank Paul Beckerman, Heraclio Bonilla, Peter Evans, Albert Fishlow, Jeffrey Frieden, Charles Kindleberger, Clark Reynolds, and Rosemary Thorp. At the University of California Press, the enthusiasm of Stephen Krasner and Naomi Schneider provided the necessary encouragement for making the seemingly endless final revisions.

INTRODUCTION

By the end of 1985, Latin Americans owed their foreign creditors $368 billion. That is nearly $1,000 for every man, woman, and child between the Rio Grande and Tierra del Fuego. The debt represents more than half (54 percent) of the region's gross domestic product, and interest payments alone consume 36 percent of export revenues. If profits are added to interest, and the total compared to new capital inflows, the drama of the situation becomes clear: a real resource transfer from Latin America is under way. Almost one peso or cruzado or austral of every twenty produced in the region goes to enrich the advanced industrial countries. Obviously, the funds being exported cannot be used to improve the standard of living of the population, but neither can they be employed to increase production so as to enable the debt to be serviced.[1]

More than three-fourths of Latin America's debt is owed to several hundred commercial banks with headquarters in North America, Europe, and Japan. Some $82 billion is held by banks from the United States alone. Although many small and

---

[1] Figures on the total size of the debt vary according to source. The $368 billion is the amount reported both by the U.N. Economic Commission for Latin America (United Nations 1985a) and the IMF's *World Economic Outlook* (1986). It includes all debt, public and private, long-term and short-term. Other data in the paragraph come from these same sources and the Interamerican Development Bank's Annual Report (1985).

medium-sized banks own a portion of the U.S. total, most is concentrated in the largest institutions – the so-called money-center banks. The top nine account for $53 billion. The importance of that amount can be understood by comparing it to the total capital of the nine, which is only $42 billion. In other words, these banks have lent more than their entire capital and reserve base to Latin America, and Latin American interest payments each year exceed the banks' total profits.[2]

These are the essential elements of the debt crisis that burst upon the world scene in August 1982 when Jesus Silva-Herzog, the Mexican minister of finance, announced that his country could not continue to service its debt. The implications of a Mexican default were dramatic, especially if other debt-burdened countries were to follow. The loss of capital could bankrupt some of the major banks and put the entire international financial system into jeopardy. On the Latin American side, the loss of trade credits resulting from a default would throw the domestic economies into chaos and probably cause large-scale political disruptions as well. To head off such an

[2] The data on debt owed to U.S. banks, and the banks' capital, are from the *Country Exposure Lending Survey* for December 1985. The percentage of total debt that is owed to the banks varies by source. The World Bank's *World Debt Tables* (1986) and the IMF's *World Economic Outlook* (1986) both indicate that more than 80 percent of the debt is owed to the banks as calculated by summing public-sector long-term debt to financial institutions plus private-sector long-term debt and all of the short-term debt. A somewhat different picture emerges if the Bank for International Settlements figure for bank claims on Latin America ($236 billion as of December 1985) is compared to the $368 billion total debt used above. In this case, only 64 percent is private bank debt. Similarly, Morgan Guaranty's *World Financial Markets* (February 1986) indicates that 67 percent of the debt of the ten largest Latin American borrowers is held by the banks. For a comparison of the various sources that provide information on capital flows and debt, see *Federal Reserve Bulletin* 72 (10):683–94.

unacceptable scenario, international financial leaders quickly put together a package of loans to patch over the immediate Mexican crisis, but it was only the beginning as multiple waves of debt problems and renegotiations came to include every major Latin American borrower except Colombia. The ultimate outcome is still in doubt.

At the same time that bankers and political leaders met at the bargaining table, academics, journalists, and even a few bankers themselves began to analyze the crisis and propose solutions of varying types.[3] Thousands, perhaps tens of thousands, of pages have been devoted to the topic in the last few years alone.[4] Most of the resulting books and articles, however, are extremely contemporary in approach and tend to become obsolete with each new round of events. Although many have an obligatory section or even chapter on historical precedents, these historical discussions do not play a serious role in the analysis. Crisis management, from a variety of ideological viewpoints, is the dominant concern.[5]

[3] For a list and discussion of the various proposals, see Bergsten et al. (1985).

[4] Some economists have analyzed the debt crisis in terms of its implications for theory (Sachs 1984; Taylor 1985; Darity 1985; Eaton et al. 1986; Devlin 1987). Others have analyzed trends from a policy point of view (Fishlow 1984; Cline 1984; Enders and Mattione 1984; Dornbusch 1985). Latin American governments and their advisors have emphasized the hardships and lost growth imposed on their countries (García 1985; Ferrer 1985; Malan 1985; United Nations 1985b). Journalists and commentators have told the "inside story" (Sampson 1982; Delamaide 1984; Makin 1984). Political scientists have tried to discern the political significance of debt and stabilization (Nelson 1984; Kahler 1985; Kaufman 1985).

[5] The more thoughtful of the recent contributions take a longer view, but they are articles and therefore cannot provide a full analysis of both historical and contemporary issues. Among those I have found most useful are Sachs (1982), Diaz-Alejandro (1983), Kindleberger (1985, chaps. 9 and 12), Fishlow (1985), and Felix (1987).

I believe that a different kind of book is needed if we are to understand the current crisis and make any viable recommendations for the future. The crucial point is to understand why the loans were made in the first place and how today's loans are similar to, and different from, those of the past. Only this kind of analytical focus has the potential to provide answers to the three principal questions that preoccupy all who are involved with the current crisis.

The first such question is what is going to happen? Will the present situation lead to a chain of defaults like those of the 1930s? This book provides an answer to that question through an analysis of the institutional changes that have occurred since the 1930s. It suggests that unilateral defaults cannot recur on any large scale because of the differences in lenders as well as the new international political-economic context. This conclusion does not mean that no serious problems are ahead but that they will be dealt with in different ways.

The second question is what kind of solutions to the debt crisis *should* be instituted? Clearly this is a normative issue, but facts can shed light on normative debates. In particular, an understanding of who was responsible for the lending that led to the current crisis may provide some leverage in devising solutions. A major conclusion of the book–unlike many other analyses–is that lending can only be understood through the interplay of both supply and demand forces. We must go beyond debtors' claims that they were enticed to borrow as well as bankers' claims that they were merely responding in good faith to Latin Americans' needs. If both were partially "to blame," together with political leaders in advanced industrial countries who encouraged the loans, then a fair solution must require sacrifices from all.

The final question is how can such problems be avoided in the future? This third question is especially important since the current situation is but the latest of a series of lending booms, followed by debt crises, that have plagued the world for several hundred years now. The book suggests a set of causal mechanisms that trigger the cycles. Only if they are understood by lenders and borrowers alike is there any hope of mitigating such cycles in the future.

The basic assumption behind the writing of this book is that the ability to deal with these three questions – what will happen in the next couple of years, what *should* happen, and how can we prevent future recurrences? – requires an examination of history and theory rather than simply current events. I hope to make a contribution to such an endeavor through investigating U.S. private bank lending to Latin America during the twentieth century as well as looking back to see the similarities and differences between twentieth-century loan cycles and those of an earlier epoch.

A historical approach is important because this is not the first time that private loans have played a major role in the finance of less-developed countries. As far back as the late Middle Ages, Italian bankers were making loans to such a borrower – wool-exporting England. As the British journalist Anthony Sampson says, England was the Zaire (or the Peru) of the fourteenth century. The Germans and Dutch followed the Italians into international banking, but the most important lenders came to be the British themselves during the nineteenth and early twentieth centuries. In this period, British capital export as a percentage of total investment reached levels never seen before or since. The peak occurred just before World War I when about half of British investment went abroad.[6] This is the context in which U.S. lending in the twentieth century must be located.

[6] This figure comes from Cairncross (1953, 2). Platt (1980) has recently cautioned that double counting and other methodological problems have inflated estimates of British overseas investment before 1870. Similar problems may exist for the 1870–1914 period as well.

The book is explicitly historical in three ways. First, it uses the literature on British lending in the nineteenth century as a source of hypotheses to explain U.S. lending to Latin America in the twentieth century. Second, it looks at U.S. private bank lending throughout the twentieth century to identify and analyze the pattern of heavy and light lending. Third, it compares the two periods of heavy U.S. lending to Latin America–the 1920s and the 1970s. In all cases, the question is the same: why did bankers lend when they did and, conversely, why did they refrain from lending in other periods?

A theoretical approach is equally important because it provides the basis for understanding why loans are offered to foreigners as well as why they are sought. Given the contemporary focus of the majority of recent studies, it is perhaps not surprising that the most relevant theoretical literature deals with earlier periods–especially British lending between 1870 and 1914. This is where I begin. Thus the individual ideas in the book are not new; on the contrary, they are specifically taken from the literature on Britain. What is new is the notion of cumulative causation to account for the recurrence of lending cycles; no single variable is sufficient. Factors on the supply side include political context, lending institutions, access to savings, and low demand for funds in the lenders' home economy. Only given these conditions can an exogenous shock set off a new lending wave which competition may drive to unsustainable heights.

It should be pointed out that some revisionist authors– Minsky, Kindleberger, Darity, Devlin–have recently begun to focus on explanations that are similar in some ways to the approach used here. I find that literature very useful and have incorporated it into the book at various points. Nevertheless, its almost exclusive concentration on supply factors has many of the same problems, in reverse, of more traditional analysts who insist that all lending is demand-driven. Despite some revisionist claims, lenders were rarely "forcing" money on reluctant borrowers either in the 1920s or the 1970s. The important point is to understand how the interests of borrowers and lenders appeared to coincide.

The methodology employed in the book combines a qualitative historical approach with a systematic quantitative data base. In fact, one contribution of the book is to bring together a significant amount of data on U.S.–Latin American economic relations in the twentieth century. Some of the data series did not exist before, while others existed only piecemeal in many different sources. The most important data series that has been constructed is that for U.S. portfolio investment in Latin America from 1899 to 1984. New series for Latin America are interest rates, premiums, and budget data for the entire twentieth century. Other Latin American data series have been "pieced together" including merchandise trade, gross domestic product, current account, and investment (from 1910, 1939, 1946, and 1950, respectively). United States data were already better centralized and standardized through the Commerce Department's *Historical Statistics of the United States from Colonial Times to 1970*. In addition to the time series, a data bank was created that includes information on each individual bond issue or loan in the 1920s and 1970s. Details on the methods for constructing these series, and the problems encountered, are found in the Appendixes.

Given the time series data, one option for analysis would appear to be use of formal modeling to trace out the causal relationships between supply of, and demand for, credit.[7] Despite its current popularity among economic historians, this option was rejected for several reasons. Perhaps the most important reason is that institutional change over the 1900–80 period

[7] For a good example of this approach, see Edelstein (1982).

means that considering parameters constant would be highly misleading. In terms of analyzing shorter periods through similar techniques, the only periods with sufficient loan volume are the two heavy-lending decades, and reliance on annual data means the number of data points is too small to permit model construction. Finally, today's interdependent economies make it extremely difficult to identify demand (Latin American) variables that can be considered independent from supply (U.S.) variables. Related problems of multicollinearity exist with multiple regression techniques. Thus, although some simple bivariate regression coefficients are reported in the footnotes of Chapter 5, the main emphasis is on identifying qualitative relationships that can be further specified through use of the time-series data.[8]

Most of the book, and most of the quantitative data, refer to Latin America as a whole. This aggregate analysis of the region is possible—even advisable—because periods of high lending activity have tended to coincide for most countries. Therefore, we can search for common characteristics to explain the coinciding trends as well as to identify divergences within the general pattern. Nevertheless, there are some kinds of questions that are best answered through a case study of a specific country. These are questions about the process involved in loan activity. How were loans initiated? How were they negotiated? For what purpose were they used? What was the role of the government and other political actors? What happened when the borrower had trouble servicing the loans? Use of a case study, of course, also provides the opportunity to verify the conclusions reached in the aggregate analysis and to specify further the mechanisms involved. The case chosen is Peru, which has been one of the

[8] Future possibilities for econometric analysis exist in data I have collected but not used: quarterly data for the 1920s and 1970s and pooling of time series and cross-sectional data from my data bank on individual loan transactions for the same two decades (see Appendix V).

larger borrowers over time and which also provides a particularly well documented history of the lending process.

The book is organized in the following manner. Chapter 1 reviews the literature on British capital export and extracts a number of potentially relevant hypotheses. Then the major differences between the British and U.S. situations are discussed in order to present a modified set of hypotheses to be investigated in later chapters. Chapter 2 has a double purpose. On the one hand, it provides a qualitative historical overview of financial relations between the United States and Latin America. On the other hand, it also shows how financial relations fit into a broader picture including direct investment and U.S. foreign policy activities. Chapter 3 presents the quantitative data on U.S. portfolio investment in Latin America, identifying two periods of heavy lending (1920s and 1970s), two periods of light lending (1900–19 and 1954–69), and a period of net negative lending (1931–53). This pattern is put into context by comparing it with total U.S. portfolio investment in all regions and by comparing U.S. portfolio investment with total international investment in the region.

Chapter 4 begins the analysis of the data by examining the long-term relationships among U.S. political-economic trends, Latin American political-economic trends, and capital export to Latin America in light of the hypotheses presented in the first chapter. Chapter 5 looks at short-term relationships by focusing on the two periods of heavy lending (the 1920s and the 1970s). It asks whether the same variables that were relevant to the long-term analysis are also important in the short term and what kind of changes occurred between the 1920s and the 1970s. Chapter 6 constitutes the Peruvian case study. As explained above, it looks at questions of process with respect to loan activity as well as reexamining, on an individual-country level, the macrorelationships discussed in earlier chapters. Finally, Chapter 7 summarizes the main findings of the study, compares them with previous theories of capital export, and discusses their relevance for understanding the international financial crisis of the 1980s.

In overall terms, then, the book contributes to the literature on international lending in three ways. First, it provides a substantial amount of quantitative data on twentieth-century U.S.–Latin American economic relations that was not available previously. Second, it uses these data as the basis for a historical analysis of U.S. private bank lending to Latin America which has not been systematically studied before. Third, it links the U.S. lending experience to that of Great Britain through the use of literature on British capital export during the nineteenth century. This third contribution, in turn, opens the way for a new interpretation of theories of international lending cycles in terms of cumulative causation and the linking of supply and demand. All three of these tasks are essential for a full understanding of the current Latin American debt crisis and any solutions that might prevent recurrences in the future.

1

Theories of Capital Export

Lessons from the British Experience

CAPITAL EXPORT is not a new phenomenon. Nor is international banking a recent innovation. The exact origins of international banking are somewhat obscure, but it was well established by the late Middle Ages. The primary center in the period was northern Italy from whence bankers moved around the European world to finance trade as well as the wars and other activities of monarchs who could not raise sufficient revenues at home (UCLA 1979, especially chaps. 3 and 4). The most prominent among these bankers were the Medici, whose bank had branches in Avignon, Caledonia, Geneva, Lyons, Bruges, and London (de Roover 1963).

At the end of the fifteenth century, the first of several major shifts in international banking occurred as the dominant role was transferred from the Italians to the Germans. The south German towns and the city of Antwerp became the principal financial as well as commercial center. Symbolic of the change was the appointment in 1490 of Jacob Fugger as the main moneylender of the Hapsburg emperor Maximilian (UCLA 1979, chap. 5), and German bankers continued to finance the Hapsburgs throughout their power struggles in Europe (Ehrenberg 1928; Van der Wee 1963). By the late seventeenth century, another shift was under way from Antwerp to Amsterdam. This move also involved a strong link between trade and finance, but ironically Amsterdam became dominant in European finance after the city had begun to lose its superiority as a commercial center. Based on the savings of their notoriously frugal compatriots, Dutch bankers financed plantation development in the Dutch West Indies as well as the continuing wars in Europe (Wilson 1941; Barbour 1950; Riley 1980).

Finally, the Napoleonic Wars hastened the transfer of international finance to the City of London. Like their predecessors, British merchant banks financed European governments, but a more significant portion of their loans went to developing economies in Asia and Africa together with the English-settled areas of North America and Oceania. Thus, for the first time, loans for productive purposes accounted for a substantial share of capital export. Other European capital markets maintained active lending operations during the nineteenth century, especially Paris and the major German cities, but London was clearly the apex of the system (Jenks 1927; Feis 1930; Platt 1985).

There have been studies of all these early centers of international banking, but it is the British experience above all that has provided the empirical basis for developing contemporary theories of capital export. Economists and economic historians have devoted major attention to Britain in the period 1870–1914, providing us with a number of different explanations of lending trends. We begin therefore by examining the most important contributions to the literature on Britain with special attention to the hypotheses suggested and tested. Having done this, we then turn to the main international and domestic differences between nineteenth-century Britain and twentieth-century United States. The final section, on the basis of these differences, modifies the British hypotheses for the U.S. case. Before beginning to look at British capital export, however, it will be useful to review the general character of capital export: the different types of capital that can be supplied, the different ways it can be financed, and the different reasons why foreign capital might be sought.

Conceptualizing Capital Export

Capital export can best be set in the context of two accounting frameworks—one specifying the components of the balance of payments and the other the national income accounts. The balance of payments identity for a lending country can be written as follows:

$$X - M - D - L_{\mathrm{pub}} - L_{\mathrm{priv}} - S + \Delta R \equiv 0 \qquad (1)$$

where X and M are exports and imports of goods and services (including net factor income), D is net direct investment, L_{pub} is net long-term loans from the public sector, L_{priv} is net long-term loans from the private sector, S is net short-term capital transactions, and ΔR is change in reserves. The specific topic of the book falls under the long-term private capital component, which can be subdivided into loans to Latin America and other regions. Long-term private loans are clearly only one type of capital export; direct investment, public-sector loans, and short-term capital are alternative forms in which capital can be supplied. The major objective here is to determine under what conditions capital will be exported and, in particular, when private loans will predominate over other forms.

If a country is to export capital, the outflows must be financed in some way. In practice, there are two primary means of financing capital export, as can be demonstrated by simplifying Equation (1):

$$(X-M) \equiv (C_O - C_I) + \Delta R \qquad (2)$$

where $(X-M)$ refers to the total transactions on the current account, which must equal capital outflow minus capital inflow $(C_O - C_I)$ plus change in reserves. One means of financing capital export, then, is through a surplus of goods and service exports (including net factor payments) over imports in the lending country. Under these circumstances, the lending country is producing more than it is consuming and exporting the remainder as a real resource transfer occurs. The other means of financing capital export is through recycling capital inflows. The current account could be negative as long as capital inflows are sufficiently large to cover both it and the capital outflows. In this second situation, the lending nation serves as an international intermediary between countries that desire to borrow and those that want to lend; it engages in *gross* but not *net* lending. The second situation is less stable since the capital inflows could dry up very rapidly if certain conditions shifted domestically or internationally.

The national income identity constitutes the other relevant accounting framework.

$$Y \equiv C + I + G + (X-M) \qquad (3)$$

where Y is total product,[1] C is consumption, I is investment, G is government expenditure on goods and services, and X and M

---

[1] Y is interpreted here as gross national product; that is, factor payments are included in that term as well as in X and M.

are exports and imports of goods and services (including net factor payments). Thus, all goods produced in the country are used for consumption or investment by the private sector, absorbed by the government, or exported. Imports must be subtracted since they provide additional resources which are used in the country but not produced there. By defining $C+I+G$ as domestic spending (E), we can highlight the relationship between the domestic economy and the current account of the balance of payments. A surplus of domestic production over spending will be reflected in a surplus on the current account.

$$(Y-E) \equiv (X-M) \tag{4}$$

Equation (4) can also be stated in another way which further disaggregates the domestic variables into public- and private-sector balances. To do this, we subtract net payments to the government (T) from both sides of Equation (3), rearrange terms, and substitute in the savings definition $(S \equiv Y-C-T)$. Equation (5) then says that the government balance $(T-G)$, plus the private-sector balance $(S-I)$, is equal to the current account.

$$(T-G)+(S-I) \equiv (X-M) \tag{5}$$

A surplus on the current account requires that the two domestic balances also be in surplus or, alternatively, that one is in a large enough surplus to more than offset the other's deficit.

Finally, if we combine Equations (2) and (5), the focus shifts to the relationship between the domestic economy and capital export in the lending country.

$$(T+S)-(G+I) \equiv (C_O-C_I)+\Delta R \tag{6}$$

Given the tax ratio and savings propensities, a level of income which results in an excess of domestic savings, government or private $(T+S)$, over expenditure $(G+I)$ could find its counterpart in net capital outflow; the alternative would be an increase in reserves. In symmetry with the foregoing discussion, the capital export could be accompanied by a surplus of merchandise and service exports over imports as a real resource transfer takes place and the country is a net lender.

If a country is a gross but not a net lender, a quite different relationship exists between the domestic variables and capital flows. With capital inflows sufficiently large, capital exports can occur simultaneously with an excess of expenditure over savings, accompanied by a current account deficit. Rather than the lending country transferring its own surplus savings, it acts as an intermediary in transferring other countries' savings. Once again, this recycling process is less stable because it relies on other countries' willingness to provide surplus savings, not on factors in the lender's own economy. A savings surplus will play a crucial role in explaining capital export in later chapters of the book.

In empirical terms, U.S. lending between 1913 and the late 1960s was characterized by real resource transfers. The United States regularly had current account surpluses and an excess of savings over expenditure. It was these savings surpluses that were sent abroad through direct investment, public loans, and private loans. In the early years of the century and after the late 1960s, by contrast, the recycling process was typical. Current account and domestic savings deficits meant that capital export could occur only by recycling capital inflows as the United States became a gross but not a net lender.[2]

It must be noted that U.S. transactions with Latin America are only one part of the total U.S. international accounts. Conse-

---

[2] The best historical source on the U.S. balance of payments is United States (1976, U1–25). Current data are found in the *Survey of Current Business,* whose June issues present regional breakdowns.

quently, it is not possible to identify capital export to that region with a specific situation of the U.S. current account or internal balances. These balances might or might not follow the patterns described here as long as total transactions meet the requirements of the accounting identities. For example, in the period when the United States was a net lender and therefore had an overall trade surplus, it could nevertheless have had a trade deficit with Latin America if the trade balance with other regions was sufficiently positive to offset a deficit with Latin America.[3]

The same accounting identities must hold for borrowing countries as for lenders (with the signs on some of the terms reversed). The typical situation in Latin America is a deficit on the current account, financed either by the import of capital (direct investment, public loans, or private loans) or by running down reserves. The current account deficit is accompanied by an excess of expenditure over domestic production. Another way of stating the latter is to say that there is a "savings gap" to finance as well as a current account deficit or "foreign exchange gap." Thus, borrowing can reflect different, but overlapping, needs. On the one hand, a borrowing country may need real resources (imports of goods and services).[4] On the other hand, it may

[3] In the case of Latin America, the United States continued to have an export surplus with the region through part of the 1970s. U.S. capital flows to Latin America, however, were much larger than the export surplus. Rather than purchasing additional U.S. exports, Latin America used the greatly increased loan volume in three ways: to import goods from third countries (mainly oil from OPEC nations), to service the foreign debt, and to accumulate foreign exchange reserves.

[4] In a period of debt crisis such as the 1980s, the service import category, which includes interest payments, can itself dominate the current account. In this case, capital imports may largely go toward servicing old debt. Growth clearly suffers as a consequence since new loans cannot be applied to capital formation.

simply need finance to put local resources to work (advances for purchase of local inputs, for example, or payment of wages).[5]

It should be pointed out that *gross* borrowing might take place even if there are domestic (government and private) and balance of payments surpluses. One possible reason would involve foreign borrowing to change the maturity structure of debt within a borrowing country where long-term capital is not available. For example, if a Latin American government wants long-term money, while its citizens are interested only in holding cash or short-term assets, then the government might be forced to borrow abroad even if a balance of payments surplus exists and the economy is quite liquid. This long-term capital import would be offset by the export of short-term capital, so that net borrowing is negative as long as the current account is in surplus. If there is a current account deficit, it could be either with the lending country itself or with other countries. During the twentieth century, Latin American nations have borrowed for all these reasons and simply to obtain more reserves.[6]

Literature on British Capital Export

In terms of the accounting identities just introduced, Britain in the nineteenth century was a *net* capital exporter. The nation continually had a surplus on the current account although that surplus derived from the service rather than the merchandise

[5] See Keynes (1937) for a discussion of uses of the term "savings" and the distinction between savings and finance.

[6] The best source on the balance of payments in Latin America is the U.N. Economic Commission for Latin America. Its annual economic survey, plus special studies, provide systematic data back to World War II for all countries of the region. Before that time, data are more scattered; see the discussion in Appendixes III and IV.

balance. In other words, the profits Britain earned from its foreign investments financed both a merchandise deficit and new capital exports. The counterpart to the positive current account, of course, was a surplus of domestic savings over expenditure. In large part, the domestic surplus seems to have come from the private sector since the government balance at most showed a small surplus and was often in deficit (Mitchell and Deane 1962; Deane and Cole 1967; Feinstein 1972).

Explanations for British capital export concentrate on six general areas. The first, and most extensive, is the role of rates of return in determining patterns of capital export. Other works deal with the relationship between foreign trade and capital flows, the link between labor migration and capital flows, the role of institutions in determining capital flows, the relative importance of economic versus political factors in bringing about capital export, and the cyclical pattern of capital flows with a focus on investor expectations.

The pioneering work that provoked many of these debates was Sir Alec Cairncross's book *Home and Foreign Investment, 1870–1913*. Although only published in 1953, the main part of the book had been extensively circulated since being presented as a doctoral dissertation at Cambridge in 1935. Cairncross's data showed an inverse trend between investment in Britain, especially in the construction industry, and overseas investment. He states his major finding as follows:

> The first point which I wish to make clear is that in the *long* run foreign investment was largely at the expense of home investment or vice versa. The great expansions in home investment in the late seventies and nineties, for example, coincided with stagnation in foreign investment; and when foreign investment was abnormally large, as in the eighties and after 1905, investment at home sooner or later fell away. This sensitiveness of home investment to the competition of the foreign loan market was not confined to any one

branch, although building seems to have reacted most promptly.
(Cairncross 1953, 187)

These data posed the irresistible challenge to disentangle the
causal relationship between the so-called Kuznets cycles or long
swings in Britain and overseas, especially the United States. Did
the impulse for the inverse cyclical pattern come from Britain or
from abroad, and what was the process involved? Cairncross
himself seemed to believe that the British economy was responding to forces from abroad. The causal mechanisms he posited
were multidimensional, focusing on trade and migration among
other factors, as the following sections elaborate.

Rates of Return

Differential rates of return in lending and borrowing countries
have been the main explanation for British capital export cycles.
Debate has centered on two types of questions. On the one
hand, there was the issue of whether falling rates of return in
Britain were the dominant factor ("push" theories) or rising
profit opportunities abroad were more important ("pull" theories). On the other hand, for those who stressed push arguments, there remained the problem of the mechanisms involved. One possible mechanism was based on declining
availability of attractive projects. The other was rooted in oversaving or underconsumption. While the causes underlying the
decline in profitable projects are such factors as disappearing
natural resources and falling productivity, the oversaving hypothesis is based on distribution of income and wealth within
the capital-exporting country. Specifically, it suggests that low
wages paid to workers lead to an increasing share of income to

capitalists. Capitalists, in turn, are assumed to save a much greater share of their income *regardless* of rate of return.

The antecedents to the decreasing availability of projects argument are found in classical and Marxist economic thought where declining profit rates are a central feature—meaning that capital export is necessary for the very survival of capitalism. The precise causal mechanisms varied from Smith's (1776) emphasis on competition to Ricardo's (1817) and Malthus's (1820) focus on diminishing returns to Marx's (1894) theory of the rising organic composition of capital, but all assumed that there was at least a tendency for profit rates to fall in mature capitalist economies. Lenin (1917) later linked falling rates of profit to capital export. Drawing heavily on Hilferding and on Hobson, whose related theory is discussed later, Lenin portrayed the development of monopolies and the advent of "finance capital" as leading to surplus capital which could only be invested profitably abroad.

> An enormous "superabundance of capital" has accumulated in the advanced countries.... As long as capitalism remains what it is, surplus capital will never be utilized for the purpose of raising the standard of living of the masses in a given country, for this would mean a decline in profits for the capitalists; it will be used for the purpose of increasing those profits by exporting capital abroad to the backward countries. In these backward countries profits are usually high, for capital is scarce, the price of land is relatively low, wages are low, raw materials are cheap.... The necessity for exporting capital arises from the fact that in a few countries capitalism has become "overripe" and (owing to the backward state of agriculture and the impoverished state of the masses) capital cannot find "profitable" investment. (Lenin 1917, 62–63)

Neither Lenin nor his contemporaries performed empirical tests of his theory. That job has fallen to modern economic historians who have studied nineteenth-century British capital export, and, in the process, a change in emphasis has come about in the theory. When the question of returns is taken up in the recent literature, the formulation has been limited to relative rates of return with some allowance for a risk premium. The older notion of capital export as a necessity for the survival of capitalism has thus been replaced by a theory stressing the search for better profit opportunities.[7] The change, in turn, has led to a merging of the discussions about this version of the push theories and the broader push/pull debate.

Many of the best works on relative rates of return are case studies of specific capital-importing countries and their relationship to Britain as capital exporter. Such studies exist for the United States, Canada, Australia, and Argentina among others. For the U.S. case, Jeffrey Williamson (1964) has studied various aspects relating growth cycles to the U.S. balance of payments and especially to capital imports. Although his work as a whole is very complex, his quantitative analysis of capital imports incorporates only variables representing British and American rates of return and relative levels of investment. For the rates of return equation, the coefficients on the British term dominate.[8] Michael Edelstein (1982, chap. 4) has also studied the U.S. case, using a more elaborate methodology to look at the processes determining capital export as well as measures of push and pull. Edelstein finds that push factors were most important in determining U.K. capital exports to the United States. This was especially true, he finds, for the 1874–94 period; the later 1895–1914 years were also dominated by push factors, but the balance was more even.

[7] This debate on the necessity of imperialism versus desirability from the point of view of the capitalists is an old one. In the early part of the century, it was debated by Rosa Luxemburg and Nicolai Bukharin. Recently it has reappeared; see Szymanski (1977) and Magdoff (1977).

[8] Despite Williamson's quantitative results, he generally emphasizes demand factors in his analysis. In particular, he portrays U.S. growth cycles as the main determinant of capital imports.

Studies of Canada, Argentina, and Australia emphasize the role of pull variables as the primary explanation for capital export although the various authors caution that push factors must not be forgotten. In the Canadian case, Gerald Meier (1953) looks at capital imports for the period 1900–13, the main years of Canadian borrowing from Britain. Stating that the willingness of British investors to subscribe to Canadian issues depended on interest rate differentials between the two countries, he then provides data showing that investment in Canada was more profitable. Nevertheless, Meier adds that the fall in British home investment after 1904 increased the volume of loanable funds available to take advantage of Canadian profit opportunities and helped to account for the high levels of investment from 1905 to 1913.

The Argentine case has been most extensively studied by A. G. Ford (1971). Political as well as economic variables are included in his analysis as he stresses the importance of military expeditions in 1878–81 to put down the Indians and make the pampa safe for cultivation, together with the assumption of power of a strong central government (the Roca government of 1880–90) "capable of maintaining law and order and safety of property." Given these political preconditions, Ford goes on to investigate economic factors determining Argentina's attraction for foreign capital. In a series of regression analyses, he finds that the most important factor is profit rates in Argentina. Although a variable representing volume of domestic investment in Britain is found to be insignificant, another measuring the London market's general willingness to lend abroad is about as important as the Argentine variable.

Finally, a study of Australia and the London market is provided by A. R. Hall (1963). Basing his work on a detailed qualitative study of trends in the Australian economy between 1870 and 1914, Hall emphasizes the role of pull factors in

Australia as providing the initial stimulus for heavy lending in the 1870s and for the cessation of British lending at the end of the 1880s. In the meantime, however, he says that Britain's willingness to lend had to change for momentum to build. Two special factors should be noted. First, Hall pays more attention than other analysts to the interrelationship of activities in Britain and Australia in explaining lending trends.[9] Second, he puts a good deal of emphasis on competition for funds between Australia and other borrowing countries in addition to competition with domestic investment in Britain. Arthur Bloomfield's (1968) quantitative analysis for Australia in 1870–1914 suggests that British and Australian variables were of approximately equal importance.

Moving from case studies to a more general level, Edelstein (1981) distinguishes between the relative importance of push and pull factors in different periods. He concludes that during the 1850s and 1860s, the latter were probably most relevant for three reasons: high demand for social overhead capital coupled with small local savings in many areas abroad; simultaneous movement of home and overseas investment (this was prior to the Cairncross relationship, which only began in the 1870s); and similar investment patterns in England and continental Europe. For the 1870–1914 period, two important findings emerge: there was a secular decline in return on both home and overseas

[9] This view is clearly expressed by Hall (1963, 199). He says: "It is misleading as has sometimes been the case amongst Australian economic historians to regard Australia's economic destiny to have been largely shaped within Australia. If one's gaze is concentrated upon the Australian scene, this will almost inevitably be the judgement of the historian. . . . If, however, one stands back from the scene, it becomes increasingly clear that it is events abroad that are most important. There is truth in both points of view. What is wrong is to regard one as exclusive of the other."

investment, but they alternated in terms of which was higher. The pattern was similar to the Cairncross cycles discussed above. Edelstein thus concludes that "to the extent that British investors based their decision to lend abroad on rates of return, these data provide an ample motive for overseas capital investment" (ibid., 81).

The other version of push theories, the oversaving hypothesis, also has its antecedents among classical and Marxist theories of the nineteenth century, all of whom (unlike their neoclassical successors) were vitally concerned with questions of distribution. The best-known classical economist who adopted an underconsumptionist analysis was, of course, Malthus (1820) in his attack on Say's law. In Marx's (1894) work, the basis for an underconsumptionist position is found in the second kind of crisis he identifies – the realization crisis.

In the late nineteenth and early twentieth centuries, the oversaving or underconsumption hypothesis was specifically related to capital export by John Hobson in his books *The Evolution of Modern Capitalism* (1894) and *Imperialism* (1902). Hobson argued that unequal distribution of income led to oversaving by the rich in nineteenth-century Britain and that the resulting lack of demand pushed capital abroad. One notes in the quote from Lenin cited above that there are elements of this same argument in his analysis even though he attacked Hobson's views. The basic difference did not concern oversaving per se but whether oversaving was an inherent characteristic of capitalism or a problem that could be alleviated through government economic policy.

Again there was no empirical evidence brought to bear on this hypothesis until recently. Hall (1963, 142) mentions the phenomenon in discussing the Australian loans. In a critique of a study by J. H. Lenfant, who suggested that the 1904 redistribution of income toward profits in Britain can explain the upturn in overseas lending, Hall points to the earlier shift toward profits between 1875 and 1882. Since this earlier income shift was *not* accompanied by higher overseas lending, Hall suggests that income shifts in and of themselves do not affect foreign investment unless they are accompanied by a high propensity to import overseas securities as an independent factor. This propensity, he says, was not an invariable characteristic of the British upper classes.

A much more extensive test of the Hobson hypothesis for nineteenth-century British capital export is provided by Edelstein (1982, chap. 8). He begins by pointing out that Hobson is not clear on many of the details of his oversaving hypothesis, so it is necessary to look at various possible formulations. The simplest would be that shifts toward nonwage income would be correlated with high overseas investment (implying that the oversaving phenomenon was limited to the pre–World War I period). Unlike the data on which Hall and Lenfant were basing their analyses, Edelstein's data show no shift in 1904 and, in general, a *falling* share of nonwage income over the 1870–1914 period.[10] Looking at more complex formulations of the oversaving hypothesis involves the investigation of the volatility of nonwage income and the business cycle. Neither offers much support for the hypothesis.

Nevertheless, Edelstein does eventually find some support for Hobson's theory by looking at the difference between *desired* (predicted from econometric models of savings behavior) and *actual* savings rates during the periods immediately preceding the two overseas investment surges of the 1870–1914 years: 1877–79 and 1903–5. At these points, models of gross private

[10] The data used by Lenfant (and Hall) were from Prest (1948, 57). Edelstein's data were from Deane and Cole (1967, 247) and Feinstein (1972, 4–5).

savings made their worst predictions as predicted desired savings rates exceeded actual rates. Furthermore, domestic investment trends were also declining. Edelstein suggests that the balance between desired saving and desired domestic investment took the form of overseas investment. In terms of the accounting identities discussed earlier, the argument suggests that a fall in the level of activity consequent upon the rise in the propensity to save led to a fall in imports with a resulting increase in net foreign lending. Thus, Edelstein finds some support for the relationship between oversaving and capital export but not, as he points out, for the reason that Hobson had in mind.

Trade and Capital Export

Theories on the link between trade and capital export are sometimes related to the push/pull debate just discussed. That is, high merchandise export value in a borrowing country, which is thought to encourage capital export, can be seen as a type of pull factor. In addition, however, there are at least two other trade arguments that stand apart from the push/pull debate. One focuses on terms of trade, arguing that deteriorating terms of trade lead to capital export. The other is a more complex structural approach that attempts to trace the interrelationship between exports, imports, and capital flows.

Cairncross (1953, chap. 7) is probably the analyst most closely associated with the terms of trade argument in explaining nineteenth-century British capital export, although he does not claim credit for the more general formulation of the hypothesis. The basic assumption underlying his analysis is that Great Britain was primarily an exporter of manufactured goods and an importer of raw materials. These raw materials, in turn, were produced and sold by countries to which Britain lent money. Given these facts, his argument runs as follows:

> One would expect to find, therefore, that during, or immediately after, a fairly long period in which the terms of trade were relatively unfavourable to Britain there would be heavy investment in the countries supplying her with imports. A scarcity of raw materials or a series of bad harvests in Europe would be likely to improve the credit of Argentina and the United States. On the other hand, when capital goods were expensive and foodstuffs were in oversupply, the continuance of a rapid opening up of agricultural countries would be distinctly surprising. (ibid., 189)

In other words, capital export should follow a deterioration in the terms of trade for lending countries and vice versa.

To test his hypothesis, Cairncross presents data on terms of trade in Britain and several capital-importing countries and compares them with trends in capital export. In general, the evidence seems to support his proposition with the important exception of the 1880s when increased capital export was accompanied by an improvement in the British terms of trade. Through the use of various ad hoc explanations, he convinces himself (though not all of his critics) that there are logical reasons for this exception and concludes his discussion with a strong statement: "It was on investment – home and foreign – that income and employment ultimately depended; and it was upon the terms of trade that the distribution of investment between home and foreign, as well as the course of real wages, ultimately depended" (ibid., 208). Cairncross follows up his general argument with a case study of Canadian capital imports. On the basis of these data, he specifically comments on the causal relationship between terms of trade and capital flows. Remarking that people formerly believed that the latter caused the former, he argues that the Canadian data show bursts of investment occurring only *after* terms of trade moved against Britain (ibid., chap. 3).

Hall (1963, 141–42) also discusses the terms of trade argument in the Australian case. Agreeing that there does appear to be an association between the two sets of variables, he nevertheless cautions against attributing too much importance to the fact. Brinley Thomas (1958) goes further, casting doubt on the relationship between terms of trade and capital flows altogether. Insofar as they are correlated, he says, terms of trade are probably a consequence rather than a cause. A third critique of the Cairncross model is by Stone (1971), who says that Cairncross provided an adequate long-run function but one which is incomplete in the short run, especially in times of financial crisis.

Other authors are interested in going beyond the terms of trade question to investigate the general relationship between trade and capital flows. One suggestion is that there is no direct relationship but both merchandise *and* capital imports move together because both are determined by a third variable, namely national income movements. Thus Williamson (1964, chaps. 2–4) argues for income swings as the basic determinant of all kinds of imports in the United States, while exports are seen as less important. Others, such as Meier (1953) on Canada and Ford (1971) on Argentina, believe that value of merchandise exports was a key determinant of capital exports since high merchandise exports would give British investors confidence and thus attract their funds.

Ford (1965) is also interested in tracing the process underlying the trade and capital relationship. To do so, he constructs a series of models differing with respect to how funds are raised in the lending country and how they are spent in the borrowing nation. These models are closely related to the two accounting identities discussed at the beginning of the chapter. Trade is affected most when investment funds in the lending country are obtained at the expense of consumption, leading to a fall in imports, and where the borrower uses the money either to pay for imports directly or to increase domestic spending which will indirectly stimulate imports. When money comes from otherwise idle funds in the lending country and is used simply to increase reserves in the borrowing nation, trade flows are affected less. Obviously, the stronger the trade links between borrower and lender, the more relevant these relationships become; the ideal is a "two-country world." These models have not been estimated with empirical data.

Migration and Capital Export

The relationship between migration and capital flows appeared as an obvious candidate for research about nineteenth-century Britain because many of the major capital-importing countries were also recipients of large numbers of British migrants. The United States, Canada, Australia, New Zealand, and South Africa are well-known examples. There was a significant British colony in Argentina as well. The essence of this hypothesis is that migration either causes capital export, by increasing demand for investment, or that migration is an important component of a multifactor model explaining capital export.

As in the case of other hypotheses, Cairncross (1953, chap. 8) was one of the early exponents of the migration/capital flow relationship. Pointing out that trends in the two variables coincided, both in terms of periodicity and amplitude, he then goes on to suggest a possible process behind the correlation. It is only at this point in his analysis, with the addition of migration, that the full scope of his argument becomes apparent. Specifically, Kuznets cycles or long swings in Britain are tied causally to capital outflow, rather than home and foreign investment simply being described as exhibiting an inverse relationship.

To explain the process, Cairncross focuses on the construction industry (although saying that many others could be similarly analyzed). Favorable trends in the terms of trade in borrowing countries led to more construction activity there which increased wages and employment opportunities, thus attracting British workers. The emigration left houses empty in Britain, rents fell, recession descended, and investors began to prefer foreign bonds rather than real estate or other investment in Britain. A panic abroad was enough to change investors' predilections and, as foreign investment fell, so did emigration, thus reversing the process just described. The role of terms of trade in triggering migration flows links Cairncross's migration argument with his analysis of terms of trade as the stimulus for capital export. Clearly a change in terms of trade could substitute for the panic suggested as a reason for the turnabout in investor preferences.

The analyst most often associated with migration as the main causal factor in explaining economic trends is not Cairncross but Brinley Thomas (1973). Thomas differs from Cairncross in attributing the role of independent variable to migration rather than terms of trade. His version of the capital flow/migration/domestic investment cycles runs as follows. A large population outflow from Britain to a borrowing country, caused by overpopulation and exacerbated at certain points by agricultural disasters, induced a wave of investment for housing and transportation there. The investment was financed by loans from Britain; it also stimulated exports from Britain. A construction boom in the borrowing country and an export boom in Britain led to inflation in the former and terms of trade thus moving in its favor. The process ended when the cycle in the borrowing country began to encounter bottlenecks, leading to lower profits and a turn of investment back toward British construction. The flow of migration slowed accordingly, and the process reversed itself.

Thomas submits his basic model to both statistical and historical tests (ibid., chap. 10). One key test was an examination of the lag structure between immigration to the United States and investment there. In general the model stands up fairly well, especially with respect to investment in construction; only the 1869–79 period finds construction investment preceding immigration. With respect to railroad investment, the Thomas hypothesis holds up for the early part of the period, but in the last two decades of the nineteenth century this type of investment preceded immigration flows. Thomas also uses detailed historical evidence to buttress his model and concludes, on the basis of both kinds of tests, that "in each case the pace of the major component of American investment was governed by mass immigration from the overpopulated rural areas of Europe" (ibid., 163).

Institutions and Capital Export

A fourth important set of hypotheses on British capital export deals with the role of institutions. This has been a prominent topic in the debates on capital export, but it has generally been formulated in a fairly narrow way. That is, the debate on institutions has tended to focus almost exclusively on the bias and efficiency of the London market. The broader issue of the development and change of the market over time has not been considered. Presumably the reason is embodied in the conclusion reached by Hall after finishing a historical analysis of the market between 1870 and 1914, as follows:

> It seems fairly clear from the above account . . . that there were
> relatively few changes in the basic mechanism of the London capital
> market between 1870 and 1914. Eventful as the history of the

London Stock Exchange had been during these years, there were no significant changes in its structure. Professional promoters and professional directors were more important in 1914 than they had been in 1870, but they were not newcomers at the earlier date. The relative importance of the various types of overseas issuing houses had changed and home issuing houses were beginning to emerge, but the method of issuing remained much the same. (Hall 1963, 82–83)

Hall's explanation for the lack of institutional change—surprising at first sight, he says, in view of great changes going on in the financial organization of industry in Britain—was that the vast majority of the borrowers remained the same over the period. These were foreign borrowers, local governments, and railroads. Local industry, he argues, except for large firms, did not have close contact with the market, which, in any case, already had long experience in dealing with the needs of joint-stock companies. Davis (1966) reinforces this idea, saying that industrial expansion in Britain produced less strain on the financial system (and therefore less change) than did such expansion in the United States.[11]

For these reasons, then, the question of prime concern for analysts of British lending was the existing bias of the market. Specifically, was there a bias in the structure of the market that led it to favor overseas issues in comparison to home issues in general and industrial issues in particular? This question was part of the larger debate on the weakness of British industry and its causes. It seems fair to say that the majority of analysts did see a bias toward foreign issues in the market, although most of them

[11] Fishlow (1985, 399) also notes the lack of institutional change involved in British lending, although he does not explain why this was the case. "Britain required no major institutional innovations, like the French Credit Mobilier or the German Great Banks, to compete. Merchant banks fulfilled the function."

also discount this bias as the major cause of the problems in British industry.[12]

Much of the discussion refers back to a survey of the British capital market by Frederick Lavington (1921). Dealing with the period 1911–13, Lavington concludes that the capital market was a relatively unimportant source of funds for home investment. Many others endorsed this view. Charles Kindleberger's (1964, 62) memorable phrase is typical: "Capital flows in channels, and these had been dug between London and the far reaches of the empire, but not between London and the industrial north." Cairncross (1953, 96) is more specific when he says: "It is clear that even in times of boom not more than about ten percent of real investment at home was financed through new issues on the London Stock Exchange by industrial concerns and that of this ten percent the proportion raised by new companies averaged under a third."[13]

Various mechanisms are cited as contributing to the alleged bias of the market. One is the experience of the institutions acting in the market. Thus, Cairncross (ibid., 90) argues that the major issuing houses—such as Rothschild's, Baring's, Schroeder's, and Hambro's—were nearly all founded by foreign families that came to England as merchant bankers and developed large international acceptance businesses. These firms did not have the background necessary to float local industrial issues but were "admirably placed" for the handling of foreign loans. This process tended to feed on itself as such houses floated more foreign

[12] See, for example, Kindleberger (1964), Hobsbawm (1968), Landes (1969), and McCloskey (1970). On the current problem of British industrial weakness, see Singh (1977).

[13] See also the debate on this subject between Hall (1957, 1958) and Cairncross (1958). This debate represents a difference in Hall's position as discussed earlier in the chapter since he argues that industry did have access to the market.

loans and their expertise became even more biased. A second mechanism has to do with the alleged size bias and its relationship to foreign and domestic securities. That is, the unit cost of floating an issue was much higher for a small than a large issue, and, since local industrial issues tended to be small, this priced them out of the London market (Saville 1961).

A third mechanism involves legislation. As Herbert Feis (1930, 93) put it, "British capital was directed toward British dominions and colonies by the Colonial Stocks Act." By this he meant that British government statutes determined where trustees could invest trust funds if no specific instructions were given in the documents establishing the trust. In 1900 colonial securities that fulfilled certain requirements were added to the admissible list; India had previously been on it.

A final mechanism concerns investors themselves. A growing preference for marketable securities among wealthy investors increased the share of investment going through the London Stock Exchange rather than real estate or direct investment in partnerships. Given this preference for stock exchange securities, which was reinforced by the increasing importance of institutional investors, the investor was more likely to purchase overseas issues than British industrial securities because such were the offerings on the exchange (Hall 1963, 59–60).

Many analysts, however, deny that the markets were biased or deny the importance of any bias that did exist. The most extensive rebuttal is provided by Edelstein (1971). His argument can be divided into two parts. First is a qualitative analysis centering on the availability of finance for small- and medium-sized firms. In the first place, he agrees with the charge that the large issue houses tended to specialize in large foreign issues. But, he says, this was a perfectly rational thing for them to do. They would have been much less efficient (thus raising the costs to all borrowers) if they had tried to engage in floating various types of issues. Second, Edelstein marshals a great deal of evidence about alternative sources of finance for British industry. He cites the existence of smaller houses and brokers that specialized in floating issues for industrial firms but stresses that most of these issues appeared on provincial stock exchanges rather than in London. Later, as firm size increased, London is said to have responded fairly quickly. Addressing the point that the smaller size of British firms in comparison to American and European firms could be attributed to market bias, Edelstein goes so far as to say: "It appears it was the very adequacy of Britain's long term external financing institutions for both modest and large scale borrowers that helped to yield the relatively small scale of its enterprises, not the hypothesized rigidities" (ibid., 95).

The second part of Edelstein's critique of the bias theory is a quantitative analysis using mean–standard deviation models of portfolio choice. Here he tests for the existence of bias according to domestic/overseas status and according to size. On the basis of the tests, he concludes that the scale of issue and regional biases did not significantly affect the pricing of assets. Nevertheless, there was a "weak and unstable" preference for large and overseas issues in the 1870–89 period. From 1890 to 1914, he found a somewhat less stable bias for domestic issues together with a very weak bias for large issues (ibid., 95–102).[14]

Politics Versus Economics in Capital Export

A fifth debate has only recently been joined, but it is nevertheless important to mention it briefly. The question is the broadest of all those discussed in the chapter: was British capital export

[14] For criticisms of Edelstein's results and his methodology, see McCloskey (1971, 106–11).

basically an economic or a political phenomenon? Many of the early analyses explicitly emphasized the political context of lending, while the later studies have implicitly assumed that economic questions were the only ones at stake. Albert Fishlow (1985) has called attention to the issue and suggests that the apparent inconsistency arises from failure to differentiate among capital-exporting countries.

The claim for the political nature of capital export came mainly through the association of state-sponsored imperialism and private lending. That is, lending was considered to be part of the process of founding and maintaining the British Empire. The political link was seen as both cause and effect: lenders obtained government support for their business ventures, while governments received private cooperation for their expansionary activities. The process can be viewed as an extension of Lenin's analysis of the falling rate of profit and Hobson's discussion of oversaving as leading to capital export. The conclusion of both arguments was that capital export was directly connected with the political process of imperialism.

The importance of the connection for Lenin (1917) was such that two of the five elements in his very definition of imperialism involved capital export and the political division of the world among the major powers. "Colonial possession alone," he says, "gives complete guarantees of success to the monopolist against all risks of the struggle with competitors" (ibid., 82). This competition could involve raw materials, but in addition the "necessity of exporting capital also gives an impetus to the conquest of colonies, for in the colonial market it is easier to eliminate competition, to make sure of orders, to strengthen the necessary 'connections,' etc., by monopolistic methods (and sometimes it is the only possible way)" (ibid., 84).

Hobson (1902) was even more emphatic about the relationship between capital export and political expansion. Having argued that trade was not a very important part of national income and therefore could not account for the large-scale expenditures to maintain the empire, he goes on to identify the foreign investor as the main beneficiary.

> It is not too much to say that the modern foreign policy of Great Britain has been primarily a struggle for profitable markets for investment. . . . What was true of Great Britain was true likewise of France, Germany, the United States, and all other countries in which modern capitalism has placed large surplus savings in the hands of a plutocracy or of a thrifty middle class. (ibid., 53–54)

The relationship was argued in both directions. On the one hand, investors want to get public assistance: "The classes who enjoy [profits from foreign investment] have had an ever-increasing incentive to employ the public policy, the public purse, and the public force to extend the field of their private investment, and to safeguard and improve their existing investments" (ibid., 54). On the other hand, governments must get the consent of the financiers to expand abroad: "Every great political act . . . must receive the sanction and the practical aid of this little group of financial kings. . . . Does anyone seriously suppose that a great war could be undertaken by a European State, or a great State loan subscribed, if the house of Rothschild and its connections set their face against it?" (ibid., 57).

Several decades later, a similar argument was put forth by a quite different source. Writing in 1930 under the auspices of the Council on Foreign Relations, Herbert Feis also expressed the view that capital export in the period up until World War I could only be understood through its interconnection with politics and diplomacy. Although admitting that British capital had greater independence from its government than did capital in France or Germany, he nevertheless summarized his overall argument as follows:

> In short, the financial transactions between western Europe and other areas were an important element in political affairs. They

became all the more important because the official circles of lending countries gradually came to envisage the foreign investments of their citizens, not as private financial transactions, but as one of the instruments through which national destiny was achieved. . . . The lines of political division in pre-war Europe, the situations which were created and which led ultimately to the War, can be understood only by taking account of the borrowing-lending relations which existed. On the other hand, the action of capital, seeking return, can be understood only by taking account of the national influences to which it was subject. (Feis 1930, xv–xvi)

Although Feis's book is widely cited by most economists and economic historians writing on British capital export, virtually no one has challenged his view of the political connection. They have simply ignored it as – more predictably – they have ignored Lenin and Hobson. Only Fishlow (1985) argues that Feis had gotten his point wrong: "[His] vision, without denying the validity of the conclusion, is only partial. Moreover, it impedes rather than facilitates our understanding of capital flows not only then but especially in comparison with the 1920s and 1930s and with the 1970s and 1980s" (ibid., 386–87).

Fishlow goes on to suggest that Feis had confused British lending practices with those of France and Germany. There were actually two lending processes going on, he says. One was "market-oriented foreign investment," largely undertaken by Britain and directed to the resource-rich, European-settled countries of the periphery. The other type of investment, carried out by France and Germany, was directed toward Europe as well as China, Turkey, Egypt, and some African colonies. "Here political considerations clearly played a part" (ibid., 392).

Expectations and Lending Cycles

The sixth hypothesis takes us back to where this section started – with a discussion of lending cycles. In this instance, however, the cycles are different in important ways from those of Cairncross. They are less regular and less well behaved, and the causal mechanisms are based as much on psychological as on economic factors. This body of literature has been heavily influenced by a single scholar: Charles Kindleberger. Drawing on numerous individual studies of national and international financial crises, plus the work of Hyman Minsky (1964, 1982, 1986) on corporate finance, Kindleberger (1978) has presented a model of international lending that relies heavily on investor expectations. The other key element is a central monetary institution which is important both for conducting monetary policy and potentially acting as a lender of last resort. Much of the criticism of Kindleberger's work has focused on the importance attributed to the lender of last resort (see, for example, Moggridge 1982), but Minsky's underlying model is also very controversial (see, for example, Minsky 1982).

The Kindleberger model of international financial crises has five stages. The cycle starts off with an exogenous shock whose nature can vary widely. Examples include a political shock such as the end of a war, an economic shock such as an invention, or a financial shock such as a particularly successful set of transactions. The exogenous shock, rather than being smoothly absorbed by the system, creates such strong positive expectations ("euphoria") among investors that the price of certain assets is bid up very quickly, setting off a period of speculation. The speculation is manipulated by bankers and facilitated by credit expansion. A high volume of debt is run up.

The next phase of the model is "financial distress." Again, expectations are the key element, but this time it is falling expectations as the speculative euphoria ends. This period could last for a long or short time, depending on whether all investors change their expectations simultaneously. If the financial distress is not dealt with adequately, a financial crisis will ensue as investors try to get out of the asset in question. The catalyst again can be any number of events from bankruptcy to scandal to revolution. Prices plummet and no additional funds are made available to previous borrowers. The model may stop at this point, with only a mild crisis mediated by a lender of last resort. Without such an actor, however, the crisis will result in default as debtors cannot (or will not) meet their payments. The consequence of default is a long period of "financial revulsion" when the borrowers cannot regain access to the market. Kindleberger is not particularly concerned with the periodization of the cycles, but there is at least an implication that a new generation of lenders must emerge before the process can be repeated.

Evidence for the existence of the cycles and their underlying mechanisms is adduced by Kindleberger from looking at many historical cases from the eighteenth to the twentieth centuries. Among these cases are the nineteenth-century British loans to Latin America. Those of the 1820s, for example, are said to have been stimulated by the successful wars of independence, those later in the century by the extension of the railroads (Smart 1911; Jenks 1927). In each case, a boom followed as lenders became highly enthusiastic about the possibilities for growth in the region. Speculation was fed by competition and manipulation on the part of bankers, as indicated by the House of Commons' Foreign Loan Investigation of 1875, which detailed the corrupt activities of lenders. As expectations fell, crisis and default resulted. All Latin American borrowers except Brazil were in default in the late 1820s (Jenks 1927, 57–58). Another wave of defaults occurred in the 1870s, but the most spectacular was the Baring crisis of 1890, which threatened the British banking system itself (Felix 1987). Apart from the lender of last resort issue, criticisms of the Kindleberger model focus on its supposed inapplicability during the twentieth century (McClam 1982). That question is addressed in later chapters.

Summary

Based on a review of the literature on British capital export, six main hypotheses have emerged:

1. The largest group of empirical studies focuses on rates of return as an explanation for British capital export. Two sub-hypotheses are involved. The first postulates that *differential* rates of return constitute the primary explanatory factor. Strong support was found for this hypothesis, although evidence differs on whether low rates in Britain or higher rates in borrowing countries were more important. The second subhypothesis argues that oversaving, due to a regressive redistribution of income, was the major cause of capital export. Some support was found for a version of this hypothesis in certain periods.

2. A second set of hypotheses centers on relations between trade and capital export. Some evidence exists to support the idea that capital export was inversely related to terms of trade between Britain and borrowing countries. Moreover, the value of the borrower's merchandise exports has been found to be correlated with its ability to attract foreign capital.

3. A third hypothesis stresses the relationship between migration and capital export. The strong version of this hypothesis, backed by some historical evidence, says that population pressures led to migration from Britain; this migration then attracted foreign capital to the borrowing country as a complement.

4. A fourth hypothesis concerns the role of institutions in biasing the London market toward overseas issues. The most extensive analysis of the question points to a very weak bias in favor of foreign issues in one period and a weak bias against them in another. That is, institutions were apparently not a major factor in the British case.

5. A fifth hypothesis deals with the relationship between

politics and economics in motivating capital export. The most convincing evidence suggests that British lending, unlike that of France and Germany, was primarily brought about by bankers' search for profits rather than being part of the foreign policy process.

6. Finally, the role of expectations is suggested as an explanation for capital export. This hypothesis is embedded in the notion of lending cycles. The process begins with an exogenous event which stimulates lender "euphoria" and leads to an unsustainable level of debt which is often followed by default. Numerous historical examples attest to the validity of the cycle if not necessarily the mechanisms posited.

These six hypotheses, then, represent the main elements of a theory of British foreign lending in the nineteenth century. The question of primary interest is whether these hypotheses, based on events of a previous epoch, are still valid. Can we simply accept them, or do different conditions require modified–or even completely different–explanations? It is to these questions that we now turn.

Nineteenth-Century Britain Versus Twentieth-Century United States

The reason for using hypotheses about British capital export in the nineteenth century in a study of U.S. capital export during the twentieth century is that basic similarities exist between the two cases. The most important of these similarities is that each country, in its respective period, was the dominant power within the world economy. The dominance was reflected in many areas including banking, monetary policy, direct investment, and military power. For the purposes of this study, however, the most important similarity is the role of the two countries in the two periods as dominant international lenders. There are also some striking parallels to the way in which Britain and the United States attained their dominant positions. The role of the Napoleonic Wars in hastening the shift of the world capital market from Amsterdam to London, and the effects of Britain's increasing economic capacity during the war, sound very familiar to those who have read of the impact of World War I on the rise of New York as the principal financial center. Nevertheless, there are also important differences between nineteenth-century Britain and twentieth-century United States that need to be explored.

Characteristics of Lenders

The size of the two lending countries, and the resources available to them, were clearly different. The resource differential enabled the United States to be much more self-sufficient than Britain, a country heavily dependent on trade. This dependence was especially crucial in two major areas: raw materials and food (Deane and Cole 1967, 32–33). In contrast, the United States has traditionally been a net food exporter with food imports limited mostly to luxury items. Self-sufficiency in raw materials has generally been the pattern as well, although some crucial minerals have been imported (United States 1963b). As a consequence, international transactions in general were more important for Britain than for the United States. The difference can be seen over a variety of indicators. Trade, calculated as the sum of exports plus imports, constituted 50 to 60 percent of national income in Britain between 1855 and 1910 (Mitchell and Deane 1962, 283–84, 367–68) but only 6 to 18 percent in the United States between 1900 and 1980 (United States 1976, F1–5; Appendix II). Likewise, in approximately the same two periods, net foreign investment accounted for 45 percent of total investment in Britain (Cairncross 1953, 169, 180) but never more than 8 percent in the United States (United States 1976, U1–25; *International Financial Statistics,* 1982 Yearbook).

A second difference concerns flows of population and labor rather than capital and goods. During the nineteenth century, Britain was a net exporter of people. Figures available for the period 1843–1913 show an annual out-migration of around 215,000 people, meaning that about 15 million people left Britain during those seventy years (Thomas 1973, 57). The United States, by contrast, was importing people during the twentieth century. The objective and subjective opportunities offered by the U.S. economy and society attracted people from all over the world. In spite of quotas limiting the number of immigrants allowed to enter the country, about 30 million arrived between 1900 and 1980 (*Statistical Abstract of the United States,* 1980, 91).

A third difference concerns the relative rigidity or fluidity of the structure of wealth and income. This topic is important to an analysis of capital export because evidence shows that those who bought securities were a small group of wealthy individuals as well as the main financial institutions (Hall 1963, 39; Cairncross 1953, 82; Morrow 1927; United States 1947). The weight of the latter increased in both countries during their respective periods as dominant capital exporter, but the role of individuals was nevertheless important, especially in the early years. Statistics on factor distribution show a fairly stable trend in Britain between the mid-1850s and 1914, with about 48 percent of national income going to labor. The share to rent fell slightly (from 14 to 11 percent), while profits and mixed categories accounted for the difference (Deane and Cole 1967, 245–48). The meager data on personal distribution of income in the nineteenth century show only a very small decline in inequality in the five decades preceding World War I. The share of the top decile fell from 52 to 50 percent, while that of the top 5 percent went from 47 to 44 percent (Williamson 1985, 68).

U.S. data on factor distribution, by contrast, show a sharp rise in the share of national income going to labor—from 53 percent in the decade of 1910–19 to 71 percent in 1960–65. Income from self-employment and rent fell correspondingly, while the profit and interest share remained fairly constant at about 15 percent of national income (Atkinson 1975, 163). From that time on, shares have varied little (*Survey of Current Business,* January 1980, pp. 42–43). Data on personal distribution in the United States also show significant variation in the post–World War I period. A regressive redistribution in favor of the very top groups took place during the 1920s with the top 5 percent increasing its share from 24 to 34 percent. From the early 1930s through the end of World War II, that share fell steadily (Kuznets 1953, 637).[15] Again, there has been little change in the postwar period (United States 1981, 54).

A final difference focuses on financial institutions. Britain's institutions were developed early, well before the main period of capital export (1870–1914) began, whereas in the United States institutions were still emerging when World War I converted the country into the major capital exporter. The City of London—that complex web of institutions that constitutes the basis of British financial operations—began to develop in the late seventeenth century while the main international financial center was still located in Amsterdam. The Bank of England, owned by City merchants but serving many of the functions of a central bank, was chartered in 1694 (Clapham 1966). The Stock Exchange was formally established in 1773 (Morgan and Thomas

[15] Williamson and Lindert (1980) support the Kuznets interpretation of the income distribution patterns of the 1920s and say that the same trends occurred in the distribution of wealth. Smiley (1983), however, questions the concentration figures for the beginning of the decade although he provides no alternatives.

1962). Although joint-stock banks did not develop until the mid-nineteenth century, the merchant banks–much more important for international transactions–were beginning to appear in the late eighteenth century. Baring's was established in 1772, Rothschild's and Schroeder's in 1804, and Brandt's, Anthony Gibbs, and Brown Shipley later in the same decade (Corti 1928; Baster 1935; Hidy 1949). They became experts in acceptances which formed not only the basis of British international trade but that of the rest of the world as well.

The case of the United States in 1915 was quite different. Various stock exchanges, of which the New York Stock Exchange was the most important, had long been in existence, but they dealt almost exclusively with domestic issues (Dice and Eiteman 1926). The structures of an international money market were only beginning to emerge; in fact, New York had only fairly recently established its dominance as the national money center of the United States (Goodhart 1969). A central bank was not created until the passage of the Federal Reserve Act in 1913 (West 1977), and this same law gave nationally chartered banks authority to establish branches abroad and accept bills of exchange. Prior to this time, only the generally smaller state-chartered banks could establish foreign branches, of which twenty-six existed. The state banks also engaged in a limited amount of trade finance, but the lack of a central bank to rediscount their acceptances put these U.S. institutions at a disadvantage with respect to their London competition (Phelps 1927; Carosso 1970).

Characteristics of Borrowers

The second type of dissimilarity focuses on borrowers rather than lenders. According to the most reliable source of information, British capital export during the 1870–1914 period was divided as follows: North America 34 percent, South America 17 percent, Europe 13 percent, Asia 14 percent, Australasia 11 percent, and Africa 11 percent (Simon 1967, 40).[16] This distribution means that the majority of Britain's borrowers were nations with a fairly high level of economic development as evidenced by per capita income levels and more importantly by industrialization and economic institutions. Looking at development in this way, differences between Britain's borrowers in the nineteenth century and the United States' Latin American borrowers in the twentieth century become clear.

Britain's largest borrower (the United States) already had a large industrial sector in the latter part of the last century and was even beginning to challenge Britain's former monopoly in industrial exports (Maizels 1965, 432–33). The same could obviously be said of Britain's major European borrowers. Canada and Australasia were more reliant on agricultural exports, but these were the kinds of exports that created the basis for industrial development.[17]

Latin America, during most of the twentieth century, was quite different. On the one hand, there was less of an industrial base; especially important was the lack of a heavy-industry sector. Industrialization began in a major way in the largest countries in the region in the 1930s and 1940s, but it was based on the production of light consumer goods via so-called import substitution industrialization (Furtado 1976, chaps. 10–12,

[16] See also Feis's (1930, 23) estimates, which show Europe 8 percent, United States 20 percent, Latin America 20 percent, British Empire 47 percent, and other countries 5 percent.

[17] See Furtado's (1976, 47–49) distinctions among the side effects of various kinds of primary exports. Grain exports, he says, produce high profits from the start and necessitate the development of an extensive infrastructural system plus agricultural technology. Such an economy is likely to result in an overall high standard of living based on high productivity and wages. Tropical agriculture and mining exports do not have these beneficial side effects.

15). High tariff barriers made most Latin American industry quite inefficient and thus incapable of competing on the international market. On the other hand, the agricultural exports produced by many countries in the region were characterized by low skills and little need for sophisticated infrastructure and backward or forward linkages (ibid., 47–49). As the post–World War II period wore on, of course, these characteristics began to change, especially in the largest Latin American countries.

A second type of development indicator is institutional infrastructure. Focusing especially on financial institutions, important differences can again be seen between the major borrowers from Britain and the Latin American borrowers from the United States. The former had domestic capital markets so that they had an alternative to foreign capital import. This is not meant to deny the importance of foreign finance for the United States, Canada, and Australasia, not to mention less-developed areas of the British Empire. Nevertheless, there were various regional stock exchanges in the United States from the late eighteenth century and in Canada and Australia from the mid-nineteenth. Although formal government bill markets were not well organized, the private banking system assumed many of the functions that central banks would later perform (Spray 1964). In Latin America, by contrast, even today no long-term sources of local capital are available in most countries. Some of the larger countries do have capital markets, but these are mainly sources of short-term funds. For long-term purposes, then, foreign capital continues to be crucial (Basch and Kybal 1970; United Nations 1970, 1971; Maxfield and Armijo 1986).[18]

---

[18] Studies of domestic capital markets in Latin America since the early 1970s are difficult to find since the bulk of attention has been focused on international markets. There seems little doubt, however,

Political-Economic Context

A third dissimilarity between Britain and the United States concerns the context, domestic and international, within which the two nations operated. The greatest difference in terms of domestic context was the role of the government. Specifically, the vast majority of the years of U.S. domination were those of growing government intervention in economic affairs. The nineteenth century, by contrast, was characterized by a much greater degree of laissez-faire, although this does not mean that the government played no role. The difference can be seen in several policy areas.

The first aspect concerns the use of fiscal and monetary policy to smooth cyclical patterns. As is well known, this governmental function became important in both Britain and the United States after World War II as the influence of Keynesian analysis spread (Winch 1969). Demand management has played a key role in the U.S. economy during most of the last forty years, ending the extremely sharp business cycles of the past.[19] In the nineteenth and early twentieth centuries, when no comparable government intervention occurred, business cycles were sharper (Schumpeter 1939; Lewis 1978), and economic growth in many countries was characterized by longer fifteen- or twenty-

---

that Brazil has done the best job in creating a voluntary market for government debt although even Brazil does not have a significant domestic market for long-term private finance. See Baer (1983, chaps. 9–10). For a recent, very critical, survey of Latin American capital markets, see *World Financial Markets* (April–May 1986).

[19] In the United States, in no year between 1946 and 1980 did national income fall by more than 1.8 percent. See *Survey of Current Business* (January 1980 and December 1981).

year swings as well (Kuznets 1952; Abramovitz 1959; Thomas 1973).

A second area in which a greater government role is evident is in regulation of economic activity. The period of British capital export coincided with the reaction against governmental controls prevalent during the mercantilist period. Britain itself took the lead in moving toward greater laissez-faire in the nineteenth century, and the movement was more complete there than in other countries that saw a strong government as a way of catching up with Britain (List 1856, chaps. 11, 26–27). As was the case with demand management policies, the depression of the 1930s also brought about a significant change in regulation. Two examples in the United States affected capital export. Investment and commercial banking were divided, and restrictions were placed on foreign securities floated in New York (Carosso 1970, chaps. 17–18). Later, from 1963 to 1974, capital controls were imposed to limit the volume of capital export (Hawley 1977, chaps. 4–6; Mendelsohn 1980, chaps. 30–31).

A third aspect of the greater governmental role during the current century involves bilateral loans and grants to foreign governments. Such government expenditure is not completely new; in particular, Britain and other colonialist governments had to spend money to maintain their empires. The British government, however, expected its colonies to finance themselves as far as possible, with the consequence that inflows and outflows more or less balanced each other (Edelstein 1981, 95–96, table 4-4). For the United States in the twentieth century, net government outflows eventually became the accepted pattern. Such a trend appeared briefly in connection with World War I. Later, during the 1930s, the Export-Import Bank was set up to help finance trade. Massive military and economic aid during World War II was then continued after the war through the Marshall

Plan, the Alliance for Progress, and other military and economic "aid" programs. (For data, see *U.S. Overseas Loans and Grants,* various issues.)

In terms of the international context, greater interdependence brought about a number of changes. One was the establishment of a group of multilateral agencies that provide finance to Third World countries. The most important are the International Monetary Fund (IMF) and the World Bank, which were established immediately after World War II. Later a number of regional development banks were set up. The IMF is especially important among the various financial agencies because, in addition to providing loans, it also attempts to coordinate economic policies across countries (Stallings 1979, 219–31).

On the private level, the Eurocurrency market—the first international capital market—has provided a new type of capital flow with the banks lending their own deposits rather than acting as intermediaries between governments wanting to borrow money and individuals willing to purchase bonds. The development of this market in the 1960s came about in an attempt by the banks to escape narrow national boundaries and regulations (Mendelsohn 1980; Bell 1974). As we shall see in later chapters, the switch from bonds to commercial bank loans was perhaps the single most important factor in determining the characteristics of the lending process and its outcomes.

Finally, the international context in the twentieth century has been marked by large shifts in international distribution of income in contrast to the continuities of the Pax Britannica. In the nineteenth and early twentieth centuries, Britain had a large and growing current account surplus, while most of the borrowing countries had matching deficits. Europe both borrowed and lent, thus playing an intermediate role (Deane and Cole 1967, 28–38; de Cecco 1974, chap. 1). This pattern persisted up to the turn of the century, when the United States began to move into a very small current account surplus. Beginning with World War I, the continuities disappeared. The war and its destruction in Europe led to an abrupt swing in international income distribution in favor of the United States. A similar shift occurred as a result of World War II (United States 1976, U1–25). In the late 1960s, a third shift began – away from the United States, toward recovering Europe and advancing Japan – although it did not become really significant until a decade later (Block 1977, chaps. 6–7). This long-term change was exacerbated by short-term fluctuations resulting from the oil price increases (Bacha and Diaz-Alejandro 1981).

Modification of Hypotheses

Given the differences outlined above, another look at the British hypotheses is in order to see where they need to be reformulated. The role of politics and economics in motivating capital export is, in many ways, quite similar for Britain and the United States. Despite the differences in institutional structure and the greater economic role of governments, there is little indication that private lending in the United States came under closer governmental control than it did in Britain. The U.S. government did not and could not compel banks to lend as part of a foreign policy stance. Foreign policy initiatives were better aided by public-sector lending agencies, and the proliferation of such agencies after World War II made such a link possible. Therefore, if loans were made, private incentives had to bring them about, just as they had in the British case. Nevertheless, more emphasis needs to be put on the role that the U.S. government did play in creating the context for foreign lending. In particular, large-scale lending meant that the government had to refrain from public loans that could crowd out more expensive private credits and regulations that would hinder private lending. Moreover, some kind of implicit guarantee of government backing might be required in case problems arose. In other words, saying that economic motives were paramount is true but insufficient.

Moving to the specifics of the lending process, more differences emerge. A major example concerns the role of institutions. In the British case, an already highly developed set of institutions underwent no major changes during the principal period of capital export (1870–1914) and did not seem to have a strong effect on the timing of loans. Thus, institutions could generally be said to play a minor role in the process of explaining long-term cyclical trends in capital export. The same was certainly not true for the United States in the twentieth century. The newness of the activity of capital export, and the lack of developed institutions at the beginning of the period, meant that changes in institutions could be expected to play a key explanatory role in the U.S. case. Other differences between the two periods reinforce this expectation. For instance, the greater role of governmental regulation should increase the role of institutional factors. Likewise, the creation of new financial institutions – bilateral aid agencies, multilateral agencies, and especially the Euromarket – suggests a larger role for institutions.

Which of the other factors might be expected to be important? The clearest need for modification concerns the relationship between migration and capital flows. In spite of its apparent relevance in Britain, migration can quickly be ruled out for the U.S.–Latin American case since emigration from the United States to Latin America was almost nonexistent. In net terms, there was a strong inflow of people from Latin America to the United States. There are also good reasons to discount the effect of trade factors in the U.S. case. First, trade represented a very small portion of U.S. gross national product – only 6 to 18 percent for exports plus imports between 1920 and 1980. Second, the close interrelationship between trade and investment that characterized British lending did not exist for the United States; as Brown (1940, 559) said, any such link was "fortuitous." Third, the lack of a trade/investment link, plus the minimal importance of trade, together meant that the key trade variable in the British literature—terms of trade—would be of little relevance in the U.S. case.[20]

Other factors, however, cannot be ruled out a priori. Relative rates of return, as well as factors underlying these rates (such as growth rates in both the United States and Latin America), should be relevant for the United States as well as Britain. Nevertheless, it should be noted that the lesser role of international transactions in the United States might wipe out any sharp trends such as the inverse cycles that Cairncross found for Britain and various borrowing countries in the nineteenth century. Oversaving, by contrast, could be more relevant for the United States than it was for Britain, given the greater fluidity in income distribution both nationally and internationally. Because of the ambiguity noted earlier in the oversaving hypothesis, it will be specifically defined as a shift of income toward high savers that results in slow growth of domestic demand and thus lack of attractive investment opportunities at home.

Finally, there is no reason to think that the cyclical pattern of lending should end, although the change in institutions and the

[20] Discarding the trade variables may be controversial. In the aftermath of both the 1920s and 1970s lending periods, bankers claimed that supporting U.S. exports was a major reason for their loans. See, for example, United States (1932, 1983a, and 1983b). Their after-the-fact testimony, when they were being attacked for neglecting the domestic market, must be viewed with some skepticism, however. Clearly, trade policy has been important in a *negative* way in contributing to the debt crises of the 1930s and 1980s, but the lack of a *positive* link between trade and lending has been a prominent feature of international capital flows since World War I.

increased role of governments should substantially moderate the cycles. In particular, the defaults and "loan revulsion" should be eliminated. Moreover, the precise mechanisms suggested in the literature on financial crises need to be reconsidered. The heavy reliance on psychological factors leading to "euphoria" and "distress" should be supplemented by analysis of competition among bankers. Competition is mentioned in the literature on Britain, but its crucial role needs to be stressed.

A set of modified hypotheses, then, can be stated as follows:

1. U.S. lending to Latin America was motivated by the search for profits on the part of banks rather than being an aspect of U.S. foreign policy. Nevertheless, the government had to provide an adequate political context in order for large-scale lending to occur.

2. Institutional development in the United States was crucial in determining the form in which Latin American demand for foreign capital was met. Specifically, institutional changes, together with political context, determined when portfolio investment would predominate over public-sector loans and direct investment.

3. Large-scale capital export required transfers of income from low to high savers to provide the necessary resources to lending institutions. Whether these transfers were at the national or international level depended on the characteristics of the institutions involved.

4. Relative rates of return were important—either through low or falling rates in the United States encouraging banks to lend abroad or through high rates in Latin America serving as a source of attraction for foreign capital. Moreover, underlying variables, especially growth rates, reinforced the influence of rates of return or played an independent role in stimulating capital export.

5. Once the lending process got under way, due to the

political and economic characteristics described above, heightened expectations and competition among bankers pushed it forward to the point of "financial distress." Whether or not a crisis actually occurred depended on political and institutional factors.

The remainder of the book is devoted to examination of these five hypotheses. They will not be tested in a statistical sense, but they will be rigorously examined in the historical setting of U.S. lending to Latin America in the twentieth century. The changes already made in the hypotheses in the course of this chapter demonstrate that a theory of capital export based on the nineteenth-century British experience cannot simply be adopted for the U.S. case in the twentieth century. Further evaluation of the hypotheses through the empirical material in later chapters will surely produce other changes as well.

Another goal of the empirical research will be to consider the interrelationship among hypotheses rather than leaving them as separate, or even competing, explanations as they are in the literature on Britain. The aim will be to combine the five hypotheses into a unified theory which will show how political, institutional, and economic factors are linked. The resulting theory will be more complex than its predecessors, but the additional complexity should pay off in terms of increased understanding.

Finally, at a more practical level, study of the similarities and differences between U.S. and British lending—and changes within the U.S. period itself—will provide a better basis for understanding and dealing with the crisis that has characterized the international financial system since August 1982. Much of the literature on Britain is embedded in the notion of capital export cycles, and U.S. lending has proceeded in a similar way. If such cycles are to be avoided or at least moderated in the future, we need to know much more about their causes.

2

U.S.–Latin American Financial Relations

A Historical Overview

AT THE CLOSE of the nineteenth century, Great Britain was still the dominant economic power in Latin America. Its dominance could be seen in trade and direct investment as well as finance. Britain was the chief supplier of industrial goods to Latin America and the main purchaser of the region's primary exports. British citizens invested in railroads, public utilities, and mining, and they were the principal holders of Latin America's public debt (Rippy 1959; Platt 1968; Stone 1968, 1977). Furthermore, sterling was the currency of Latin America's international transactions that were financed through bills of exchange drawn on London and facilitated by Britain's vast network of branch banks abroad (Joslin 1963; Jones 1977). These relationships were long standing, stretching back to the time of British participation in Latin America's struggle for independence from Spain and Portugal.

Despite their relative strength, the British did have rivals who became more important in the years after 1870. Both France and

Germany began to export significant amounts of capital to Latin America in the last quarter of the nineteenth century. A large volume of Latin American bonds was floated on the Paris bourse, and some French companies also increased their direct investment activities in the region. The Germans likewise expanded their Latin American activities, particularly in banking (United Nations 1955, 1965; North 1962; Fishlow 1985). Britain's most important rival, however, was the United States. The United States had declared its intention to move into the region as early as 1823 with the proclamation of the Monroe Doctrine in the aftermath of the independence struggles. At the time, the country had neither the economic nor the political strength to back up its statement of intent, but the situation had begun to change by the late 1800s.

This chapter picks up the story at the turn of the century and presents a general overview of the increasing economic role of the United States in Latin America after 1900. Various actors were involved, including direct investors, exporters, and the U.S. government, but the focus here is on the private banks. The banks' activities were neither constant over time nor gradually evolving but assumed a cyclical pattern marked by sharp institutional changes. In many ways, the two U.S. banking cycles constituted a continuation of British lending history in the nineteenth century, but as we shall see there were also significant differences.

The chapter focuses on three main issues. First, the characteristics of the cyclical pattern of banking activities are identified. The relative importance of various kinds of capital export, as well as the cyclical pattern, are summarized in Figure 1. Second, the institutional changes in portfolio investment–especially the shift from bond issues to commercial bank credits–are highlighted. Third, the relationships between the banks and other U.S. actors are examined to see if the banks were initiators or followers. This chapter concentrates on developing a qualitative

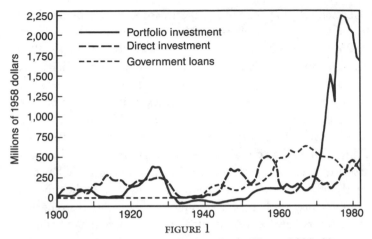

FIGURE 1

U.S. Capital Export to Latin America by Types: 1900–82
(Five-Year Moving Averages)

source: Appendix I.

description of trends in the eighty-five-year history of U.S. lending to Latin America. Chapter 3 then adds extensive quantitative data to provide greater specificity on the trends that have been identified.

Throughout the book, portfolio investment is defined to include bond issues and bank credits, both over one-year maturity. Investment is measured net, which is defined as U.S. investment minus amortization. Direct investment is that made by a company in which citizens of the lending country own more than 10 percent of equity. For further details on definitions, see Chapter 3 and Appendix I.

The Transition Period in International Finance: 1897–1919

The years up through World War I witnessed most of the initial steps necessary to prepare the way for the emergence of the

United States as the major financial power in Latin America. U.S. banks began to displace their British rivals in terms of loans to governments and corporations in the region, although these activities were basically limited to areas near the U.S. borders. In South America, the banks took the first steps toward the formation of a branch banking network to support U.S. exporters and direct investors, and of course to increase their own profits at the same time. Perhaps most important, the United States had set up a central bank that strengthened the domestic banking system and gave institutional support to the new movement to expand abroad. In this early period, the activities of U.S. banks were closely linked with those of other U.S. economic and political actors. The initiative for expansion abroad often came from direct investors, exporters, and government officials who seemed to have a clearer vision than the bankers of the potential in Latin America.

As was logical in terms of proximity, the initial U.S. ventures in Latin America were in Mexico and the Caribbean area including Central America. The earliest types of economic activity there involved direct investment and trade. U.S. companies built railroads in Mexico and Central America and established plantations to raise fruit and sugarcane in Central America and the Caribbean. Mining, including petroleum, was also important in Mexico as well as Chile and Peru (Lewis 1938; Wilkins 1970, chaps. 6–7, 9). As direct investment increased, so did U.S. government activity. Government support for U.S. oil interests in Mexico has been well documented, as has intervention in various Caribbean countries including Cuba, Haiti, the Dominican Republic, and Nicaragua (Nearing and Freeman 1925; Munro 1964). Later we shall examine the significance of these activities.

At the same time, important changes were occurring in U.S. production and therefore trade. Up until the late nineteenth century, the United States had been an exporter of raw materials and an importer of industrial goods, but as industrialization progressed, the pattern began to shift. By 1897 more than half of U.S. exports were industrial goods (United States 1976, U213–24). Furthermore, industrial capacity in general seemed to be growing faster than the domestic market, so businessmen were looking abroad for markets. Latin America and the Far East were seen as the best possibilities (Williams 1959, 32–35; LaFeber 1963, chap. 4; MacKaman 1977, chaps. 2–3). It was through trade links, then, that the United States first reached into South America. The early investments in that continent were largely in the establishment of sales operations (Lewis 1938, 575–607). Both the direct investment with its political links in Mexico and the Caribbean, and the trade expansion in South America, led to involvement by U.S. banks.

In the case of Mexico and the Caribbean, the banks became active in two ways. On the one hand, U.S. investment banks floated bonds and sold stock to raise capital for investment abroad by American companies. The earliest such issue appears to have been in 1897 for a U.S. firm investing in Mexican railroads. Between that year and 1919, some 118 issues were floated by a variety of banking houses of which the most important were J. P. Morgan, Kuhn Loeb, Brown Brothers, J. and W. Seligman, and Lee Higginson. The main borrowers were U.S. railway construction companies in Mexico, U.S. sugar companies in Cuba, the United Fruit Company with holdings throughout Central America and the Caribbean, and a few U.S. mining and petroleum companies in Mexico and elsewhere (Dickens 1933, 205–34; United States 1930a, 58–74). On the other hand, the banks were also involved in floating bonds for governments in these same areas. Mexico was the largest borrower, and the central government, several state governments, and the National Railways of Mexico were all in the market (ibid).

The phenomenon of government/bank relations in the Caribbean is usually referred to as "dollar diplomacy." The case of the Dominican Republic was quite typical of the process. In 1907 the U.S. Senate approved a treaty between the two countries that provided for the issuance of $20 million in bonds to pay the Dominican Republic's public debt and the collection of its customs revenues by a U.S. government appointee in order to guarantee the servicing and repayment of the debt. Following up on these financial manipulations by President Roosevelt, his successors (Taft and Wilson) ordered direct military intervention—ranging from the dispatch of several hundred Marines to full-scale military control beginning in 1916—to protect American financial and "security" interests. Meanwhile, the military government floated bonds through U.S. banks in the name of the Dominican Republic. Military control ended in 1924 when the Dominicans agreed to ratify a treaty providing for U.S. control of customs, treasury, army, and police (Nearing and Freeman 1925, 124–33).

The other way in which bankers became involved in Latin America was through the expansion of U.S. trade and direct investment. U.S. trade had traditionally been conducted using sterling as the currency of transaction with British banks as intermediaries. As long as the United States was mainly exporting primary products, and thus not in competition with Britain, this system was acceptable to all parties. Once the export of manufactured goods began, however, the use of British banks was called into question, and U.S. exporters began to push for the country's own banks to provide trade finance.

From the exporters' point of view, as Phelps (1927, chap. 4) explains, there would be several advantages to the entry of U.S. banks into the Latin American market. First, U.S. exporters suspected that the British banks were passing information about their activities to their British competitors; the only way to avoid this practice would be to use U.S. banks. Second, many British loans were formally or informally tied to the use of British equipment; by acquiring U.S. finance, the exporters thought they could gain additional customers. Third, banks have traditionally served as providers of information for their clients, and American banks were considered to be more reliable for this task. The exporters thus undertook a campaign to persuade the banks to move into Latin America and other areas being penetrated by U.S. industrial exports. As allies they enlisted the U.S. government.[1]

At the same time, many U.S. firms with direct investments were also trying to lure the U.S. banks into Latin America. Such companies as U.S. Steel, Du Pont, W. R. Grace, International Harvester, Armour, and Standard Oil offered U.S. bankers substantial amounts of business if they would establish branches in the region. These corporations wanted the banks to finance their foreign inventories, provide local credit, transfer money, and supply other services that had previously been provided by British banks (Cleveland and Huertas 1985, 76–78).

There were two obstacles to these plans. First, nationally chartered banks in the United States, generally the largest banks, were prohibited by law from establishing branches abroad. Second, the bankers themselves were rather hestitant to engage in what they considered to be a highly risky venture (Mayer 1968, chap. 4). Both of these obstacles were removed in large part through the efforts of the National City Bank, which was to become the world's premier international bank. Under the leadership of Frank Vanderlip, National City Bank became an aggressive institution. It was the largest commercial bank in the

[1] Key U.S. political and economic officials – including Presidents Roosevelt, Taft, and Wilson – saw expansion of U.S. trade as a top priority in the early twentieth century. Branch banking was considered to be essential for trade. For a summary of these views and government activities to promote trade and banking, see Mayer (1968, chaps. 3–4).

United States but was nevertheless very much in the shadow of the investment bank of J. P. Morgan. The House of Morgan was the unofficial central bank of the United States and also the representative of most European governments in New York and Washington; in addition Morgan had the lion's share of major U.S. corporations among its clients (Corey 1930; Parrini 1969). National City was thus fenced in. It could not make much headway in gaining new corporate clients; it could not move into other states because of U.S. laws against out-of-state banking; and it could not break into the European market. If the bank was to grow, the only solution seemed to be a move into international areas where Morgan was not already entrenched.[2] Latin America, together with Asia, provided the key to this strategy (Mayer 1968, 30).

Like other major New York bankers, Vanderlip had long been a proponent of the establishment of a central bank for the United States. These bankers saw the need for greater stability through central control of currency issue and a lender of last resort (Kolko 1963, 150–58, 181–89). Furthermore, if U.S. banks were to be viable in trade finance, there had to be a central bank to discount acceptances. During a secret weekend on Jeckyl Island, Georgia, the bankers drew up a plan for a central bank that was presented to the U.S. Congress by Senator Nelson Aldrich (Vanderlip 1935, chap. 21). After extensive changes in the initial proposal, the Federal Reserve legislation eventually emerged (Kolko 1963, 217–54).[3] One of its clauses gave U.S.

[2] The recent inside history of Citibank (Cleveland and Huertas 1985) puts a greater stress than do other authors on the cooperative ventures between National City Bank and Morgan. For example, compare Cleveland and Huertas with Parrini (1969).

[3] Kolko reports that the banking community was divided in its opinions about the Glass Bill, which eventually became the Federal Reserve Act. The major New York bankers, especially Vanderlip, preferred the Aldrich Plan which they had written, but most preferred the Glass Bill to no legislation at all.

banks the right to establish branches abroad. Vanderlip had been pushing for this measure and preparing for it for some time. He had decided on Argentina as the site for National City's first branch, which was opened in November 1914, less than a year after President Wilson signed the Federal Reserve Act into law (Mayer 1968, chap. 5; Cleveland and Huertas 1985, chap. 5).

The British and German preoccupation with the war in Europe made this a highly propitious time for U.S. banks to expand into Latin America. National City Bank, having initiated the branching drive, continued to maintain the lead. As of 1919 it had forty-two branches in nine Latin American countries (Phelps 1927, 142–49). The only other commercial bank to establish a branch of its own during the war was First National Bank of Boston, which opened an office in Buenos Aires in 1917. National City's main competition came from two banking corporations that were jointly founded by a number of investment banks, commercial banks, and trust companies.[4]

One banking corporation was the Mercantile Bank of the Americas, which was organized in 1915 with Brown Brothers, J. and W. Seligman, and Guaranty Trust as the major owners. The main function of the Mercantile Bank was to promote trade; in order to do so, it established a number of affiliated corporations. The first was opened in 1916 in Peru with six local offices, and affiliates in seven other countries soon followed. The other banking corporation was the American and Foreign Bank-

[4] The two banking corporations are said to have been established under the regulations of the Edge Act, an amendment to the Federal Reserve Act that made banks exempt from U.S. antitrust legislation for the purpose of forming cartels for activities outside the country (Parrini 1969, chap. 4). In fact, the two were set up under state legislation before the Edge Act was passed in December 1919. Although the Edge Act was expected to be an important instrument in promoting international banking activities, it never had much effect.

ing Corporation (AFBC), organized in 1917, under the leadership of Chase National Bank. During 1919 and 1920, AFBC established seventeen foreign branches and acquired two others; the majority were in Latin America (ibid., 154–57). By 1920 there were ninety-nine branches of U.S. banking institutions in Latin America, providing a firm basis for the lending boom of the next decade.

The First Lending Boom: 1920–30

If U.S. bankers had been relatively timid about setting up a branch network in Latin America, the same was not true with respect to lending to the region. Furthermore, the very process of establishing branches gave them greater familiarity with Latin America and thus more confidence in making loans. Once the U.S. government's wartime lending ended, the banks moved in rapid fashion to displace their British rivals in underwriting bond issues for Latin American governments. Far from having to encourage them, the U.S. government made some weak attempts to limit lending through regulation. Despite a potential complementarity between loans, trade, and direct investment, the bankers resisted any effort directly to link the various activities, preferring to go their own way in the highly profitable venture. Competition among the banks drove the process forward until the defaults of the 1930s brought it to a sudden halt.

World War I brought a historic shift in international economic and political relations. The trend toward greater U.S. importance had been clear previously as the gap between Britain and the United States narrowed, but Germany had been catching up too. It was the war that pushed the United States out in front as demand for its products rose rapidly. The trade surplus went from an average of $230 million in the three years before the war to an average of $3.13 billion between 1915 and 1919 (Appendix II). U.S. business and government leaders believed that if the country wanted to maintain productive capacity at the level achieved during the war, it would have to maintain its merchandise exports. Since there was strong opposition to increased imports,[5] foreign loans were seen as the essential means to provide finance (MacKaman 1977, chaps. 2–3). Little concern was evidenced about the implications of this combination on borrowers' capacity to service the resulting debt.

Despite a general consensus about the need for trade and lending, disagreement arose over the precise nature of the relationship. Exporters wanted the connection formalized through loan contracts that would require borrowers to spend at least 20 percent of the proceeds on U.S. goods, a practice they claimed was similar to that prevailing in Britain. Herbert Hoover, then secretary of commerce, favored a weaker clause to guarantee U.S. firms equal opportunities in bidding for contracts and supplying materials under such loans. The bankers, although acknowledging the importance of loans for trade, opposed specific restrictions on their activities (Parrini 1969, chap. 7; Wilson 1971, chap. 4). In the absence of any agreement, the bankers' view prevailed, and the various U.S. economic activities went forward in a parallel but uncoordinated fashion.

The year 1920, the peak of the expansion drive, witnessed the largest number of branches to exist until the 1960s. Several problems arose for the infant banking industry in Latin America in the early 1920s. First was the return of Britain, and to a lesser extent Germany, to Latin American banking; this competition

[5] Tariff policy during the 1920s was highly controversial and divided the business community between protectionists and internationalists. The leading bankers generally favored the internationalist position of low tariffs as did the major exporters. On the tariff debates, see Parrini (1969, chap. 7) and Wilson (1971, chap. 3).

put considerable pressure on the new institutions (Parrini 1969, chap. 7). Second was the postwar economic crisis. This was especially difficult for the Mercantile Bank, since the drop in commodity prices made it impossible for many of its customers to meet their obligations, and the corporation was disbanded in 1921. It was reorganized on a more modest scale the following year as the Bank of Central and South America. In spite of new capital and some important new partners, including J. P. Morgan and several New York commercial banks, the corporation failed and was sold to the Royal Bank of Canada in 1925 (Phelps 1927, 158–60). The American and Foreign Banking Corporation also fell before the increasing competition and economic difficulties in the early 1920s and closed all its Latin American offices except the two in Panama and the one in Cuba. These were acquired by Chase National Bank to begin its own branch network (ibid., 157). A third problem confronting the new branches was the lack of trained personnel. It was this factor, together with economic problems, that led to a cutback in National City Bank's growing branch system. Between 1920 and 1924, it closed fourteen of its fifty branches though still maintaining its presence in all major countries except Colombia (Citicorp Annual Report, various years). In the case of National City Bank (NCB), the retrenchment of the early 1920s was only that. Unlike its competitors, it survived these difficulties and went on to enlarge its network during the latter half of the decade. Figure 2 shows the number of U.S. bank branches in operation during the 1914–30 period.

The problems with branch banking did not dampen enthusiasm for the main activity of the U.S. banks during the 1920–30 period—the flotation of securities issues. Although there were clear connections between new securities issues and the U.S. trade position, on the one hand, and direct investment expansion, on the other, lending was nevertheless an autonomous

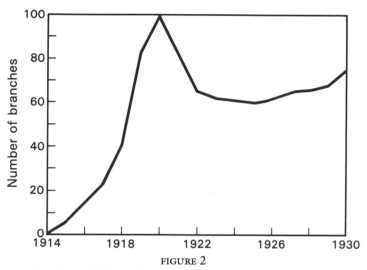

FIGURE 2

Number of U.S. Bank Branches in Latin America: 1914–30

SOURCE: Phelps (1927, chap. 9); Citicorp, *Annual Report*.

activity of the banks. If they had to be pushed into branching abroad, providing loans was something with which they were familiar and in which they were eager to get involved.

Corporate securities, providing funds for direct investment, continued to be issued for the Latin American region. Direct investment as a whole almost doubled, rising from $2.0 billion in 1919 to $3.7 billion in 1929. The main growth area was South America, where direct investment rose by more than 160 percent. In Mexico, which was recuperating from the 1910 revolution, investment increased by only around 10 percent. The Caribbean and Central America fell in between with a growth in investment of 88 percent. This average masks a very high growth rate in Cuba, the only country that could compete with the attractions of South America (Lewis 1938, 575–607).

In the Caribbean area, the banks themselves sometimes became direct investors. In Haiti, for example, National City Bank owned the main railroad as well as the national bank (Nearing and Freeman 1925, 133–51; Mayer 1968, 186–89). In Cuba, after the price of sugar plummeted in 1920, the banks took over many of the sugar companies when they could not meet payments on their loans (Jenks 1928, 281–88; Smith 1960, 29–33; Cleveland and Huertas 1985, 104–12). By sector, the highest growth area for U.S. foreign investment was public utilities, mostly accounted for by a large influx of capital into South America in the last half of the 1920s. Other high-growth areas were petroleum and manufacturing, although the latter still represented only a small fraction (7.5 percent) of all U.S. investment in Latin America (Lewis 1938, 575–607).

Perhaps surprisingly, the bond issues for the U.S. corporations investing in Latin America followed a somewhat different pattern than direct investment as a whole. Public utilities was the sector where the largest volume of securities was issued (about 40 percent). The next largest sectors, however, were agriculture (30 percent) and mining (23 percent). Petroleum and manufacturing lagged far behind, representing only 6 and 2 percent respectively of total corporate issues. Presumably the small share of bond finance going to petroleum and manufacturing indicates that investment in these sectors was largely being financed by retained earnings or private capital. The principal corporations that floated issues on the U.S. stock exchange for use in Latin America were copper companies operating in Chile, sugar companies in Cuba, and a few utility companies in Central America and the Caribbean. Throughout the period, small issues were floated for petroleum companies operating in Mexico, Venezuela, and Colombia, and, at the end of the 1920s, there were several large issues for utility companies in Argentina, Brazil, and Chile (United States 1930a, 58–137).

The boom area in foreign securities, however, was not corporate securities but government bonds. Latin America was no exception to this overall trend. Government bonds represented more than two-thirds of all issues floated for Latin America during the 1920–30 period. The history of the government issues during the 1920s was a varied one – depending on the year, the bank, and the borrowing country – but the general tendency was for bankers to encourage borrowers to take out larger loans than they could absorb and service (United States 1932). When export revenues fell in the 1930s, the consequence was massive default and the end of Latin America's access to the U.S. capital markets for more than a generation – a pattern of boom and bust similar to Latin America's history on the London market in the nineteenth century.

Lending to Latin American governments in the 1920–30 period can be broken down into two subperiods. The 1920–24 years saw a relatively low volume of bonds floated, compared to what would come later. The U.S. public – or rather the small portion of it that purchased securities – was not accustomed to foreign bonds and needed to be "educated" in the words of government and bank officials. This was especially true for Latin American issues. Around $400 million of Latin American government bonds were issued in New York in this half decade compared to $1.1 billion between 1925 and 1930. The Latin American increase occurred at the same time that the volume of western European government bonds was declining rapidly and Canadian issues were dropping slightly. Thus, Latin America moved from 16.6 percent of total government loans in the first half of the decade to 48.8 percent in the second (Appendix V).

More important than the difference in volume was the difference in process involved during the first and second halves of the decade. In the first half, the "normal" lending process still prevailed, whereby a potential borrower would present a loan proposal to a banking house which would then decide whether or not it was interested in the project. In many cases, the borrower was turned down. If the loan was accepted, the bankers then had to persuade the public to buy the bonds (United States 1932, 618). One banker explained it in the following way:

> It was a most difficult business because many people in our country did not know where [various foreign countries] were. We published books with pictures . . . we had a regular campaign in order to let the public know the circumstances. We got some men to make speeches and to explain to the people what the purpose of the loan was. It was quite a campaign. (ibid., 616)

In part because of these difficulties, only the most respected financial institutions were involved in these early loans (Appendix V).

In the second half of the decade, the process changed dramatically. Rather than sitting in their imposing New York offices, waiting for clients to call on them, bankers traveled around the world soliciting borrowers. No longer was it necessary to educate the U.S. public on the value of foreign bonds. As U.S. interest rates steadily declined, more and more people wanted to buy foreign issues with their higher yields. (Other explanations are discussed in later chapters.)

Competition among the banks reached unprecedented levels. At one point, for example, there were representatives of twenty-nine U.S. banks in Colombia alone trying to negotiate loans with various government agencies (United States 1932, 845–46). The bankers paid agents who could bring them business. In Peru one such agent was the son of the president of the republic; he was later convicted in a Peruvian court for "illegal enrichment." Similarly, the son-in-law of the president of Cuba was employed in the local branch of an American bank while that bank was successfully competing for Cuban loan business (ibid., 1279–80, 1949–57). Banks went against the advice of their own representatives on the soundness of potential loans

and against the advice of knowledgeable people in the borrowing
countries themselves. They claimed they were competing for
loans to satisfy "the appetite on the part of the American public
to buy foreign loans" (ibid., 1321), but they were also feeding
that "appetite" by withholding information on the true level of
risk involved (United States 1933, 2051–2124; United States
1934, 124–50).

What role did the U.S. government play in this process? The
best description of its position was passivity. The State Department was clearly interested in getting U.S. banks into Latin
America as a way of eliminating potential European influence,
but it did not want to guarantee bank loans against political risk.
Its policy was a compromise that required bankers to inform the
government of loans that were being considered so that those
thought to be against the national interest could be vetoed (Feis
1950; Tulchin 1971, chap. 5; MacKaman 1977, chaps. 4–9). At
the Commerce Department, Herbert Hoover wanted the government to take a stronger role, trying to ensure that loans were
made only for productive purposes.[6] Although this infighting
left the bankers confused about government policy, by late 1922
it became clear that there would be little interference except
where countries owed money to the U.S. Treasury or had expro-
priated property of U.S. citizens (Parrini 1969, 189–90; Wilson
1971, 105–8).

In general, the U.S. government pulled back from dollar
diplomacy in the 1920s, but a special situation existed with
respect to Mexico and Central America. Mexico had been the
largest Latin American borrower in New York before the 1910
revolution, and for several years thereafter it continued to float

[6] Hoover's proposals actually went further than mere concern with
productive use. He wanted the U.S. government to rule on the economic viability of proposed loans as well as their political acceptability,
but he was unable to persuade the State and Treasury Departments to
accept his plan.

bonds in the U.S. market. By 1913, however, President Wilson embarked on a collision course with the new government, and a financial blockade was imposed. Recognition was withheld until 1923, and hostilities continued even afterward because of expropriations of U.S. property and lack of receptivity toward foreign investment. The bankers were more conciliatory, agreeing to make new loans to the Mexican government if it would resume payments to bondholders. An International Committee of Bankers on Mexico was formed to negotiate, but little was accomplished, in part because of U.S. government hostility (Turlington 1930, chaps. 7–8; Smith 1972; MacKaman 1977, chap. 13).

In Central America, long considered an area of special interest to the United States, the government maintained its policy of dollar diplomacy. As the war ended, the State Department proposed a plan whereby the U.S. government would guarantee bonds floated by U.S. banks in order to refinance Central America's European loans. This plan would "place the control of the financial affairs of the Western Hemisphere in the hands of the American government" and thus eliminate the "distressing complications" of the past (quoted in Tulchin 1971, 156–57). The Treasury Department vetoed the proposal, but the United States nevertheless gained control over several countries' financial affairs via military occupation of Cuba, Nicaragua, Haiti, and the Dominican Republic. The bankers profited from the occupations by floating bonds under implicit U.S. guarantee. Such politically linked loans, however, were only a small portion of the total during the 1920s.

Default and the Private Bank Retreat: 1931–54

The defaults of 1931–32 brought a virtual end to the bond underwriting activities of U.S. banks in Latin America. Individual investors – the ultimate purchasers of the bonds – were highly disillusioned even though settlements of the defaults were eventually reached, and their disillusionment was increased by the U.S. government's refusal to take more than minimal steps to help. Likewise, the banks' branch network shrank as the industry cut its foreign ties. Other types of capital flow were also negative throughout the Depression, but direct investment and government loans picked up during the war and immediate postwar period although U.S. concern about Europe limited the amount of foreign capital available to Latin America.

In 1930 depression came to Latin America as to most other parts of the world. Exports fell by 65 percent between 1928 and 1932 (Appendix III), and economic growth fell with them.[7] The trade problem was exacerbated by the sudden end to foreign lending, and the combined effect meant that Latin American governments had great difficulty in servicing their foreign debts. Most decided that their scarce foreign exchange reserves should be husbanded for imports and thus informed creditors in Europe and the United States that they were suspending interest and sinking fund payments (Thorp 1984). In January 1931 Bolivia defaulted on its loans and was followed later that year by Brazil, Chile, the Dominican Republic, and Peru. In 1932–33 defaults were declared by Colombia, Uruguay, various Central American countries, and the state and municipal borrowers in Argentina. Thus, by the end of 1933 every Latin American country that had borrowed was in default except Haiti, although Argentina and some Central American and Caribbean countries maintained partial debt service (Foreign Bondholders'

[7] Precise data on declining economic growth rates cannot be provided since GDP was not calculated for most Latin American countries until after World War II. In Brazil and Argentina, for which GDP data are available, the fall was 31.5 and 22.8 percent respectively between 1929 and 1932; see Appendix IV.

Protective Council 1936; Winkler 1933; Madden et al. 1937, chaps. 6–14; Mintz 1951, chap. 2; United Nations 1955).

The logical response by U.S. investors was to stop all new loans, although it is unlikely that many would have been forthcoming in any case, given the disorder of the financial system. Stock prices plummeted and many investment banks, as well as individual investors, went into bankruptcy. Trade too declined sharply–total U.S. exports fell by 69 percent between 1929 and 1932–which probably had the effect of dampening demand for loans (Kindleberger 1973, chaps. 5–6; Chandler 1970, chap. 5).

The most tempestuous aspect of U.S.–Latin American economic relations during this period involved the banks. On the one hand, the branch network was cut back substantially. From seventy-seven branches in Latin America in 1930, the number dropped to a low of forty in 1945 before beginning a slow turnaround (*Bankers' Almanac and Yearbook,* various years). On the other hand, the value of U.S. bond holdings collapsed as borrowers defaulted. Table 1 shows that loans of $1.6 billion out of a total of $1.9 billion were in default as of December 31, 1935. It also shows the variation by debtor country.[8]

The U.S. government's reaction to the defaults was less supportive than bondholders would have liked. In 1932 Secretary of State Stimson denied any government responsibility.

---

[8] Defaults on Latin American bonds were the highest of any region except eastern Europe. Calculation of a "default index" (ratio of defaulted loans to all loans) shows that western Europe and the Far East defaulted on no bonds, Canada on 4.1 percent, Latin America on 71.8 percent, and eastern Europe on 88.4 percent. The international average was 35.3 percent. The default index also showed a difference between bonds issued in the first and second halves of the decade. The overall index for 1920–24 was 17.5 percent compared to 49.5 percent in 1925–29. Latin America's index for 1920–24 bonds was 55.2 percent, whereas its 1925–29 index was 79.4 (Mintz 1951, chap. 2).

TABLE 1

Outstanding Publicly Offered Latin American Foreign Dollar Bonds: 1935, 1945, and 1952
(millions of dollars)

Country	Principal Outstanding[a]			Amount in Default[b]		
	1935	1945	1952	1935	1945	1952
Argentina	$351.2	$183.8	–	$ 95.9	$ 0.8	–
Bolivia	59.4	59.4	$ 59.4	59.4	59.4	$ 59.4
Brazil	349.2	217.4	128.5	349.2	69.8	8.0
Chile	308.0	170.2	115.9	308.0	150.6	9.1
Colombia	156.1	148.7	74.2	156.1	105.8	6.4
Costa Rica	8.8	8.1	8.1	8.8	8.1	8.1
Cuba	123.8	97.1	69.6	103.2	9.4	7.1
Dominican Republic	16.3	12.1	–	16.3	4.3	–
El Salvador	12.6	8.8	5.9	12.6	8.5	0.3
Guatemala	2.2	–	–	2.2	–	–
Haiti	9.8	6.7	–	–	6.7	–
Mexico	295.5	273.6	200.3	295.5	238.6	11.1
Panama	18.6	15.8	–	14.4	1.1	–
Peru	91.3	85.7	64.5	91.3	85.7	17.0
Uruguay	63.4	49.7	40.0	63.4	1.7	0.6
TOTAL	1,866.3	1,337.1	766.7	1,576.4	750.5	127.2

SOURCE: United Nations (1955, 157).

a Nominal value.

The Department of State has not passed on the security or the merits of foreign loans . . . and the public has been made to understand that the department's action carried no implications as to government approval of loans. In fact, it may be said that no foreign loan has ever been made which purported to have the approval of the American government as to the intrinsic value of the loan. (cited in Winkler 1933, 163)

A standard reply to bondholders who asked for help was to say that "our historic policy has been one of noninterference in transactions between private citizens and foreign governments" (Wilson 1971, 181). At the same time, the government did provide help to large commercial firms that had their credit lines frozen in various Latin American countries. The main reason was the government's view that trade with Latin America was the key to the recovery of the entire export trade of the United States. A major priority of the New Deal was thus to devise new tactics to stimulate exports (ibid., 182–83). One such tactic was the establishment of the Export-Import Bank, of which more will be said later. The main effort to help bondholders was the formation in 1933 of the Foreign Bondholders' Protective Council, a quasi-official organization to help in negotiations with debtor countries.[9] It was through the intermediation of the council that agreements were eventually made on resumption of payments.

Three basic forms of agreement can be identified. First, the three countries that had maintained at least partial debt service (Argentina, Haiti, and the Dominican Republic) gradually eliminated their debt by amortization at par or close to it. Second,

[9] The council was patterned after the British Corporation of Foreign Bondholders. It was authorized as part of the Securities Act of 1933, whose relevant provisions are reprinted in Winkler (1933, 173–78). Beginning in 1934, the council issued an annual report that discussed its own activities and provided data on all countries with defaulted bond issues.

most countries that had suspended debt service (Bolivia, Chile, Colombia, Costa Rica, Cuba, El Salvador, Guatemala, Panama, Peru, and Uruguay) offered settlements calling for interest rate reductions and longer maturities but no change in the amount of principal due. In addition to the provisions just outlined, some of these countries repurchased their bonds on the open market at well below par. Third, Mexico and Brazil asked for reductions in interest rates *and* amount of principal. Mexico proposed a reduction of 80 percent in principal. Brazil offered two alternative plans. One provided for a reduction in principal with partial cash payment, while the other called for a lowering of interest rates and extension of maturity with principal maintained (Foreign Bondholders' Protective Council, various years; United Nations 1965, 30).

As a result of the resumption of service payments plus substantial repurchase of bonds on the open market, the amount of dollar bonds outstanding fell throughout the period. As Table 1 indicates, the total declined from $1.9 billion in 1935 to $1.3 billion in 1945 and then dropped sharply to $767 million by 1952. These amounts represent nominal totals (that is, the face value of the bonds); the actual market value was only about half these amounts.[10] The amount in default dropped much more rapidly than amounts outstanding, going from $1.6 billion in 1935 to $751 million in 1945 to $127 million in 1952. The other side of the drop in outstanding bond issues was a capital *inflow* from Latin America to the United States during the entire period.[11]

[10] The estimate of market value is an average for Latin America for the year 1951 as reported in United Nations (1955, 157). It was undoubtedly lower in earlier years and was lower for those countries that were still in default even in 1951.

[11] In the fifteen years after World War II, bond transactions provided an annual average capital flow *from* Latin America *to* the United

Apart from the formation of the Foreign Bondholders' Protective Council, the main U.S. government initiative during the 1930s with respect to international finance was to try to regulate the behavior of the banks. The opinion was widespread, especially in the Congress, that the bankers had acted irresponsibly in the way they issued foreign bonds. Testimony in Senate hearings certainly seemed to support this view (United States 1932, 1933). The solutions proposed were of three types. First, the structure of the banking system was changed through the Banking Act of 1933 (the Glass–Steagall Act), which prohibited a firm from engaging in both commercial and investment banking. Second, the process of issuing securities was changed so that certain types of information had to be presented to the Securities and Exchange Commission before a security could be listed on a stock exchange (Carosso 1970, chaps. 17–18). Third, the percentage of foreign securities that institutional investors could hold in their portfolio was limited (Diaz-Alejandro 1976, 195). A fourth provision – from which Latin America was exempted – was the Johnson Act, which prohibited loans to countries in default to the U.S. government (Wilson 1971, 294).

These regulations, even though many of them were not directly aimed at foreign securities, had the effect of limiting the possibilities of foreign securities being issued in the U.S. market. This was especially true for Latin America and other Third World countries for whom the added cost of meeting the disclosure requirements was great.[12] This fact, together with the perception that huge losses had been incurred on Latin Ameri-

---

States of about $37 million. This figure represented $14 million from amortization over new bond issues and $23 billion from purchase of outstanding securities. Calculated from *Survey of Current Business* (June issues).

[12] For the Latin American view on these problems, see Organization of American States (1973).

can bonds,[13] has prevented Latin American countries from regaining large-scale access to the U.S. bond market to this day.

Like portfolio investment, direct investment also declined during the Depression but by a fairly moderate amount. The book value of direct investment fell steadily from $3.5 billion in 1929 to $2.7 billion in 1940. The decline ended during the war, however, and the total even began to edge up slightly (Appendix I). The movement of direct investment was influenced by Latin American governments' attempts to exercise strict control over their economies. Taxes, labor legislation, tariffs, and limits on profit remittance all had their effect, although they were often contradictory in direction. Little new money came in, but earnings that could not be sent home were reinvested. At the same time, some investments were written off or their value written down (United Nations 1965, 33–34; Thorp 1984).

In the early postwar period, direct investment grew further. This was one area where Latin America managed to profit by the lull in Europe while direct investors waited for government-financed reconstruction to produce a propitious investment climate. Other than Canada, Latin America was the largest recipient of direct investment between 1946 and 1955 as book value of investments rose from $3.0 to $6.4 billion. The largest Latin American investment sites were Brazil and Venezuela fol-

[13] The perceptions of large losses on the 1920s bonds have been crucial in terms of Latin American access to the U.S. capital markets, but they are not necessarily correct. Calculations have been made for the various regions as of December 31, 1935 (that is, *not* including any of the later repayments). Taking into account the market value of the bonds (especially low in 1935) and previous payments of interest and principal, the total loss was $58 million out of $1.9 billion or about 3 percent. These losses were clearly eliminated by later repayment agreements, although some individuals may have sold their bonds at a loss before the agreements were made. See Madden et al. (1937, 138–65).

lowed by Mexico and Chile. This country division reflected the sectors where investment was heaviest – mining/petroleum and manufacturing (Mikesell 1962c, 55; United Nations 1965, 213–15).

The other large source of foreign capital for Latin America in this period came from the Export-Import Bank, the organization founded by the U.S. government in 1934 to stimulate trade (Elsasser 1954; Adams 1968). Although Latin America had been the major Exim client during the bank's initial years, its share of loans dropped sharply during the 1946–50 concentration on Europe. During this period, more than 70 percent of all Exim loans went to Europe while Latin America had to settle for a mere 14 percent. (The absolute amounts going to Latin America nevertheless more than doubled in constant dollars.) The 1950s then saw another turnabout such that Latin America again accounted for about half of Exim loans (Mikesell 1962a, 288).

Although all government lending in the postwar period was strongly motivated by the desire to maintain U.S. exports at high levels, and thus stimulate U.S. domestic economic activity, Exim loans had an especially close relationship to trade. In general, Exim credits were given only for the purchase of U.S. goods for specific projects, but some exceptions were made in the late 1950s when the bank provided a number of general-purpose loans to Latin America (Mikesell 1962b, 472–74). Other than Exim loans, Latin America received very little government money during these years. The economic focus was on Europe, where the Marshall Plan and the Mutual Security Act were channeling large amounts of capital (Price 1955; Block 1977, chap. 4). U.S. interest in Latin America was centered on political relationships in terms of the Cold War.

Nonbank Capital Flows: 1955–69

By the mid-1950s, the U.S. preoccupation with Europe had diminished since the reconstruction process was well under way, and a new set of priorities gave Latin America increased access to U.S. capital. Measured in constant dollars, total U.S. capital flows to Latin America between 1955 and 1969 more than tripled with respect to the previous fifteen years as direct investors and the U.S. government poured funds into the region. Other public lenders—the multilateral agencies—also became important actors. Portfolio investment, by contrast, continued to languish, apparently doomed to play an increasingly irrelevant role in Latin American finance. Under the surface, however, processes were in motion that would soon catapult the private capital markets to a position of prominence overshadowing even their role in the 1920s, although the institutional framework would be quite different from the earlier period.

U.S. corporations had been increasing their investments in Latin America throughout the postwar period, but the trend accelerated after the mid-1950s. A particularly large amount was invested during the latter half of the decade due to special circumstances, especially the Suez Canal crisis. The crisis led to increased petroleum investment in Latin America, spurred on by new investment policies in Venezuela, the region's major oil exporter. During the period 1956–60, petroleum and mining accounted for 55 percent of new U.S. investment (including reinvested earnings), while manufacturing was second with 23 percent. Venezuela and Brazil continued to receive more than half of these investments and Mexico was in third place (United Nations 1965, 213–15).

In contrast to the late 1950s, the early 1960s saw a drop-off in investment as businessmen reacted to the nationalizations in Cuba and fears about possible repetitions elsewhere in the hemisphere (Levinson and de Onis 1970, 71–73).[14] In specific terms, Venezuela and Brazil, the two major sites for direct investment in the 1950s, were both seen as problematic. Venezuela had a new democratically elected government that, while favorable to capitalist development, nevertheless tried to regulate the behavior of foreign investors. Compared to the military dictatorship of the previous decade, the atmosphere probably appeared cool and contributed to the large investment outflow from Venezuela during the early 1960s (Tugwell 1975). Brazil also seemed less than desirable as an investment site in this period as the Quadros, and especially the Goulart, regimes moved to the left (Skidmore 1967). There were some reinvested earnings in Brazil but very little new capital inflow. Argentina and Mexico thus became the two largest recipients of direct investment.

In the second half of the decade, direct investment picked up as political conditions appeared more favorable. Country distribution was more diverse. Mexico and Brazil were the largest recipients, followed by Peru and Argentina. Venezuela continued to have a net investment outflow, but it was much smaller than during the first half of the decade. Throughout the period, there was an increased emphasis on investment in manufacturing rather than the extractive industries. In the 1950s only 19 percent of investment was in manufacturing; in the 1960s the share rose to 91 percent.[15] The industrial investment was mainly

[14] Businessmen were also annoyed at having been ignored in the formulation of the Alliance for Progress, even though direct investment was expected to play a large part in the Alliance's strategy. It was only at the very last minute that a business delegation was invited as observers to the Punta del Este conference. This does not imply, however, that businessmen were generally opposed to the Alliance per se. Some were, but the most internationally oriented businessmen were in favor of the overall policy; see Levinson and de Onis (1970, 71–73).

[15] Calculated from United States (1963a, 178–82) and *Survey of Current Business* (various issues). Data represent net capital outflows

for import substitution that was taking place in all of the larger Latin American countries. Foreign investors played an important role – in part because tariffs and other forms of protection made it much harder for them to export industrial goods to Latin America.

U.S. government loans to the region also began to increase in the late 1950s, but it was the next decade when this form of capital export became the dominant one. In fact, historical accounts of U.S.–Latin American economic relations will surely portray the 1960s as the decade of the Alliance for Progress. In terms of money, as well as rhetoric, the decade was dominated by the U.S. government as attempts were made to carry out the grandiose plans of the Kennedy administration.

The Alliance for Progress is one of the most controversial topics in the history of hemispheric relations (Lowenthal 1974). Conceived by the Kennedy team as a response to the Cuban Revolution, it embodied the idea that socioeconomic reform was essential if Latin America was not to turn to socialism. As promised by Treasury Secretary C. Douglas Dillon at the Punta del Este conference in 1961, the Alliance was to provide $20 billion over the next decade to promote economic development (Levinson and de Onis 1970, chap. 4). Military assistance would also be increased in order to provide a "stable environment" in which socioeconomic change could take place (Klare and Arnson 1979, 139–58). An examination of quantitative data on government aid during the main Alliance for Progress years (1962–69) reveals that it fell far short of the $20 billion discussed at Punta del Este. Summing economic and military aid, together with Export-Import Bank loans, the total was around $8.5

---

only; reinvested earnings are not included. For a general discussion of direct foreign investment in Latin America in this period, see Diaz-Alejandro (1970b).

billion. Of that total, economic aid represented 72 percent, military aid 10 percent, and Exim loans 18 percent. Exim loans not only fell in relative importance compared to the previous period, but they also dropped in absolute amounts (*U.S. Overseas Loans and Grants*, 1976).

Both the country distribution and the purpose of economic aid funds under the Alliance for Progress differed from those encountered in the private capital markets or even Exim loans. The reason, of course, is that political criteria were much more important. Thus, although Brazil was the largest recipient of aid funds, the other countries among the top five were less familiar. They included Colombia, Chile, the Dominican Republic, and Bolivia (ibid., 34–65). The last three were countries where the U.S. government was trying to create showcases of capitalist development. The Alliance's loans were more socially oriented than those provided by the banking sector. Housing, schools, and health facilities were prominent, although economic infrastructure was important as well.

Some U.S. aid funds were also channeled through multilateral agencies. The most important for Latin America were the International Bank for Reconstruction and Development (the IBRD, one part of the World Bank system) and the Interamerican Development Bank (IDB). Although established in 1945, the IBRD was more concerned with reconstruction than development prior to the 1960s. At that point, it stepped up its activities in Latin America, providing $2.9 billion between 1960 and 1969 compared to $1.2 billion between 1946 and 1959. The IDB, which was founded in 1960, had loaned $3.5 billion by 1969 (Interamerican Development Bank 1980, tables 8–9).

While bilateral, multilateral, and direct investment flows were increasing rapidly in this period, portfolio investment lagged behind. In fact, until 1953 portfolio investment flows remained negative in net terms. The change came about as a result of a new kind of portfolio investment – direct loans by commercial banks. These loans had begun on a small scale during the war, but they were basically stagnant until 1953 when they began to increase rapidly.

Between 1953 and 1959, medium- and long-term claims of U.S. banks on Latin American customers jumped from $62 million to $785 million – almost a twelvefold increase (United States 1963a, 228–29). To put these sums in perspective, however, it is useful to remember that they were only about 50 percent of the portfolio investment claims on Latin America resulting from bonds issued between 1920 and 1930. Little is known about these bank loans. In terms of country distribution, the main borrowers were Brazil ($269 million in claims in 1959), Mexico ($175 million), Argentina ($64 million), Cuba ($59 million), and Chile ($48 million) (ibid.). Some of these loans were part of cofinancing arrangements with the World Bank and the Export-Import Bank,[16] and most went to finance the purchase of capital goods.

Only in the 1960s did Latin American bond issues begin to appear on the market again, although in small amounts compared to the 1920s. The total for the decade was less than $1 billion. Bank loans were almost as important as bonds early in the decade, but they became negative in net terms near the end. It would appear that they had been crowded out of the market

[16] The earliest record of private bank participation in World Bank loans was in 1954. Between that year and 1960, private banks assumed some $30 million out of total World Bank loans to Latin America of $1.1 billion. The most active banks were Bank of America, First National City Bank, Chase Manhattan, Chemical, and Grace National Bank. The procedure was for the private banks to take the earliest maturities, while the World Bank retained the later ones (World Bank Annual Reports). No data are available on cofinancing with the Export-Import Bank.

by the more traditional forms of portfolio investment (that is, bonds) and "soft" government loans. With respect to bonds, the big news was the return of Mexico to the markets. *The New York Times* heralded the event with the following comments:

> An old friend is returning to the public bond market here this week after an absence of 53 years. The Government of Mexico plans to sell publicly Wednesday four bond issues that total $40,000,000 through an underwriting syndicate headed by Kuhn Loeb and the First Boston Corporation. The offering would be the first public dollar bond offering by Mexico here since $20,000,000 of 4 percent external gold obligations were floated in 1910. . . . Mexico's return to the public bond market here, however, is considered a milestone in that country's recent financial history, far more important than the borrowing. (*The New York Times*, 7/14/63)

Mexico thus regained its status as major borrower for the first time since shortly after the revolution, with several government agencies (Nacional Financiera, Petroleos Mexicanos, and Banco Nacional de Obras Públicas) floating public bond issues and making private placements. Argentina, Colombia, and Venezuela were less important borrowers in the 1960s (World Bank 1972a, 1972b). It should also be added that Latin America became an indirect borrower on the U.S. capital market in the 1960s as the IBRD and the IDB obtained much of their funds, a good portion of which were then lent to Latin American borrowers, from bonds floated in New York. Almost $2 billion was raised in this way, $400 million for the IDB and $1.4 billion for the IBRD (ibid.).

Despite the interest generated by Latin America's return to the bond market, it was not the most important development for U.S. banking activity in the region. Two other trends were the crucial ones in paving the way for the banks' new role in the 1970s. The first was taking place in London, where a new international capital market–the Eurocurrency market–was emerging.

The Eurocurrency market consisted of a group of banks in London and other financial centers that took deposits and made loans in currencies other than that of the local economy. The Euromarket flourished because it could pay higher rates for deposits and charge lower rates for loans than its domestic competitors in Europe and the United States. Smaller margins existed for several reasons. First, the Euromarket rarely made loans of less than $1 million, and economies of scale meant lower unit costs. Second, there was greater competition in the Euromarket than among domestic banks (Bell 1974; Mendelsohn 1980). Third, restrictions that curbed domestic banks were absent in the Euromarket. On the supply side, the lack of reserve requirements meant that Eurobanks could lend out a greater percentage of their deposits than could domestic banks. Regulations in domestic markets–the best known at the time being Regulation Q, which placed a ceiling on the interest rates U.S. banks could pay on time deposits–led to a smaller supply of money available to lend out. Until recently, U.S. banks could not pay interest on deposits of less than thirty days' maturity. On the demand side, U.S. regulations also helped the growth of the Euromarket. For example, the Interest Equalization Tax, which existed from 1963 to 1974, effectively closed the New York market to foreign borrowers. Moreover, the Voluntary Foreign Credit Restraint Program (1965–68) and the mandatory controls on capital export (1968–74) meant that U.S. corporations wanting to invest abroad had to secure capital outside the United States (Hawley 1977).[17]

[17] This discussion has concentrated exclusively on the Eurocurrency market. Although it has not been very important for Latin America, there is also a bond sector of the Euromarket. Since the 1960s, the bond market has been divided into foreign bonds (denominated in one

The second trend that would facilitate Latin America's access to the U.S. capital market in the 1970s took place in Latin America itself. This trend was a new surge of branch banking, the first since the early years after the Federal Reserve Act legalized the establishment of foreign branches. As Figure 3 shows, the number of branches fell during the Depression and World War II; in the immediate postwar period, from 1945 to 1959, the trend reversed itself and branching began to pick up slowly.[18] It was not until the 1960s, however, that the second branching wave of the century took place. From 57 in 1960, the number rose to 75 in 1965 and then doubled to 149 in 1970. This second wave saw the incorporation of new countries into the U.S. branch network (Bolivia, the Dominican Republic, El Salvador, Honduras, and Nicaragua), but more important in quantitative terms were the incorporation of new cities in countries where branches already existed and the multiplication of branches in major cities.

Part of the new thrust came from Bank of America's large-scale entry into the region and some increase in the number of branches belonging to Chase Manhattan and First National

---

currency and sold in the respective country) and international bonds (denominated in several currencies and sold in several markets simultaneously). For Group of Ten countries, bonds (foreign and international) provided $111 billion of finance between 1972 and 1980 compared to $106 billion of Euroloans. For Latin America during the same period, the amounts were $11 billion and $96 billion respectively (calculated from Appendix V).

[18] The biggest post–World War II setback for the branch bank network occurred in 1960 when the new Cuban government nationalized the seventeen branches remaining on the island and declared that it would not repay the money borrowed by its predecessors. Nevertheless, the banks ended up gaining more than they lost since the Cuban government had more money on deposit with the New York banks than it owed them. The deposits were frozen, and a lawsuit has been pending for a number of years to try to recover these funds.

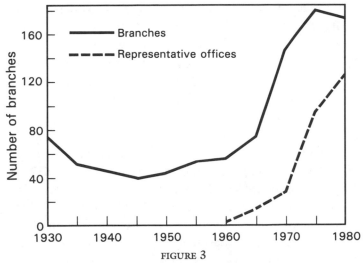

FIGURE 3
Number of U.S. Bank Branches in Latin America: 1930–80
SOURCE: *Bankers' Almanac and Yearbook* (various years).

Bank of Boston. Most of the growth, however, came from the continued expansion of First National City Bank, which had 102 branches in 16 countries in Latin America by 1970 (*Bankers' Almanac and Yearbook;* Citicorp Annual Report, various years). Moreover, a trend that would mushroom in the 1970s began to appear in the 1960s. This was the establishment of representative offices that could not engage in banking activities but gathered information and made contacts about loans and other services. In certain countries branching was no longer allowed, so the only way to enter the market was through representative offices. Mexico was the most important case. The only U.S. bank with branches in Mexico was First National City;[19] others

[19] First National City Bank enjoyed a privileged position in Mexico for historical reasons. It had established a branch in 1929 and was

had to settle for representative offices, of which there were eleven by 1970. Venezuela likewise closed its market to branches so that seven banks had set up representative offices in Caracas by 1970. In other countries, some banks set up representative offices even where branches were still allowed.[20]

Chase and a few smaller banks tried a third strategy – buying partial ownership in local banks (affiliates). During the 1960s Chase acquired a presence in six Latin American countries in this way. Its acquisitions included Banco Mercantil y Agrícola (49 percent), Venezuela's third largest bank; Banco Lar Brasileiro (51 percent), a medium-sized Brazilian bank; Banco Continental (51 percent), Peru's fourth largest bank; Banco Atlántida (51 percent), Honduras's largest bank; Banco de Comercio (48 percent), Colombia's fourth largest bank, and Banco Argentino de Comercio (70 percent), a medium-sized Argentine bank (Goff 1976, 6). The Chase strategy had several advantages: it permitted entry where branches were not possible, it provided a low profile in a period of growing nationalism, and it offered an immediate deposit base which a branch would have to build up.

Like the earlier period, the 1960s branching wave does not

---

considered to have helped Mexico through hard times when other banks were not interested. As a consequence, it was allowed to maintain branches in Mexico City even after regulations prohibited foreign branches in general (Interview 1118).

[20] The issue of branch banks appears to be a sensitive matter among bankers. My interviews generally found that bankers see branches as advantageous, especially in terms of breaking into the private-sector market. For participation in large public-sector loans, branches are less relevant. Some bankers, however, claim that branches are more trouble than they are worth because of greater regulation by governments. In any case, they seemed to feel that they had lost the opportunity to enter the market by the late 1970s. Chase officials' perceptions along these lines led them into the different strategy described below (Interviews 1107 and 1108).

seem to have originated with the banks themselves. In this case, the crucial factor was the relationship between banks and their multinational corporate clients. The latter were beginning to move abroad in ever greater numbers, and the banks followed to avoid being replaced by local credit sources. There was even the fear of losing corporate clients within the United States itself if they began to work with other banks abroad. An additional factor spurred the branching wave–once some banks expanded abroad, others felt they too had to follow (Odjagov 1977). Whatever the reasons, the increased representation of U.S. banks–via branches, representative offices, or affiliates–greatly facilitated the 1970s lending. Together with the institutional structure of the Euromarket and the corresponding instrument of Eurocredits, the new acquaintance with Latin America provided by the branching wave of the 1960s laid the foundations for the new surge of loans.

The Second Lending Boom: 1970–80

The 1970s finally saw the return of portfolio investment to the position of dominance in Latin American finance that it had occupied in the 1920s and in the previous century. Even after taking inflation into account, there was a twentyfold increase in U.S. portfolio flows to Latin America of which three-quarters consisted of Eurocredits. The other quarter was credits from the banks' U.S. offices; less than 2 percent was bond financing. Direct investment and U.S. government loans fell dramatically in importance as competition among banks drove loan volume to new highs. The increased supply of funds after the oil price rises stimulated the process already under way.

The Eurocurrency market was, in many ways, an extension of the U.S. capital market. About 80 percent of deposits and loans in the early period were denominated in dollars–hence the shorthand term "Eurodollars." Figure 4 shows the rapid growth of the market and the dollar share. The dominance of the U.S. currency was paralleled by the dominance of U.S. banks. Through 1978 U.S. banks managed 45 percent of total Eurocredits, and the top five banks were all from the United States–Citibank, Chase Manhattan, Morgan Guaranty Trust, Bank of America, and Manufacturers Hanover. For Latin America, U.S. banks were even more important than these figures indicate, as they handled 53 percent of Latin American loans between 1970 and 1978 (Appendix V). After the latter date, however, this dominance began to decline as European and Japanese institutions became more active in Latin American lending.[21]

In the 1960s Eurocredits were almost exclusively short-term loans, primarily working capital for U.S. and European multinationals, but during the 1970s the pattern changed. Comparisons are difficult because of the lack of data before 1970, but in that year 9 percent of publicized Eurocredits went to Third World countries; this proportion increased to 33 percent by 1973. In 1974 there was a dip as advanced countries took out large loans to finance balance of payments deficits caused by the increase in oil prices,[22] but by 1975 a majority of all Eurocredits were going to Third World countries with Latin America as the most important region (ibid.).

[21] The main reason for the decline was the partial withdrawal of U.S. banks from the market because of ever-lower spreads. The lower spreads, in turn, were due largely to increased competition from European and Japanese banks which could accept lower spreads either because they were state-owned banks or because European private banks generally have lower overhead costs.

[22] Such a dip did not exist for U.S.-managed Euroloans in 1974. The vast majority of increased European borrowing in that year was done through European banks (Appendix V).

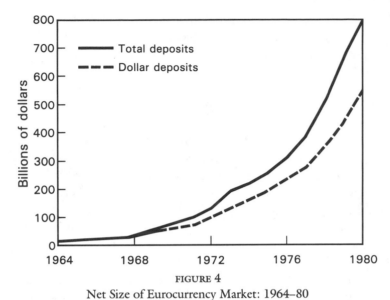

FIGURE 4

Net Size of Eurocurrency Market: 1964–80

source: Bank for International Settlements, *Annual Report*.

The reason for the change can be traced to events outside Latin America itself. In the early part of the decade, for the first time since the 1930s, business cycles in the United States and Europe coincided on the downswing. As a consequence, multinational corporations slowed their borrowing, and the banks began to look around for new clients in order to maintain their loan volume and thus their profit rates (Kuczynski 1976). In this context, certain Third World countries began to seem increasingly attractive. The banks' problems were greatly exacerbated by the 1973–74 oil price rises as a serious recession hit the advanced capitalist world, further dampening loan demand, and the OPEC countries deposited the majority of their new revenues in U.S. banks. Faced with a potential falling rate of profit if they could not loan out this money at an adequate interest rate, the banks increasingly turned to Third World clients.

As had happened in the 1920s, the banks' need to make loans generated a fierce competition for borrowers. The British journalist Anthony Sampson (1982) portrays a process that, as he himself indicates, was remarkably similar to the earlier experience.

> In the early years of the Eurodollar the raising of international loans was a sedate and gentlemanly business. The borrower, whether a corporation or a foreign government agency, would approach its customary bank or a specialized bank, which would then arrange the syndicate. But as it became more lucrative and competitive, the loan officers of banks began—around 1970— to solicit business, and to telephone or visit corporations and government agencies on their own initiative. Some of the banks were no longer acting simply as intermediaries between a surplus and shortage of funds: they were now actively selling loans—as they had done in the twenties and earlier. (ibid., 116)

In the 1970s there was a peculiar combination of cooperation and competition among the banks. Cooperation arose because the large loans were syndicated. A lead manager brought together a group of banks, which could number in the hundreds, and each took a piece of the loan and shared the risk. Competition entered as the largest banks vied for the "mandate" to organize syndicates and obtain the front-end fees that were more lucrative than interest payments. Thus, the lone investment banker traveling to a Latin American city in the 1920s in hopes of selling a $50 million loan was replaced by "pin-striped salesmen [who] crowded each other in Interconti hotel lobbies and the reception rooms of finance ministers" (Delamaide 1984, 43) in order to offer $500 million. Also unlike the 1920s, U.S. banks were joined in the competitive fray by European and Japanese institutions as the 1970s moved on. The resulting fall in profits eventually drove many U.S. banks out of the market or substantially lowered their participation.

The rapid increase in Eurocredits to Latin American customers was reflected in the jump in the number of representative offices in the region. While branching activity slowed substantially in the 1970s, and the total number actually declined during the last half of the decade (see Figure 3), representative offices increased fourfold. In 1970 there were 30; by 1975 the number had increased to 95; and it continued to rise to 127 in 1980. The number of banks involved also rose, going from 13 in 1970 to 41 in 1980, as more banks began to regard Latin American countries as important customers. Most of these representative offices were located in Brazil, Mexico, and Venezuela, since they were the largest borrowers and had restrictions on branch banking (*Bankers' Almanac and Yearbook,* various years).

At the same time that new banks were entering the Latin American market via representative offices and participation in loans to central governments, the more established banks were penetrating deeper into the market. This process included loans to local governments and government corporations and agencies as well as loans to the private sector. In the case of the largest bank and the largest borrower, Citicorp had only about 20 percent of its Brazilian portfolio in government assets in the late 1970s (Hagerman 1977, 53). Bank of America's government loans also declined as a percentage of the total as finance for the private sector increased (Interviews 1116 and 1117). Private-sector loans carried higher interest rates—because they were considered to be higher risks—but only banks with long experience and a large number of employees in the region had the ability to evaluate the loan proposals. The major banks also broadened the types of services they offered to include leasing, brokerage, investment banking, and credit cards (Citicorp, Bank of America, and Chase Manhattan annual reports, various years). Many of these were activities from which the banks were legally barred in the United States.

Even direct investment showed a tilt toward finance in the 1970s. The trend toward an ever-increasing share in manufacturing reversed itself in the second half of the decade, and the prime competitor was the financial sector. Between 1975 and 1979, some 52 percent of U.S. direct investment was in manufacturing compared to 20 percent in finance. The latter was up from about 13 percent in the early 1970s, while the former was down from around 90 percent.[23] If investment in the English-speaking Caribbean, increasingly considered as part of Latin America, is included, then the trend toward direct investment in finance was much more pronounced. Indeed, the majority of direct investment in this broader definition of Latin America was in finance during the 1975–79 period. It should also be added that investment in the Caribbean area was greater than in all the nineteen Latin American republics combined.[24] In terms of country distribution, Brazil remained the largest recipient of U.S. direct investment with over 60 percent for the decade as a whole. Peru was in second position, followed by Mexico and Argentina, while Venezuela continued to have an investment outflow. In general, there was greater diversity in the second half of the decade as Brazil's dominance lessened in response to that country's economic difficulties (*Survey of Current Business,* various issues).

[23] *Survey of Current Business* (various issues). Figures are for net capital outflows only; reinvested earnings are not included.

[24] Much of this investment in the English Caribbean was probably connected with the operation of various financial centers located there – places with very few regulations where the banks establish "shell" offices. Loans are then formally booked from these offices as a way of avoiding taxes and other regulations.

Although U.S. government lending to Latin America increased in nominal terms, from an annual average of $652 million in the 1960s to $787 million in the 1970s, it actually declined by 25 percent in real terms (Appendix I). The Alliance for Progress was widely considered to be a failure. Growth rates were high in many countries, but the gap between rich and poor had widened. Liberals thought that problems were due to errors in implementation; radicals blamed the very nature of the program itself (Lowenthal 1974). Lacking any alternative vision, the U.S. government pulled back and advised Latin Americans to open their doors to private enterprise. Those who rejected this advice found the Nixon–Kissinger White House trying to force them to do so. For example, economic boycotts and CIA manipulations harassed the Velasco government in Peru (Einhorn 1974) and helped overthrow Allende in Chile (Petras and Morley 1975). The private enterprise attitude was reflected in the makeup of those government funds that were available. Whereas Export-Import Bank loans (aid to U.S. exporters) had constituted only 10 percent of government economic flows in the 1960s, more than half of government money was from this source a decade later (*U.S. Overseas Loans and Grants,* various years).

The Carter administration changed the rhetoric, and in some cases the substance, of U.S. policy toward Latin America with its human rights focus (Feinberg 1980). Aid was cut off to the most repressive regimes in the region, and ties were strengthened with the social democrats. Nevertheless, the enormous bank credits propped up the same governments that official policy was ostracizing. Chile was the principal example, but Argentina and Brazil were similar cases (Stallings 1982). There was also a second sense in which private banks' actions hindered the human rights policy. The counterpart to the bank loans was the accumulation of huge debts by many Latin American countries, the service of which was causing or exacerbating balance of payments problems. In line with postwar practice, the International Monetary Fund stepped in to give short-term loans to stave off crises. The quid pro quo was the so-called stabilization program whereby recipient governments were obliged to cut expenditures, thus causing economic hardships and often requiring political repression to enforce the policies.[25]

As they looked into the 1980s, bankers had mixed opinions about the future of Latin American lending. On the one hand, the loans had helped to prevent the banks from falling into the recession and profit squeeze that most of the world economy had suffered during the second half of the 1970s.[26] On the other hand, the rising debt burden of borrowers was causing some nervousness. Calls began to go out from bankers and government officials alike for more collaboration between private banks and multilateral agencies. Statements about the need for more government assistance increased significantly after the second oil price rise in 1979 as new recycling problems were foreseen.[27]

[25] In one case, the banks were more directly involved. When Peru ran into a financial crisis in 1976, the government went to the banks rather than the IMF for a balance of payments loan. The banks then briefly assumed the IMF's traditional role of setting targets and monitoring the economy until problems led them to retreat. See Chapter 6.

[26] An indication of the importance of international lending is the fact that the international share of profits of the top ten banks rose from 17 percent in 1970 to 46 percent in 1980. In the case of Citibank, South American profits went from less than 2 percent of total profits in 1971 to 25 percent in 1980—with Brazil alone accounting for 11 percent. The high point for all these trends was actually in the mid-1970s before the U.S. banks began to slow their international lending. In 1977, for example, international earnings were 51 percent of the total, and Brazil represented 20 percent of Citibank's profits. See the banks' annual reports.

[27] See, for example, the remarks of Federal Reserve Chairman Arthur Burns (1977). The banker who was most vocal in calling for collaboration was Gabriel Hauge, chairman of Manufacturers Hanover; see *Financial Times* (6/10/77). For the IMF reaction, see Reich

Although the rate of increase of U.S. lending to Latin America slowed–for a variety of reasons that are discussed in Chapter 5– European and Japanese banks became more active. The 1980s would bring a new phase in lending history.

Epilogue: The 1980s

Although the statistical analysis in the book ends with 1980, some brief comments must be added to bring the historical chronology up to date. Figure 1 has been extended through the early 1980s, as well. Large-scale lending to Latin America continued through 1981, but a watershed occurred in August of the following year when Mexico announced that it would be unable to continue servicing its debt without substantial outside assistance. Many other countries soon followed suit, and the potential for a 1930s-style chain default clearly existed. Such an outcome has thus far been avoided for reasons already discussed.

Most important, the private bank portion of the Latin American debt–estimated at some $230 billion at the end of 1982 (calculated from OECD 1985)–was held by the banks themselves rather than individual investors.[28] This, of course, was the consequence of the switch from bond to bank lending. Since the

---

(1977). After the second oil price rise, David Rockefeller, chairman of Chase Manhattan Bank, and Jacques de Larosiere, executive director of the International Monetary Fund, were especially active in calling for a larger public role to limit the pressure on the private banks. See the report of Rockefeller's views in *New York Times* (6/14/79). De Larosiere's opinions are found in various issues of the *IMF Survey;* see especially 7/7/80 and 11/10/80.

[28] This figure includes long- and short-term debt to the public and private sectors held by private banks. Bond issues constitute an additional $14 billion.

debt of Argentina, Brazil, and Mexico alone represented 113 percent of the capital of the nine largest banks in the United States (United States 1983a, 76), a series of defaults could seriously jeopardize the international financial system. Thus, as a consequence of the Mexican crisis, the U.S. government abandoned its nonchalant view of the debt problem and quickly helped put together a rescue package consisting of $4 billion from the U.S. Exchange Stabilization Fund and the Bank for International Settlements (BIS). Part of the BIS loan, and any large-scale debt relief from the private banks, were made contingent on Mexico's signing an agreement with the IMF.

The IMF's role, however, changed substantially as the managing director called the leading bankers to New York and told them that he would not recommend approval of an IMF loan unless the banks guaranteed their participation in the rescue operation. The required actions included restructuring the Mexican debt and a new loan representing a 7 percent increase in each bank's exposure. The large banks realized that such a process represented their best hope of weathering the crisis, but many of the smaller ones wanted out. Such a withdrawal was prevented by the persuasive efforts of Paul Volcker, chairman of the Federal Reserve, and the large banks themselves (Stallings 1983b).

The Mexican package became the model that, with some modification, was followed in reschedulings that eventually involved all major Latin American borrowers except Colombia. Since one-year reschedulings were obviously not sufficient to deal with the problem, Mexico again took the lead in negotiating a multiyear package. All in all, three rounds of negotiations have been carried out with terms increasingly favorable to the borrowers. Nevertheless, a real resource transfer from the region continues if interest payments are included (United Nations 1985b).

Opinion differs substantially on whether the debt crisis is now under control or only awaiting future eruption. Some economists and policymakers (such as Cline 1984) argue that further case-by-case negotiations are sufficient. Others (Rohatyn 1982; Kenen 1983; Weinert 1983; Fishlow 1984; Lever and Huhne 1986) insist that a more generalized approach is needed to provide enough breathing space for a return to acceptable growth rates in the debtor countries. The Baker Plan, proposed by the U.S. government in 1985, is an intermediate step (*The New York Times,* 10/3/85, 10/9/85; *World Financial Markets,* February 1986). One of the crucial variables is international trade. Growth rates in the advanced industrial countries, and the outcome of the struggles for increased protectionism, will have an important influence on the debt crisis. Likewise, the availability of new loans will play a significant role.

Opinion also varies on who is responsible for the current debt crisis. Congressional hearings (United States 1983a and 1983b) were held that had strong parallels with the 1932 Senate hearings discussed earlier. Politicians made similar charges of mismanagement, bad judgment, greed, and lack of concern for the U.S. domestic economy. Bankers responded, as they had in the 1930s, by saying that foreign lending was necessary to stimulate trade which was very important for maintaining growth rates and employment in the United States. Despite the similarities, however, it was clear that the power of the bankers in 1983 vis-à-vis their congressional critics was substantially greater than in 1932. Thus, there are striking similarities – but even more important differences – between the situation of the 1930s and the 1980s.

Conclusions

After this brief examination of the history of U.S. banking activities in Latin America, we conclude by returning to the three issues mentioned in the introduction to the chapter. First of all, it is apparent that banking activities were not spread evenly across the century but took place in cyclical fashion. This conclusion pertains to both branching and lending. The first branching wave occurred from 1914 to 1920. It was immediately followed by the first lending boom during the 1920s. Both processes went into decline during the Depression, World War II, and the immediate postwar period. A second branching wave took place in the 1960s and was again followed by a new surge of lending in the 1970s. Both ended in the early 1980s.

A second point to emerge from the historical data is the importance of institutional change in the operation of U.S. banks. Although two lending cycles did indeed occur and many similarities existed between them, there were also profound differences. In particular, the form of portfolio investment changed from the flotation of bonds by U.S. investment banks to the extension of credits by U.S. commercial banks and especially U.S. banks operating in the Eurocurrency market. This institutional change–and others such as the increased role of international agencies–had significant effects on the outcome when borrowers got into difficulties in servicing their loans, as can be seen by comparing events in the 1930s and 1980s. The unilateral defaults of the 1930s have been replaced by negotiated reschedulings in the 1980s.

Finally, the analysis suggests that important but changing relations existed between the private banks and other U.S. actors. The two branching waves were encouraged and stimulated by nonbank actors; the banks themselves did not take the lead. The early branching wave was due largely to U.S. exporters and direct investors; the U.S. government was also enlisted to help. The later wave came about as the banks followed their multinational corporate clients abroad. The lending booms, by contrast, owed more to the banks' own initiative. As alternative sources of loans disappeared and adequate institutions were created, the banks moved rapidly into large-scale lending. In each case—branching as well as lending—competition among banks was an important force in driving the process forward until outside events brought it to a halt. All of these topics will be explored in greater detail in later chapters.

3

Characteristics of U.S. Portfolio Investment in Latin America

Tʜᴇ ꜰɪʀsᴛ U.S. portfolio investments in Latin America were made in 1899 when U.S. citizens purchased a $20 million bond issue from the Mexican central government and a $500,000 issue from the Mexican state of Jalisco (Dickens 1933, 211–70).[1] Eighty years later, such investments had multiplied to 104 transactions representing $6 billion per year—a three hundredfold increase (Appendix V). Even after taking inflation into account, a thirtyfold rise had taken place. The increase did not come about through a smooth upward trend but in a cyclical pattern over time. Five subperiods will be identified in this chapter. U.S. portfolio investment in Latin America will be located with respect to total U.S. private investment abroad (portfolio plus direct) and total U.S. capital flows (pri-

[1] The 1899 date refers to the first Latin American issue floated on the U.S. market. Individual U.S. citizens had purchased Latin American bonds floated in Europe earlier in the nineteenth century.

vate plus public). Portfolio investment in Latin America will be compared to total U.S. portfolio investment in all regions, and U.S. portfolio investment in Latin America will be located within total international portfolio investment in the region. Data will also be presented on who was obtaining loans in Latin America, what they were used for, and the terms that accompanied them. Before proceeding, however, a brief digression is necessary on portfolio investment and the data used in the book.

Notes on the Data

Portfolio, or indirect, foreign investment is a term used in contrast to direct foreign investment. The latter exists where nationals of one country hold controlling interest in an investment in a second country; the former occurs when the investors have only a small minority interest.[2] Unlike direct investment, portfolio investment can be either long or short term. Short-term capital flows, usually defined as those with less than one-year maturity, are *not* included in this study, for the focus is long-term portfolio investment. There are two main reasons for

[2] The term "controlling interest" is very ambiguous. Some studies claim that a foreign firm can control decision making with as little as 5 or 10 percent equity ownership. The U.S. government's definition of direct investment, for example, is investment in a foreign affiliate in which a single U.S. firm owns at least 10 percent of the equity (*Survey of Current Business,* August 1981, 29). This distinction between direct and portfolio investment leads to the exclusion of loans to U.S. corporations operating in Latin America from the data base on U.S. portfolio investment in this study and their inclusion as direct investment. Even though the purchase of stocks or bonds from such a company is portfolio investment from the viewpoint of the individual purchaser, it is really a way of financing direct investment by the company.

excluding short-term flows. First, data on the subject are very difficult to obtain since short-term capital enters a country under many guises and often stays a very brief time. Second, short-term capital appears to follow quite different patterns than long-term investment and thus needs to be investigated as a separate topic. It is more volatile and often involves speculative motives in addition to conventional trade finance. In quantitative terms, short-term capital flows to Latin America since World War II have been at least as large as long-term flows and thus are clearly an important topic for future research.[3]

The traditional kind of long-term portfolio investment involved the purchase of securities, either stocks or bonds. In the Latin American case, stock purchases were practically nonexistent, so until the 1940s long-term portfolio investment meant bond issues. During the 1940s, a new kind of long-term portfolio investment arose in the form of bank credits. Until 1970 these credits were made by the banks' head offices in the United States; after that, they were mainly Eurocurrency loans issued by the U.S. banks' European or other foreign offices.

Another type of private long-term investment also appeared

[3] The source for this estimate is the *Survey of Current Business* (June issues). It includes both public and private loans from U.S. sources. The *Country Exposure Lending Survey* (various issues) indicates that about half of U.S. bank claims on Latin America have been short term. Under "normal" conditions, short-term debt is mainly trade credits. According to one estimate (Kuczynski 1982), the amount at any given time should be roughly equivalent to three months of imports after deducting capital goods financed on a long-term basis. In periods of crisis, short-term debt may increase, either for speculative purposes or to substitute for longer-term credits which may become unavailable. Kuczynski's estimates for Latin America as of mid-1982, for example, suggest that total external debt was about $295 billion of which $75 billion was short-term. This figure compares to $30 or $40 billion for normal periods as defined above.

in the post–World War II period–suppliers' credits or credits from nonbanking institutions. Suppliers' credits are also excluded from the current study since they are directly tied to U.S. trade. In this study, the goal is to analyze nontied loans. The exclusion of long-term suppliers' credits is never of major quantitative importance. It had the greatest effect in the 1950s and 1960s when suppliers' credits constituted 6 percent of total private investment; the figure was less than 2 percent in the 1970s (Appendix I). Prior to World War II, long-term suppliers' credits were virtually nonexistent.[4]

The main data series used in the book consists of *net* long-term portfolio investment–that is, gross bonds and credits minus amortization payments. The reason for choosing the net series is basically a practical one: data limitations make it impossible to construct a gross series for the entire period 1899–1980.[5] Gross data are available for most of the period, however, and these are used in some parts of the analysis. When gross or net is not specified, the reader should assume that the net series is being used. A further clarification about the term "net" is needed. For balance of payments purposes, net is generally defined as the result of aggregating U.S. capital flows to another region (corrected for amortization) minus capital flows from that region to the United States (corrected for amortization).

---

[4] Keep in mind that the vast majority of suppliers' credits are short-term loans. The only kind of trade that is likely to be financed by long-term suppliers' credits is capital goods (including weapons). Such credits can come either from public or private sources.

[5] The appropriateness of gross or net data depends on the question being asked. Thus the ideal situation would be to have both available for the entire period. What is missing is gross data for bank credits from home offices because data on bank credits are collected from the banks in the form of claims at the end of a period rather than credits granted during the period.

These latter flows are *not* included in this study, which focuses on the behavior of U.S. capital exports.[6]

U.S. capital exports to Latin America have substantially exceeded flows in the opposite direction. The average figure for capital import from Latin America as a percentage of capital export to the region since World War II is 32 percent (*Survey of Current Business,* June issues). Little information is available on flows to the United States, but the majority appears to have been Latin American governments' foreign exchange reserves held in short-term assets. There were also, of course, private capital flows from Latin America to the United States, both long and short term. Since many of the private flows are illegal (registered as "errors and omissions" in U.S. and Latin American balance of payments), they are exceedingly difficult to quantify.[7]

[6] The procedure of considering only long-term flows to Latin America, ignoring reverse flows, clearly loses information. One example is the Brazilian government's policy during much of the 1970s of building up reserves (held abroad as short-term deposits) in order to increase the country's creditworthiness in the eyes of the banks. This kind of transaction is missed in this study.

[7] The only source that deals specifically with Latin American capital flows to the United States is the *Survey of Current Business* (June issues), which breaks down U.S. balance of payments transactions by regions of the world. On the basis of these figures, direct foreign investment and securities purchases by Latin Americans in the United States constituted about 8 percent of all Latin American capital flows to the United States between 1960 and 1980. Many of the other categories are aggregated, but a best guess is that reserve assets constituted the largest single category. The U.S.–Latin American balance of payments has a very large errors and omissions category, sometimes positive and sometimes negative. Recently, *World Financial Markets* (March 1986) published data on "capital flight" for ten Latin American countries between 1976 and 1985. Their estimate was $123 billion over those ten years compared to an increase in gross external debt of $270 billion. The figures have been challenged by Latin American central banks, but they

In general, the deflated net series, specifically data put into 1958 dollars, is used. Although the cyclical pattern does not change whether current or constant prices are used, the amplitude of the cycles does vary. For the long-term analysis, five-year moving averages are employed rather than annual data since the focus is on long-term trends rather than year-to-year fluctuations. In the short-term analysis, however, it is precisely the fluctuations that are of interest, so the annual data are maintained.

This note must end with the warning that the data series on portfolio investment should be taken as a first approximation only. The book is an initial attempt to draw together data from a wide variety of sources, some more thorough and reliable than others. (For more details on sources, calculation methods, and problems, the reader should consult Appendix I.)

Periodization of Portfolio Investment

The five periods found in U.S. portfolio investment in Latin America have thus far followed a cyclical pattern that resembles British loan cycles in the nineteenth century. The first period includes the twenty years from 1900 to 1919 that witnessed the initial U.S. forays into the international capital markets as a lender.[8] In overall terms, the United States was still a net borrower, as more capital was imported than exported, but the trend was beginning to change. By the end of World War I, the

---

clearly indicate that flows from Latin America to the United States have become increasingly important. For a more extensive discussion of capital flight, see Lessard and Williamson (1987).

[8] Periods are based on changes in the annual data; thus they are slightly different from those that would result from using moving averages to define periods.

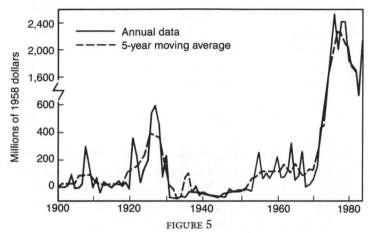

FIGURE 5

U.S. Portfolio Investment in Latin America: 1900–84

SOURCE: Appendix I.

United States had displaced Britain as the major capital-exporting nation. From the perspective of Latin American borrowers in the U.S. market, the years 1900–19 were a prelude, a small-scale beginning, as can be seen in Figure 5. The average yearly loan totals were only $11 million ($37 million in 1958 dollars).[9] From 1900 through 1905, loans averaged about $5 million per year. This figure increased to $25 million from 1906 through 1910, only to drop back again to $13 million from 1911 to 1918. With the end of the war, the 1919 total jumped, previewing what would occur during the 1920s.

It was the decade of the 1920s that constituted the first period of large-scale U.S. lending to Latin America. The average yearly total for the decade was $133 million ($260 million in 1958

[9] All figures in this section on average yearly loans are calculated from data in Appendix I.

dollars), a sixfold increase from the early part of the century. The 1920s lending reached a peak in 1926–28 of almost $400 million (1958 dollars) per year that would not be repeated until the early 1970s. With the U.S. stock market craze and the onset of the Depression, lending fell in 1929–30, and net lending to Latin America became negative with the chain of defaults in 1931–32. By 1933 all Latin American countries except Haiti were in at least partial default.

The third period, then, is made up of the twenty-three years of net negative lending that lasted from 1931 through 1953. The average yearly figure for the period was –$30 million (–$60 million in 1958 dollars). The defaults dominated this period with the consequence that no new bond issues were floated, while partial amortization payments on outstanding debt and repurchases by Latin Americans led to a net inflow of capital into the United States. During this period, a new kind of portfolio investment – bank credits – became increasingly important for Latin America. It was the bank credits that brought about the shift from negative to positive lending in the early 1950s. Bond transactions remained negative until the early 1960s.

The year 1954 started the fourth period as bank credits led to a new upswing in U.S. portfolio investment in Latin America. Lending during this period, however, never matched the record levels set in the 1920s. The yearly average was only $129 million ($124 million in 1958 dollars compared to $260 million in the 1920s). In many ways, this fourth period was analogous to the first in being a prelude to the large-scale 1970s investments. This was especially true with respect to bank credits that were just getting started in the post–World War II years as bonds were getting started between 1900 and 1919.

The final period begins in 1970 and lasts until the present, although quantitative data in the book are generally presented only through 1980. Figure 5, however, like Figure 1, has been extended through the early 1980s. This second period of heavy-lending activity far exceeded the loan volume of any other period, including the 1920s. Average yearly U.S. portfolio investment in Latin America between 1970 and 1980 totaled $3.2 billion ($1.5 billion in 1958 dollars). In constant prices, this was more than six times the 1920s average. The annual data peaked in 1976, and a slightly lower loan volume prevailed during the latter half of the decade. The decline continued into the 1980s. Of the three types of portfolio investment referred to previously—bond issues, bank credits from home offices, and Euro-loans or bank credits from foreign offices—it was the third type that was principally responsible for the spectacular increase in portfolio investment during the decade.[10] Bond issues actually declined, reaching net negative levels in 1978–80, while home office credits increased but at a fairly slow rate.

Comparisons with Other Types of Investment

In order to determine the relative importance of U.S. portfolio investment in Latin America, it must be compared to various other investment aggregates. We shall do this for the century as a whole as well as the subperiods described earlier, focusing on yearly averages for different kinds of investment in different periods.

A first comparison addresses the question of how important portfolio investment has been within total U.S. capital export to

[10] In spite of their large volume, Eurocredits are actually underestimated by the data used here, which are based on publicly announced credits. Since there is no legal requirement to disclose credits, not all are known. The World Bank, which collects data both on publicly announced credits and on actual capital inflows into member countries, estimates that about 85 percent of Eurocredits are made public.

TABLE 2
U.S. Portfolio Investment in Latin America as Percentage of Total
U.S. Private Investment in Latin America: 1900–80
(millions of 1958 dollars, annual averages)

Period	Portfolio Investment	Private Investment	Portfolio/ Private
1900–19	$ 37.0	$186.6	19.8%
1920–30	260.1	483.7	53.8
1931–53	−59.5	41.0	−
1954–69	123.7	454.4	27.2
1970–80	1,520.5	1,782.4	85.3
AVERAGE	258.5	455.2	56.8

SOURCE: Appendix I.

Latin America. The question is first examined from the perspective of private capital flows, which include direct investment and suppliers' credits as well as portfolio investment (bonds and credits). As Table 2 shows, portfolio investment has accounted for over half of total private U.S. investment in Latin America during the twentieth century; the exact figure is 57 percent. There are large variations, however, once the focus shifts to the subperiods.

As one would expect, portfolio investment represented a much larger percentage of total private investment during the two decades identified as heavy-lending periods – the 1920s and the 1970s. In the 1920s portfolio investment was 54 percent of total private flows, meaning that direct investment was 46 percent since suppliers' credits were of minimal importance in this period. In the 1970s the dominance of portfolio investment became much more pronounced and accounted for 85 percent of all private flows. This left about 15 percent for direct investment, since suppliers' credits were again a minor factor. Note that the dominant position of portfolio investment in both the

1920s and the 1970s derived mainly from the large increase in portfolio investment itself, since direct investment varied less, as can be seen in Table 3. During the two light-lending periods, portfolio investment was much less important: in 1900–19 it represented only one-fifth of private flows, while in 1954–69 it accounted for about one-fourth.

A second measure of the importance of portfolio investment in Latin America leads to a comparison with total U.S. capital flows to the region – public and private. The results for the entire period, also shown in Table 3, indicate that portfolio investment was 41 percent of total capital flows. Government long-term loans accounted for another 27 percent, and direct investment plus suppliers' credits together provided 32 percent of total flows.

Again there was substantial variation among subperiods. The first two were identical to the previous analysis since there was no significant U.S. government lending to Latin America until the late 1930s. The 1931–53 period had the largest government participation in percentage terms, but this was due to negative portfolio flows rather than to large government loans. It was in the 1954–69 period that government loans became the crucial component of total U.S. capital flows to Latin America. This period included the Alliance for Progress years when "foreign aid" reached its peak of popularity in the United States. Portfolio investment dropped to a mere 14 percent, while government loans accounted for half of the total. Direct investment was 34 percent and suppliers' credits 2 percent. To preview an argument that is presented later, it might be suspected that government loans were displacing private credits as the former supplied the majority of the capital requirements of Latin American governments. Thus, the slack deriving from lack of U.S. investor confidence in Latin America after the 1930s defaults was taken up by the public sector, both in the United States and, at the international level, by the World Bank and the Inter-

TABLE 3

U.S. Portfolio Investment in Latin America as Percentage of Total U.S. Public and Private Capital Flows to Latin America: 1900–80

(millions of 1958 dollars, annual averages)

Period	Portfolio Investment	Direct Investment	Private Investment[a]	Government Loans	Total Capital Flows[b]	Portfolio/ Total Capital
1900–19	$ 37.0	$149.5	$186.5	$ 0	$186.5	19.8%
1920–30	260.1	223.6	483.7	0	483.7	53.8
1931–53	–59.5	117.4	41.0	84.8	125.7	–
1954–69	123.7	304.8	454.4	449.2	903.5	13.7
1970–80	1,520.5	241.1	1,782.4	433.4	2,215.8	68.6
AVERAGE	258.5	193.6	455.2	171.6	626.8	41.2

SOURCE: Appendix I.

[a] Private investment is sum of portfolio plus direct investment from 1900 to 1945; after 1945, it also includes suppliers' credits.
[b] Total capital flows are sum of private investment plus government loans.

TABLE 4

U.S. Portfolio Investment in Latin America as Percentage of Total
U.S. Portfolio Investment: 1900–80
(millions of 1958 dollars, annual averages)

Period	Latin American Portfolio Investment	Total Portfolio Investment	Latin American/ Total Portfolio Investment
1900–19	$ 37.0	$466.7	7.9%
1920–30	260.1	881.5	29.5
1931–53	−59.5	−68.4	87.0
1954–69	123.7	848.3	14.6
1970–80	1,520.5	6,531.7	23.3
AVERAGE	258.5	1,270.1	20.4

SOURCE: Appendix I.

american Development Bank. In the 1970s, however, portfolio investment regained its importance, accounting for 69 percent of all U.S. capital flows. Government loans dropped to 20 percent, while direct investment fell to 11 percent.

Another kind of comparison focuses on the relative importance of Latin American portfolio investment within total U.S. foreign portfolio investment. Table 4 provides some data for this analysis and shows that, over the period as a whole, portfolio investment in Latin America was about one-fifth of total portfolio investment. There was less variation within subperiods in this comparison, although Latin American participation tended to increase in heavy-lending periods. Thus, the Latin American percentage was 30 percent in 1920–30 and 23 percent in the 1970s. By contrast, it was only 8 percent in 1900–19 and 15 percent in 1954–69. The 1931–53 percentage was very high, but it really meant that Latin America accounted for a large portion of the negative capital flows during the 1930s and 1940s.

In addition to overall portfolio investment, it is important to

TABLE 5

U.S. Bank Credits and Securities Issues for Latin America Compared to All Regions: 1900–80
(millions of 1958 dollars, annual averages)

Period	Latin American Bank Credits	Total Bank Credits	Latin American %	Latin American Securities	Total Securities	Latin American %
1900–19	–	–	–	$ 37.0	$466.7	7.9
1920–30	–	–	–	260.1	881.5	29.5
1931–53	$ 5.2	$ 16.9	30.8	–59.5	–75.2	79.1
1954–69	72.5	157.3	46.1	50.0	694.6	7.2
1970–80	1,481.8	4,823.1	30.7	38.5	1,708.6	2.3
AVERAGE	351.6[a]	1,119.2[a]	31.4[a]	42.7	582.8	7.3

SOURCE: Appendix I.

[a] Average for 1931–80.

separate bank credits from securities transactions for the period after 1940 when bank credits began. Table 5 shows that Latin America was much more important in the former category than the latter. In 1931–53, Latin America accounted for 31 percent of all bank credits to foreign customers; in 1954–69, the figure increased to 46 percent, returning to 31 percent in 1970–80. For securities transactions, the picture was very different. Latin America represented only 7 percent of all foreign bond and stock issues between 1954 and 1969; the figure dropped to 2 percent in the 1970s. (The apparently high percentage in 1931–53 again results from Latin America accounting for a large share of the negative flows in that period.) The low participation in the bond market in the postwar period is an especially dramatic demonstration of the fact that Latin American countries never regained the confidence of the investing public in the United States. The banks, by contrast, saw the region in a more positive light for reasons that are discussed in the next chapter.

Finally, to conclude this section, we look at the relative importance of U.S. portfolio investment in Latin America compared to portfolio investment by other nations. These comparisons are somewhat less systematic due to lack of data, but the general trend is clear: non-U.S. portfolio investment was important in the first and last of the five subperiods, but it practically dropped out of the picture in the intervening years.

Table 6 shows Latin American external public debt at the end of 1914 by lending country – the cumulative result of a century of lending. Great Britain accounted for the vast majority (68 percent) of the debt, while France was a distant second with 14 percent. The United States held only 4 percent of Latin America's debt at this point. During the first years of the twentieth century, the pattern began to change. Of new securities for Latin American governments between 1900 and 1913, some $724 million (55 percent) were issued in London, $361 million (27

TABLE 6
Latin America's External Public Debt by Lending Country: 1914

Lender	Amount (millions)	Percentage of Total
Great Britain	$1,481	67.8
France	302	13.8
United States	93	4.3
Germany	47	2.2
Others	262	12.0
TOTAL	2,185	100.0

SOURCE: United Nations (1965, 16).

percent) in Paris, and $238 million (18 percent) in New York.[11] World War I speeded up the change that had already begun, so that the United States clearly outdistanced its rivals by the 1920s. Net European lending to Latin American governments was generally negative during the interwar period (United Nations 1965, 19) while, as we have seen, the United States provided almost $1.5 billion. Britain maintained its stock position, with a fairly high level of outstanding loans and other investments until World War II when they were rapidly liquidated, but no significant new investments were added (United Nations 1953, 4; Wilkins 1977).

In the immediate post–World War II period, Europe and Japan were involved in reconstruction and became massive *importers* of capital. Large-scale investment in Latin America was therefore out of the question until the late 1960s when both direct and portfolio investment began again. Table 7 shows the

[11] British data are calculated from Simon (1967, 39–40) for total British capital exports to Latin America and Stone (1968, 319) for percentage of government securities; French data are calculated from United Nations (1965, 11); U.S. data are from Appendix I.

TABLE 7

Portfolio Investment in Latin America by Lending Country:
1970–80

(millions of 1958 dollars, annual averages)

Lender	1970–73	1974–77	1978–80
United States	$627.6 (52.7%)	$2,173.5 (52.9%)	$3,352.5 (37.9%)
Britain	125.8 (10.6)	289.2 (7.0)	471.2 (5.3)
Germany	29.2 (2.5)	438.7 (10.7)	1,085.3 (12.3)
France	81.3 (6.8)	120.7 (2.9)	561.6 (6.3)
Japan	115.0 (9.7)	115.9 (2.8)	1,046.0 (11.8)
Canada	12.8 (1.1)	124.6 (3.0)	769.9 (8.7)
Other	198.3 (16.7)	848.6 (20.6)	1,568.0 (17.7)
TOTAL	1,190.0 (100.0)	4,111.2 (100.0)	8,854.5 (100.0)

SOURCE: Appendix V.

distribution by lending country of Euroloans and bonds during the 1970s. It is apparent that Europe began to make a comeback and partially reclaimed its former position in Latin American portfolio investment. The trend is especially marked in the later 1970s when loans and bond issues from other advanced industrial countries exceeded those of the United States by a substantial margin.[12]

Characteristics of Portfolio Investment

The final task of this chapter is to provide additional details on U.S. credits and bond issues for Latin America. We shall examine data on country distribution of loans, on borrowing institutions, on the purpose of loans, and on their terms. More complete data are available for the 1920s and 1970s, but some information can be provided for the other periods as well.

The country distribution of loans has undergone substantial variation during the eighty years covered by this study. Table 8 shows the percentage breakdown of gross loan volume by major borrowing countries for four of the five subperiods. The period of negative net lending is not included.[13] In the 1900–19 sub-

[12] Disaggregating the figures in Table 7 into bonds and credits shows that the same trend toward greater non-U.S. participation occurs in both. U.S. banks have traditionally been stronger in credits than bonds, and this trend was accentuated during the 1970s. Thus the U.S. share of credits fell from 53 to 40 percent between 1974–77 and 1978–80, while its share of bonds fell from 48 to 16 percent.

[13] The only country distribution data for the 1931–53 period are net bank credits, which give a fairly distorted view. That is, many countries had large loans during the period but, since they had been repaid by the end, they were eliminated from the final result. This is why gross figures are used for the calculation of country distribution in Tables 8 through 10.

TABLE 8

U.S. Portfolio Investment in Latin America by Borrowing Country:
1900–80

Country	1900–19	1920–30	1954–69	1970–80
Argentina	15.9%	27.9%	14.2%	8.9%
Brazil	10.7	22.1	9.4	22.1
Chile	–	17.6	3.5	5.4
Colombia	–	9.4	2.3	3.6
Cuba	13.0	6.8	0.4	–
Mexico	52.8	–	44.6	28.4
Panama	1.0	1.3	3.1	3.2
Peru	–	5.5	6.2	4.6
Uruguay	–	3.0	1.4	1.2
Venezuela	–	–	7.0	14.8
Other	6.8	6.4	7.9	7.8
TOTAL	100.0	100.0	100.0	100.0

SOURCES: Appendix V; Dickens (1933); World Bank (1972a, 1972b).

NOTE: Percentages are based on gross loan volume except for 1954–69, where the base is *net* bank credits and gross securities.

period, Mexico was clearly the dominant country, accounting for 53 percent of all loans. This pattern was to be expected since, in the early years of U.S. foreign investment, a strong preference was evidenced for countries in close geographical proximity. The same trend occurred with respect to direct investment (Wilkins 1970, chaps. 6 and 8). Furthermore, only two South American countries (Argentina and Brazil) received any large loans during this period, and together they represented a mere one-quarter of the total. With the exception of Bolivia, all of the countries in the "other" category were also from the nearby areas of Central America or the Caribbean.

During the 1920s some major changes occurred. Most notable was the fact that Mexico disappeared from the picture entirely. This was the period following the 1910–17 revolution in Mexico, and a U.S. government boycott existed with respect to private investment there until outstanding claims were settled. Mexico's absence, in turn, led to a redistribution of loan percentages toward South American countries. The distribution of loans was part of a general trend to integrate South America into the U.S. economic sphere; trade and investment links also increased as the United States replaced Britain in the region (Lewis 1938, app. D; Wilkins 1970, chap. 9). Argentina and Brazil became the countries absorbing the largest volume of loans (28 and 22 percent respectively), followed by Chile and Colombia (18 and 9 percent). If the "other" category is disaggregated, it turns out that South America received 89 percent of all loans, while Central America and the Caribbean were left with only 11 percent (most of which went to Cuba).

By 1954–69 Mexico had returned to its former dominant position, which it would not relinquish again. This time, however, Mexico accounted for only 45 percent of total loans. The second heaviest borrower was Argentina (14 percent) followed by Brazil (9 percent). Another noteworthy characteristic in this period was the first-time appearance of Venezuela as a borrower in the U.S. market. That country's oil wealth had previously made the government decide to stay out of the market, and, as other countries were eagerly borrowing during the 1920s, Venezuela was paying off its nineteenth-century debts (United Nations 1955). After World War II, however, Venezuela decided to borrow despite its oil.

Further changes occurred in the 1970s. Mexico remained as the single largest borrower (28 percent), but Brazil became a close second (22 percent). Brazil had been recognized during the 1960s as a rising international economic power and this fact, together with the Brazilian government's own economic strategy, which put heavy emphasis on foreign loans, led to its increased importance (Wellons 1974, 102–16). Venezuela also increased its borrowing, coming to account for 15 percent of total loans during the 1970s (Karl 1982). Argentina was the only country that declined significantly in its loan percentage, due largely to what investors regarded as an unfavorable political climate during much of the decade (Martel 1978, 21–38). Similar reservations existed about Chile, which received no loans until 1975 when it became a heavy borrower (Letelier and Moffitt 1978).

Another important characteristic about Latin American borrowers is the institutions seeking the funds. Borrowing institutions have been central governments (including the central banks), state and municipal governments, public corporations, and private corporations. As Table 9 indicates, there were variations over time on this factor too. Data are presented for the same four subperiods, again excluding the period of net negative lending.

In the earliest period, nearly half of all borrowing was done by the central governments of Latin America and another 13 percent by state governments. The 43 percent listed as loans to public corporations consisted entirely of loans to the Mexican National Railways, which were nationalized during the years 1903–9. This was one of the few corporations owned by governments in Latin America at that time. No private Latin American corporations (as opposed to U.S. corporations operating in Latin America) were strong enough to borrow in the U.S. market. During the 1920s, as Mexico ceased to borrow, the high percentage of loans to public corporations fell. The figure dropped to 6 percent which primarily represented loans to public-sector banks in Chile, Colombia, and Panama. Central government borrowing increased to 66 percent, and state and local borrowing became more important as well (28 percent). Loans to state and local governments were especially frequent in

TABLE 9

U.S. Portfolio Investment in Latin America by Borrowing Institution: 1900–80

Institution	1900–19	1920–30	1954–69	1970–80
Central government	44.8%	66.3%	60.4%	33.4%
State/local government	12.5	27.9	0.6	2.8
Public corporation	42.6	5.8	21.9	47.1
Private corporation	–	–	17.0	16.7
TOTAL	100.0	100.0	100.0	100.0

SOURCES: Appendix V; Dickens (1933); World Bank (1972a, 1972b).

NOTE: Percentages are based on gross loan volume.

Brazil, Argentina, and Colombia. Again private Latin American corporations were not represented.

In the post–World War II period, the pattern shifted. Between 1954 and 1969, central government borrowing maintained its importance (60 percent), but state and local governments practically disappeared from the market (less than 1 percent). Public corporations, by contrast, reappeared, accounting for 22 percent of all loans. The public corporations were again of Mexican origin – this time the National Development Corporation (Nacional Financiera) and firms dedicated to energy and industrial production. For the first time, private Latin American corporations became borrowers, although almost entirely through private placements rather than publicly issued bonds; most tended to be very small loans. The foregoing information pertains only to bond issues; no data are available on distribution of bank credits.

The 1970s witnessed only one significant change with respect to the previous period. This was a shift from central government borrowing to public corporations: the former represented only 33 percent of loans, surpassed by the latter with 47 percent. The shift was found mainly in the largest Latin American countries – Mexico and Brazil – since the smaller nations still needed to use the name of the central government to acquire funds.[14] State and local governments and private corporations maintained approximately the same proportion of lending as before. Note also that many of the public corporation loans were guaranteed by

[14] The difference between the borrowing patterns of Mexico and Brazil, compared to the other Latin American countries, is most clearly demonstrated by looking at the percentage of borrowing done by the central government. The figure is 12 percent for Brazil, 17 percent for Mexico, and 52 percent for the other countries. Percentages for public corporations are 60, 55, and 37 percent respectively. Data are for 1970–80 and are calculated from Appendix V.

the central governments; the same was true to a lesser extent for private corporations.[15]

One of the most difficult kinds of information to obtain concerns the purpose of loans. In order to maintain as much flexibility as possible, borrowers often try to avoid specifying the ways in which they will use the money. Thus, it is not uncommon for no purpose to be listed at all or for a very vague one to be given ("to be used for development projects," for example). Indeed, greater flexibility in use of loans was one of the reasons why Latin American governments turned from public agencies like the World Bank to the private capital markets. The World Bank insists on detailed specification of the projects it finances, and it monitors their progress as they are carried out. Private banks have neither the interest nor the capacity to do so. In fact, there was a debate in the 1970s among private bankers as to whether the purpose of a loan even mattered. Some preferred to lend for specific projects, while others said "money is fungible" – it is impossible to keep track of it, once disbursed, and it is easy for a borrower to substitute funds from one project to another (Interviews 1113, 1114, and 1120).

These problems should be kept in mind when examining the data on purpose of loans during the two heavy-lending periods. Table 10 shows that major changes again occurred over time. First, in terms of information availability, a significant decline occurred between the 1920s and 1970s. In the earlier period,

[15] One-fourth of all U.S. loans to private enterprises in Latin America were guaranteed, whereas 35 percent of public corporation and 40 percent of local government loans were similarly backed. The most common guarantor for the public sector was the central government, while guarantees for private-sector loans were shared between the central government, state development corporations, and other private enterprises (usually multinational corporations). These figures are calculated from Appendix V.

TABLE 10

U.S. Portfolio Investment in Latin America by Purpose:
1920–30 and 1970–80

Purpose	1920–30	1970–80
Production	–	34.0%
Infrastructure	37.6%	22.7
Refinancing	50.3	21.9
General purpose	12.1	21.4
TOTAL	100.0	100.0
Purpose unknown[a]	4.7	35.7

SOURCE: Appendix V.

NOTE: Percentages are based on gross loan volume for known purpose.
[a] These percentages alone are calculated on total loans, purpose known and unknown.

only 5 percent of all loans were for unspecified purposes (mainly in the early part of the decade); the figure rose to 36 percent in the later period. The greater lack of information in the later period is largely because 1920s loans were all bond issues for which a prospectus had to be published, whereas bank credits (which represented 98 percent of loan volume in the 1970s) had no such legal requirement.

Turning, then, to the percentages based on loans for which a purpose is known, some other differences are also clear. There were no loans in the 1920s for production, but 34 percent were so classified in the 1970s. The lack of corporate borrowers in the earlier period, whether public or private, accounted for this difference. Infrastructure and refinancing declined substantially between the 1920s and the 1970s. Infrastructure fell from 38 to 23 percent, while refinancing dropped from 50 to 22 percent. The refinancing category is probably the least reliable, since many borrowers wanted to avoid public admission of the need for refinancing for fear of lowering their credit ratings. Presum-

ably a significant portion of the "purpose unknown" category
was refinancing, and there may have been refinancing loans
disguised under other categories as well, especially in the second
half of the 1970s. The general-purpose category, which is another way of avoiding specific details regarding purpose, also
increased between the 1920s and 1970s, rising from 12 to 21
percent.

Finally, terms on loans have changed over time, mainly as a
result of the switch from bonds to bank credits. One change was
shortened maturities. The average maturity in the 1920s was
twenty-five years compared to only eight years in the 1970s.
Although this decline was largely attributable to the shorter
maturity of bank credits (the average for the 1970s was 7.6
years), it should be noted (Appendix V) that bond maturities
also shortened (the average for the 1970s was 11.6 years). The
key change in interest rates was the move from fixed rates, which
prevailed through the 1960s and are still commonly used for
bond issues today, to floating rates that are used on Euroloans.
Floating rates mean that a fixed percentage or "spread" is set
above the current deposit rate (usually the London Inter-Bank
Offer Rate, or LIBOR). The borrower then pays the combined
rate, the second part of which is readjusted every six months as
the deposit rate changes. This system guarantees that the banks
will not be caught with fixed-rate loans as interest rates rise, but
at the same time it increases the risk that borrowers will have
trouble servicing the loans.

A third difference in lending terms concerns collateral. In the
1920s a Latin American borrower would usually be asked to put
up some kind of collateral in order to obtain a loan. Three types
were generally used. One was a property mortgage, often on the
project being constructed (say, a railway or sewage plant). Eigh-
teen percent of loans in the 1920s were covered by property
mortgages. The second type was a lien on taxes. Customs duties
were often involved in Central America and the Caribbean with a

U.S. citizen placed in charge of collecting the tax; other typical liens included tobacco and alcohol duties. Thirty-eight percent of 1920s loans were covered by tax liens, and another 6 percent had collateral that was a combination of property mortgages and tax liens (Appendix V). At times the demands for such collateral became excessive, as for the Bolivian loan of 1922. This loan became a political scandal when a hard-pressed government agreed to security amounting to more than half the national income (Marsh 1928). A third form of collateral was the "negative pledge," which stated that the country would not provide collateral for any other loan without also doing so for the loan covered by the negative pledge. Loans in the 1920s covered by negative pledges amounted to 38 percent of the total (Appendix V).

Whether or not any of these arrangements increased the safety of loans during the 1920s is unclear. What is clear is that they provided no help at all after defaults occurred in the early 1930s. Lenders discovered that they could not foreclose on a country as they could on a company. In part because of this experience, and in part because Latin American governments demanded more dignified treatment, the requirements for collateral generally disappeared in the post–World War II period although negative pledges continued to be used for some bond issues. As we shall see, however, other kinds of conditionality were instituted, mainly in an effort to influence the economic policies that a borrowing government followed. In some cases, the banks tried to impose these conditions themselves; more common was cooperation with the International Monetary Fund (Stallings 1979, 1982).

Conclusions

This chapter has presented a variety of quantitative data on U.S. portfolio investment in Latin America during the twentieth century. The data have focused on three sets of characteristics about portfolio investment: the timing of investment flows, the relative importance of those flows, and the main features of the individual loans in different periods. The detailed information contained in the chapter can be summarized in the following description of the lending process:

1. Portfolio investment was concentrated in two decades of the century. More than 90 percent of total U.S. portfolio investment in Latin America occurred between 1920 and 1930 or between 1970 and 1980.

2. During those two decades, portfolio investment was the dominant type of U.S. capital export to Latin America. At other times in the century, direct investment or government loan flows were larger.

3. Portfolio investment from other countries, especially Europe, was important only at the beginning of the century (before World War I) and at the end (in the late 1970s). Otherwise, the U.S. bond market or banks were virtually the only source of private lending available to Latin America.

4. Within Latin America, portfolio investment was concentrated in a small number of countries. At the beginning of the century, Mexico was the major borrower, whereas the focus shifted south to Argentina and Brazil in the 1920s. After World War II, Mexico regained its previous dominant position and was then joined by Brazil in the 1970s. These three nations accounted for about half of all portfolio investment in the region during the various periods.

5. The main Latin American borrowers throughout the century were governments; private borrowers were in a small minority. The borrowing institutions, however, changed over time. Central governments dominated until the 1970s when public corporations displaced them, suggesting a change in the structure of Latin American governments, especially in the largest countries.

6. The reasons for borrowing changed in ways that are consistent with changes in borrowing institutions. Lending for productive purposes became prominent as public corporations emerged. General-purpose loans and even unidentified purposes increased as bonds changed to credits, where prospectuses were not required.

7. The terms on loans also changed with the switch from bonds to credits: maturities shortened, floating interest rates were substituted for fixed rates, and collateral disappeared.

These seven characteristics constitute the basic inputs for the analysis in the remaining chapters of the book. The pattern of lending over time is explained in Chapters 4 and 5. The lack of alternative lenders is crucial for interpreting supply relationships, while the identity of borrowing institutions and the reasons for borrowing are important to the discussion of demand factors. The concentration of borrowing in Brazil, Mexico, and Argentina means that special attention must be paid to these three countries to ensure that explanations based on aggregate regional data are consistent with what was happening in the three major borrowing nations. The discussion in Chapter 6 of Peru, a medium-sized borrower, provides the opportunity to examine the same characteristics on a micro level.

4

Long-Term Trends in U.S. Portfolio Investment

LONG CYCLES are the drama of economic history. Long cycles in production tend to be associated with major technological breakthroughs, sometimes with war. Foreign investment cycles in the nineteenth century were related to transcontinental migration, the bringing of new products onto the international market, and the rise and decline of industry at home. This chapter investigates the cyclical character of U.S. private bank lending in the twentieth century, where there were two decades of heavy lending (the 1920s and 1970s) in eighty years of otherwise light lending. It seeks to explain the U.S. lending pattern and to ask how it is possible to distinguish *between* heavy- and light-lending periods. Chapter 5 then discusses short-term fluctuations, focusing on some related questions about patterns *within* heavy-lending periods.

Both chapters require examination of supply as well as demand factors. Even though the 1875 British parliamentary inquiry showed that an occasional ingenious bank may have invented a fictitious borrower to bolster its profits (Jenks 1927, 47), lending normally cannot take place unless both lender and borrower desire to participate in the transaction. Thus, we need to identify the main factors that determined the actions of lenders and borrowers individually as well as discover how the two interrelate.

In technical terms, distinguishing the *ex ante* role of supply and demand is quite difficult since *ex post* statistics on lending represent the outcome of pressures from both sides. In an interrelated system, such as that between the U.S. and Latin American economies, identification of supply and demand is especially complex. Thus, the goal of the chapter is primarily to explain shifts in the jointly determined supply/demand relationship over time. Where possible, however, both quantitative and qualitative evidence are brought to bear to help assess whether there is more likely to have been an *ex ante* shift in supply or in demand during the period being examined.

The main focus of interest is an explanation for two shifts in the supply/demand relationship: the substantial increase in U.S. lending during the 1920s in comparison with the 1900–19 period and the similar increase during the 1970s in relation to the earlier post–World War II years. The period 1931–53 is not dealt with in detail because it was characterized by net inflow of capital from Latin America to the United States. The argument to be presented can be summarized as follows. During the 1920s the change was due to an outward shift in both supply of, and demand for, portfolio investment *from the United States*. The United States displaced Britain and other European countries as the major source of supply, but the total amount of capital made available did not equal that of the earlier period. Thus the change in demand was probably larger than the change in sup-

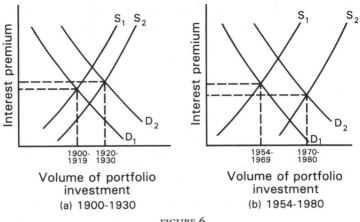

FIGURE 6

Changes in Supply and Demand for U.S. Portfolio Investment:
1900–30 and 1954–80

ply.[1] In the 1970s supply and demand again both shifted, but the change in supply was much larger than that in demand. Figure 6 expresses supply and demand as traditional curves, although this is a major simplification of the relationships involved.[2] In particular, supply and demand are not typically independent of one another as the curves would imply. Moreover, supply of, and demand for, loans cannot be seen only as functions of a single price (the premium). A much more complex analysis, including political and institutional as well as economic variables, is necessary.

[1] The relationship could also be viewed in terms of *total* capital supplied and demanded. In that case, we would have the supply curve shifting to the left while the demand curve would stay more or less in its original position.

[2] A similar approach is taken for a year-on-year analysis in the late 1970s by Fleming and Howson (1980). For a further elaboration, see Fleming (1981).

The procedure to be followed in the chapter involves three steps. First, factors on the U.S. (supply) side – political context, institutions, income distribution, growth, yield, and bankers' response – are examined to see how far they can take us in explaining the lending pattern; in this section, demand for loans at any realistic going price is assumed. Second, the assumption about demand is discussed with a focus on the general sources of demand for foreign capital in Latin America and specific characteristics on the demand side associated with the two heavy-lending periods. Finally, in the concluding section, the interrelationship between supply and demand is explored and, through its changing nature, an interpretation of the lending pattern is suggested.

Supply Factors: Characteristics of the U.S. Economy

The interdependent relationship between the United States and Latin America is a highly asymmetrical one in that the United States is much more important to Latin America than vice versa. The relative economic size of the various countries is one indicator. A more important one involves trade flows. During the twentieth century, the U.S. market has been much more important for Latin American exports than has the Latin American market for U.S. exports.[3] In terms of this study, the primary

[3] On the average, between 1910 and 1980, some 16 percent of U.S. exports were sold in Latin America while 36 percent of Latin American exports were sold in the United States (calculated from United States 1976; *Statistical Abstract of the United States* 1984; Pan American Union 1931 and 1952; Interamerican Development Bank, *Annual Report,* 1982). This difference is also magnified in two ways. First, if we consider *individual* Latin American countries rather than the region as a whole, the gap becomes much more significant. Second, Latin American trade

asymmetry is that the United States has had money to lend, while Latin America has wanted to borrow. Under normal conditions, power lies with the lender in international as well as domestic lending. These various asymmetries justify considering the development of the U.S. economic and financial system as largely independent of happenings in Latin America although it may be strongly influenced by events in other parts of the world.[4] This relative independence is crucial to an interpretation of causal relations between supply and demand. An examination of certain aspects of the U.S. economy is thus an initial step in explaining the periodization of lending to Latin America. The discussion is organized around the hypotheses presented at the end of Chapter 1.

The Political Context of International Lending

The first hypothesis discussed in Chapter 1 states that U.S. lending to Latin America in the twentieth century, like British lending in the nineteenth century, was primarily motivated by economic rather than political considerations. This is a story of profit-oriented private institutions which, during certain periods, considered it advantageous to do substantial amounts of business abroad. Although private lending to Latin America cannot be understood as an arm of U.S. foreign policy, neither can we go to the other extreme and ignore the crucial role the

---

is a larger proportion of GDP than is U.S. trade. Exports as a percentage of GDP for 1980 were 15.2 percent and 8.4 percent respectively (calculated from Appendixes II and III).

[4] Fleisig (1972) tried to quantify the feedback on the U.S. economy from Third World economies in the 1930s and found the effect to be slight. In the 1980s that effect has increased somewhat as international trade has come to account for a larger share of the United States' GNP.

government did have to play in providing the proper context for large-scale private lending to occur. In particular, the government had to avoid regulations that discouraged foreign investment, and it had to refrain from its own lending that could crowd out more expensive private loans. More controversial is the possibility that the government had to provide an implicit guarantee for the loans.

The periodization introduced in Chapter 2 is useful for understanding the political context of lending because politics played different roles at different times. It was precisely in those periods of least government involvement that private lending flourished. In the years up to World War I, most economic transactions with Latin America focused on countries of close geographical proximity—Mexico, Central America, and the Caribbean islands. It is in this part of Latin America that the U.S. government has traditionally been most inclined toward intervention, both diplomatically and militarily. Thus it is not surprising that there was a close intermingling of public and private activity at the beginning of the century through the process known as "dollar diplomacy." Secretary of State Knox encouraged lending to this area as a way of gaining political influence, and U.S. troops frequently occupied the smaller countries in order to ensure loan payments. Likewise, bond issues were floated in the name of those countries where U.S. occupation occurred with the clear implication that the bonds were backed by the force of the U.S. military (Nearing and Freeman 1925; Williams 1929; Angell 1933).

During the 1920s, the focus of lending activity shifted to South America, and concomitantly the political role of the U.S. government with respect to Latin American lending was substantially reduced.[5] It is important to note that the Latin Ameri-

[5] Several authors remark on the sharp break in U.S. foreign policy vis-à-vis Latin America in the 1920s, pointing to a new disinclination

can trend was quite different from what was happening in Europe, where politicization was at a high level because of the reparations and war debt issues.[6] In Latin America, the 1920s lending wave by the private banks existed in part because the government decided to end its own lending operations after the war. The bankers applauded this decision and vigorously argued against government regulation of investment activities. In general, government officials agreed with the bankers' position—both because dollar diplomacy was regarded as a failure and because private initiative was considered to be a superior form of organization (MacKaman 1977, chaps. 2–3).

The direct U.S. government role in the 1920s was thus limited to fairly passive supervision. Banks were to inform the State Department before making a loan, but only on rare occasions was a loan blocked. The open question is whether investors regarded the government's "failure to object" as an indication of support for the loans and how important such an implicit guarantee was in their willingness to purchase Latin American bonds. The State Department made every effort to prevent such an inference from being drawn, and banks were prohibited from mentioning the department in their prospectuses, but the assistant secretary of state admitted that confusion had resulted (Madden et al. 1937, 245). No *ex ante* evidence on investors'

---

toward intervention (Angell 1933, chap. 5; Madden et al. 1937, 239–41). Those who stress a continued political role during the 1920s focus mainly on the State Department's power to review loans (Feis 1950; Tulchin 1971, chap. 5).

[6] For a discussion of the European situation during the interwar period, see RIIA (1937), Feis (1950), de Cecco (1985), and Fishlow (1985). Among the differences concerning Europe and Latin America was the bankers' view on the U.S. government's role after the war. As indicated below, bankers wanted the government out of Latin American finance, but they were apparently of a different mind with respect to Europe. On the latter, see Abrahams (1969).

opinions is available, but the *ex post* results are clear: after the defaults of the 1930s, the government provided only minimal assistance to bondholders (Winkler 1933; Feis 1950; Tulchin 1971).

Apart from its refusal to help bondholders, the U.S. government also engaged in other activities during the 1930s that discouraged foreign lending. In particular, several restrictive regulations were introduced that affected international portfolio investment, even if this was not always their major objective. The Securities Act of 1933 required bankers to file a detailed statement with the Securities and Exchange Commission, to pay a fee, and to observe a twenty-day "cooling off" period before the securities could actually be sold; it also made them legally liable for providing inaccurate or misleading information (Carosso 1970, chaps. 17–18). The Banking Act of 1933 (Glass–Steagall Act) divorced investment from commercial banking in the United States. The relationship between this forced divorce and international portfolio investment came via the decline in funds available to the investment banks, once their ability to accept deposits was eliminated. Statistics suggest that the resulting decline in capital was more than 60 percent (ibid., 371–72). Less capital could be expected to mean less attention to marginal clients such as foreign investors. Moreover, many states limited the amount of foreign securities that banks, insurance companies, and pension funds could hold in their portfolios; 1 percent was a typical figure (Merrill Lynch White Weld 1979).

World War II again saw major U.S. government lending, and this time the activity was carried into the postwar period. Initially the primary aim was promoting European recovery but, once that was assured, attention turned to Latin America. The combination of an active government and the bond market's lack of interest in Latin America after the defaults meant that public lending became the primary source of external finance for the region. The U.S. government first supported the establishment of the Interamerican Development Bank in 1960 and then began extensive bilateral lending via the Alliance for Progress a year later (Levinson and de Onis 1970; Lowenthal 1974). In conjunction with increasing multilateral aid, U.S. bilateral funds had a negative effect on portfolio investment during the 1960s: much of the potential demand for private loans was siphoned off.

The resurgence of private bank finance in the 1970s coincided with the decline in bilateral aid to Latin America as the Alliance for Progress fell into disfavor because of its own failures and shifting U.S. geographical priorities. The Eurocurrency market provided a convenient alternative source of external finance, as we shall see, and the U.S. government aided its growth by refraining from attempts to regulate the market despite some doubts about its activities (Bench 1977; Heimann 1977; Einhorn 1978; Hawley 1984).

Again, as in the 1920s, the question arises as to whether the government also provided more positive support in the form of an implicit guarantee. In the 1970s evidence exists that bankers did *perceive* such a guarantee or "safety net" as Sampson (1982, 117) calls it. Interviews conducted for the preparation of this book confirm this impression (Interviews 1110, 1116, 2857) as do the studies of others (Gisselquist 1981, 142; McKinnon 1984, 18; Darity 1985, 43–46). At least as important was the role of the International Monetary Fund as the institution that was supposed to persuade Third World borrowers to follow economic policies that would enable them to service their debts.

Regardless of any perceived guarantee that might be called in the future, the Eurobanks' recycling of OPEC oil revenues enabled governments of advanced industrial countries as well as OPEC to avoid becoming immediately involved in financing the increased balance of payments deficits that emerged in Third World countries after the oil price increases. Only as a result of the near defaults in the early 1980s did the U.S. government reluctantly resume a strategic role in international finance, thus confirming the bankers' expectations. Its new role had an internationalized character as close coordination was carried out with the IMF (Stallings 1983b; IMF 1984). The contrast between increased government activity when a lending crisis emerged in the 1980s and the hands-off stance in the 1930s derives in large part from the different institutional arrangements of the two periods.

Institutional Framework for International Lending

The second hypothesis discussed in Chapter 1 centers on the necessity of an adequate institutional structure to support large-scale portfolio investment in foreign countries. The primary requirement is a group of banking intermediaries with access to funds which can be channeled to foreign borrowers. In historical terms, these have been either investment banks selling bonds to individuals and institutions or commercial banks lending their own deposits. Complementary financial infrastructure includes such institutions as a central bank for controlling monetary policy and a stock exchange for trading bonds. It is not coincidence that the most important financial innovations of the twentieth century took place in the years preceding the two heavy-lending periods.

For the United States to assume the major role in capital export after World War I, some important developments had to occur. A crucial step was the establishment of a central banking system via passage of the Federal Reserve Act in 1913.[7] From the

[7] This did not mean that the system had been totally decentralized before the passage of the Federal Reserve Act. Some of the worst excesses had been eliminated by the National Banking Act of 1863,

point of view of foreign lending, the Federal Reserve Act had three main consequences. First, it gave the government the power to conduct monetary policy – that is, to influence, even if not totally control, the money supply and interest rates. The liquidity of the economy can have a significant influence on foreign lending. For example, many economists suggest that the easy credit policy during much of the 1920s played an important role in stimulating foreign loans (Madden et al. 1937, chap. 4; Brown 1940, chap. 18). Likewise, Kindleberger (1985, 151–52) argues that the Federal Reserve's easy money in the early 1970s, in the face of a contrary stance by the Bundesbank, led to a pre-OPEC buildup of Eurodeposits and therefore loans. In both cases, tight money near the end of the respective periods was associated with a cutback in lending.

A second consequence of the 1913 legislation was to permit nationally chartered banks to accept bills of exchange, the traditional source of international trade finance. Previously, U.S. foreign trade had been financed by British bank acceptances. A closely related change was the Federal Reserve's capacity to rediscount the trade bills. Without such a rediscount facility, the private banks' acceptance of bills would lock up their reserves and limit the amount of credit that could be extended (Abrahams 1976, chaps. 2–3; Reynolds 1914). The Federal Reserve Act thus gave impetus to foreign banking in general which, in turn, was conducive to portfolio investment.

---

which regulated the issuance of new currency. The banking problems arising out of the 1907 panic, however, convinced many skeptics that further steps were needed. One of the difficulties in creating a central banking system in the United States, which was also the reason for the decentralized nature of the Federal Reserve, was the suspicion with which the general public viewed Wall Street. This suspicion dictated the great secrecy which shrouded bankers' participation in the drafting of the new legislation. See Kolko (1963) and West (1977).

The third important consequence of the Federal Reserve Act for international lending was the specific authorization given to foreign branch banking. Prior to 1913, only state-controlled banks could establish branches; the new legislation gave national banks the same privileges. The existence of branch networks gave the banks closer acquaintance with the personnel and institutions of foreign governments and corporations and thus more ability and confidence in making loans. Although a branch network was not a necessary prerequisite, as evidenced through the lending activities of banks like Morgan without branches, there can be little doubt that the early branching did give added impetus to the 1920s loans. Likewise, the 1960s branching wave facilitated loans in the 1970s (Odjagov 1977; Weinert 1978; Cleveland and Huertas 1985).

In addition to creation of a central bank, and a system of trade finance and international branches, innovations had to take place in the domestic banking system in order to sell foreign bonds in the U.S. market. As de Cecco (1985, 55) points out, anyone who suggested in 1913 that New York would replace London as the major financial center would have been greeted with disbelief. The New York market had none of the "technology for the 'production' of foreign bonds." Probably the only way the "technology" could have been quickly created was to sell foreign bonds the same way domestic bonds were sold. Thus, the major investment banks set up securities affiliates which either had their own retail operations or arranged with brokerage firms to distribute bonds to individual investors (RIIA 1937, chap. 11; see also Cleveland and Huertas 1985 for the example of National City Bank).[8] The U.S. public's lack of familiarity with foreign countries required the use of these bond salesmen

[8] De Cecco (1985) goes further to say that the facilities used were the ones set up to market war bonds.

as well as extensive publicity campaigns. The success of such methods – very different from those used in Britain – was seen in the ability of the U.S. market to absorb billions of dollars of bonds during the 1920s. The "improvised" nature of the new institutions (Brown 1940, 587), and their rapid emergence in a setting without significant prior experience in international finance, surely accounted for many of the problems as well.

The second set of twentieth-century institutional changes involved the development of the Eurocurrency market during the 1950s and 1960s. Although the market's inception is said to be traceable to Soviet deposits in European banks, the big growth in the new institutions in the early period came from U.S. banks trying to escape U.S. government regulations. Two such regulations were attempts to limit capital outflows. One was the Interest Equalization Tax (IET) of 1963, which had the effect of increasing the yield that had to be offered on new securities to offset the tax and thus making the New York market more expensive than its European competitors. The other was the Voluntary Foreign Credit Restraint (VFCR) program that was introduced in 1965 and became mandatory in 1968. The main purpose of the VFCR was to prevent U.S. corporations from borrowing in the U.S. market in order to invest abroad. Bank credits were also restricted with priority given to export credits in an attempt to improve the trade balance. Many observers think that the combined effect of the Interest Equalization Tax and the credit controls was a major impetus to the growth of the Eurocurrency market (Hawley 1977, chap. 7; Mendelsohn 1980, chap. 6; Makin 1984, 131–32).

Other institutional innovations provided the necessary security to make U.S. bankers – for the first time since the 1920s – willing to engage in large-scale international finance. Three such innovations were especially important. One was syndicated lending whereby a number of banks joined together to share the risk, and the profits, of a loan. The syndicates were organized by a lead-managing bank that received a front-end fee in addition to its share of interest payments. A second innovation was floating interest rates such that the major portion of the interest rate was readjusted every six months according to the banks' cost of funds, thus passing the risk of rising rates onto the borrower. Finally, cross-default clauses made it impossible for a borrower to play off one creditor against another.

These institutional developments were complemented by organizational changes within the banks themselves that further stimulated international lending proclivities. Branch offices were set up abroad to service multinational corporate clients, eventually leading to international loans to help cover the costs of the foreign offices. As a consequence, the career advancement possibilities of certain bank personnel became linked to international lending. Moreover, by the late 1960s the drive for increased earnings again became important in the banking industry, once the memory of the 1930s faded with the passing of the older generation (Weinert 1978).

As the Eurocurrency market developed, it came to have a trajectory that was substantially autonomous of the U.S. (or any other national) banking system. Without a domestic clientele, either for deposits or loans, the Eurobanks became totally internationally oriented. Growth was more rapid, and competition more intense, than in the regulated national markets. The result was greater volatility but also greater receptivity to innovative types of finance and to new clients such as Third World governments (Bell 1974; Mendelsohn 1980).

In the U.S. context, the role of the Eurocurrency market was particularly crucial. U.S. banks were having trouble even in acquiring sufficient deposits to service domestic loan demand as their supply of government securities was run down and they lost deposits to nonbank financial institutions (Winningham

1978, chap. 3; Goodhart 1984, chap. 5). These difficulties, reflected in the turn from asset to liability management in the mid-1960s, meant that the possibility of large-scale Latin American borrowing from banks in the United States was nonexistent. Since the U.S. bond market was not very receptive to Latin American issues, an institutional change was necessary for the private markets to again assume a major role in supplying capital to Latin America.

Income Distribution and Access to Savings

Once the institutions came into being, there was still the need for savings to fund foreign loans. The third hypothesis relates savings availability to certain patterns of income distribution. Specifically, it suggests that foreign lending is associated with a redistribution toward high-income groups who are assumed to be high savers. The resulting problem of "oversaving" is then alleged to limit investment possibilities at home and increase the attraction of foreign investment.[9] Income distribution data during the twentieth century support this hypothesis, although the nature of the redistribution changes from national to international over time.

Figure 7 shows the share of disposable income that accrued to the top 1 percent and top 5 percent of the income scale (that is, the high savers) in the United States between 1919 and 1946. The one period when that share increased significantly was during the 1920s. Thus, from 1919 to 1928, the share of the top income groups rose steadily. Disposable income of the top 1 percent increased from 12 to 19 percent, while the top 5 percent went from 24 to 34 percent in the same period. Thereafter, the

[9] See Edelstein (1982, chap. 2) on the lack of specificity of the "oversaving" hypothesis and possible alternative formulations.

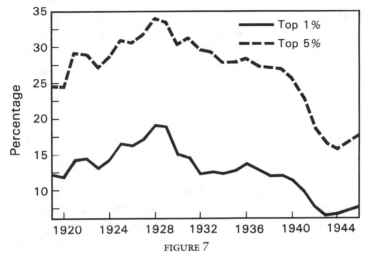

FIGURE 7

Disposable Income to Top Groups in the United States: 1919–46

SOURCE: Kuznets (1953, 637).

share of the two groups fell, reaching 7 and 18 percent respectively by 1946.[10] From that time on, shares have remained fairly stable (United States 1981, 54).

This trend in income distribution for the top groups was especially important in the early part of the century because, at that time, wealthy individuals were the main purchasers of stocks and bonds.[11] About half of all interest and dividend

[10] These data are from Kuznets (1953, 637). Williamson and Lindert (1980, chaps. 3 and 4) support Kuznets's notion that the 1920s brought increased inequality of both income and wealth in the United States. Smiley (1983) questions the trend, doubting the figures for the early part of the decade, but offers no alternative estimates.

[11] Apparently in contradiction to the analysis in this chapter–that foreign bonds were purchased by a very small percentage of the population–is the importance that de Cecco (1985), Cleveland and Huertas (1985), and others place on a "large and growing middle class" as

payments between 1915 and 1930 went to the wealthiest 1 percent of the population, while around 70 percent went to the top 10 percent (Kuznets 1953, 646–55). Furthermore, a study done by the U.S. Treasury Department in 1943 showed that foreign assets were even more highly concentrated than domestic assets.[12] For the post–World War II period, personal income distribution became less relevant because the primary purchasers of securities changed from individuals to financial institutions such as insurance companies and pension funds (Goldsmith 1958, 1968; Kotz 1978, chap. 3).

In the 1970s a quite different kind of redistribution took place, but it affected the level of foreign lending in a manner that falls within the bounds of the same hypothesis. In this case, the redistribution was international, rather than within the United States, and it transferred income toward high-saving countries. Table 11 shows balance of payments data for three groups of countries during the 1970s; they are the OECD (the advanced

---

purchasers of foreign bonds. A closer look is revealing. In support of the middle-class thesis, Cleveland and Huertas (1985, 135) say that nearly 600,000 people in the United States had incomes over $5,000 in 1922, and by the end of the decade the number had increased to 1 million. Given a population of 123 million in 1930, however, the "large middle class" represented less than 1 percent of the population. Likewise, in a widely cited article, Morrow (1927) reports on the distribution of five large foreign bond issues in the 1920s. Although he concludes that these issues were bought mainly by "small investors," his data show that the average individual sales ranged from $2,944 to $4,335. These amounts represented more than the total annual income of all except the top 1 percent of the population—hardly supportive of any commonsense notion of small investors.

[12] Individuals who owned foreign assets represented 0.1 percent of the population and, even within this group, concentration was very high. Thus, 88 percent of foreign assets belonging to U.S. citizens were owned by 0.02 percent of the population with individual holdings averaging more than $50,000 each.

industrial countries of North America, Western Europe, and Japan), OPEC (the oil-exporting nations in the Middle East, Africa, and Latin America), and the non-oil-exporting Third World countries in Africa, Asia, and Latin America. The table indicates that the 1973 oil price increase brought about a large transfer from both OECD and Third World countries toward OPEC in 1974 but that, by 1975, all of the deficit was borne by the Third World. A similar process occurred after the second set of oil price increases in 1979.

This redistribution of income affected foreign lending because of the new role of commercial banks functioning through the Eurocurrency market as has been discussed earlier. There are a number of sources of Eurodeposits, of which multinational corporations and central banks are among the most important; a multiplier of undetermined size also expands the potential lending volume (Johnston 1982, chap. 9). In 1974 an important new source of deposits came from the OPEC governments, especially those OPEC countries that did not have a very large absorptive capacity in the short run (that is, the high savers). The principal examples were Saudi Arabia, Kuwait, and the United Arab Emirates, all of which had small populations and low levels of industrialization.

The OPEC countries initially wanted to maintain a very high degree of liquidity; thus they deposited most of their funds with the largest Eurobanks in London and New York.[13] Once the

[13] The behavior of the OPEC countries indicates that a large balance of payments surplus alone is not sufficient to bring about the development of an international financial center. Surplus countries can lend through existing channels. An extension of the OPEC example suggests that the emergence of New York as the dominant financial center in the 1920s was not inevitable simply because of the U.S. balance of payments position. The political and institutional developments were crucial.

TABLE 11

Variation in Current Account Among Groups of Countries: 1973–80
(billions of dollars)

Year	Industrial Countries		Oil Exporters	Non-Oil Third World	
	All	7 Largest		All	Latin America
1973	$19.7	$14.1	$ 6.6	-$11.5	-$ 4.7
1974	-11.6	-3.7	67.8	-36.8	-13.4
1975	17.6	23.2	35.0	-46.5	-16.6
1976	-0.2	9.1	40.0	-32.9	-11.9
1977	-4.6	8.0	31.1	-28.6	-9.1
1978	30.8	34.2	3.3	-37.5	-12.9
1979	-7.8	4.7	68.4	-57.6	-20.9
1980	-44.1	-15.7	112.2	-82.1	-33.1

SOURCE: International Monetary Fund, *Annual Report* (1981, 18).

NOTE: Totals do not sum to zero because of errors, omissions, and relations with non-IMF countries.

banks accepted the deposits, they then had to find customers interested in borrowing the money and willing to pay higher interest rates than the banks were paying for the deposits. On the surface, it might seem curious that the banks accepted these deposits rather than lowering their interest rates to keep them out. The reason was competition. From the bankers' point of view, OPEC was "the hottest game in town." Refusing to accept the new deposits would jeopardize all OPEC business. If the banks could have united to agree on how to handle the deposits, the outcome might have been different, but from an individual bank's viewpoint, refusing to participate would put it at a severe disadvantage vis-à-vis its competitors.[14]

This, then, was the mechanism whereby the international income transfer increased foreign lending in the 1970s by a process analogous to the income transfer within the United States in the 1920s. The fact that Eurodeposits had very little dependence on individuals in the United States meant that U.S. income distribution and savings rates no longer had the direct importance they once had for foreign lending. In contrast, growth rates in the United States – which were closely correlated in this period with growth rates in other major industrial countries – retained their relevance, since this country was a potential site of loan placement in competition with Latin America.

[14] Although there is controversy about the banks' handling of OPEC deposits, two particularly revealing interviews with bankers (Interviews 1104 and 1114) found them saying that they probably *could* have turned down deposits but they did not and, moreover, that by the late 1970s they *had begun to discover* that they could turn them down. The latter statement implies that, in the years of highest lending, they believed they had to accept them. It should be pointed out that most bankers deny the process described here. They insist that they first looked for good loan opportunities and only then sought deposits to fund the loans. For an example of this position, see the statement by the former head of Citibank's international division (quoted in Sampson 1982, 127).

Growth Rates and Yield

The fourth hypothesis focuses on economic growth rates within a lending country. Specifically, it predicts that low growth rates will be associated with high foreign lending. Growth rates, in turn, are likely to affect, and be affected by, rates of return which may also have an independent relationship with foreign investment. The evidence that follows provides some support for this hypothesis.

Measuring trend rates of growth calls for a slight modification of the periods used elsewhere in the study. Following the methodology developed by the National Bureau of Economic Research (NBER), growth rates for the twentieth century as a whole, and for the various subperiods, will be measured between cyclical peaks. This is one way of suppressing the influence of cycles in order to examine trend movements.[15] The modifications in the subperiods involve the two heavy-lending decades; in each case, the last year of the period is eliminated since each represents a substantial downturn. Thus, the 1920s are measured from 1919 to 1929 and the 1970s from 1969 to 1979. With these modifications, it is then possible to make use of the NBER's own data series as shown in Table 12.

Both heavy-lending periods represent some fall in growth rates when compared to the previous (light-lending) periods. Low growth during the 1931–53 period was not sufficient to offset the disorder of the markets (as the government imposed new regulations) and the effect of the defaults (many of which

[15] Other ways of measuring trend include calculating moving averages or fitting a regression line to logarithms of the growth series. On the National Bureau of Economic Research (NBER) methodology, see Kuznets (1961, chap. 2) and Kendrick (1973, 36–37). The NBER growth cycle chronology can be found in Moore (1980).

TABLE 12

Volume of U.S. Portfolio Investment in Latin America Compared
to Variation in U.S. GNP: 1899–1979
(1958 dollars)

| Period | Portfolio Investment | Growth Rate | |
		GNP	GNP per Capita
1899–1919	Low	4.05%	2.30%
1919–29	High	3.10	1.60
1929–53	None	3.06	1.93
1953–69	Low	3.60	2.13
1969–79	High	3.05	1.98

SOURCES: Kendrick (1961, 79 and 84) for 1899–1953; GNP data for 1954–79 from
Appendix II and population data from *Statistical Abstract of the United States* (1982, 6).

were still unresolved). In the case of the 1920s, the fall with
respect to 1900–19 was from 4.05 to 3.10 percent,[16] while in
the 1970s the decline from 1954–69 was from 3.60 to 3.05. Per
capita growth rates show a similar pattern, although the differences are not as striking, especially in the post–World War II
period. Although the 1970s are generally regarded as a slow-
growth ("stagflation") decade, a few words may be in order
about the 1920s. The twenties are often viewed as a prosperous,
optimistic decade, but much of this impression may be based on
looking back from the speculative craze in 1928–29 (Kindleberger 1973, 61–62).[17] The decade as a whole was more somber,

[16] If the war years are excluded, the growth rate during the earlier
period increases to around 5 percent (calculated from Appendix II).

[17] Kindleberger himself takes a middle line between those who see
the 1920s as a boom era and those, like Friedman, who deny any boom
existed because of lack of increase in the money supply. Nevertheless,
Kindleberger's interpretation of the relationship between foreign lending and growth—based only on the early part of the century—is the
opposite of the view outlined here. See Kindleberger (1973, 54–56).

characterized by very uneven growth with a downward trend across peaks. Furthermore, growth was also uneven across regions and sectors as agriculture, mining, and traditional consumer goods languished (ibid., chap. 4; Brownlee 1979, chap. 14).

What do low U.S. growth rates mean in the context of foreign lending? Why are they important? The basic assumption underlying the relationship is that, all else being equal, home investment is preferred by banks as well as most other firms. Only if conditions are unfavorable there will they invest abroad. If growth is low, demand is likely to be low, as is capacity utilization. Thus, demand for credit at home will also be low. If low growth is accompanied by low rates of return, then a double reason exists for capital export.

In the 1970s the effects of low growth in the United States were magnified by trends in other advanced countries. For the first time since the Depression of the 1930s, growth rates in the advanced industrial world coincided.[18] This synchronized pattern began with a recession in 1970–71 and was followed by a boom that lasted into 1973. From 1974 through the early 1980s–with some brief interludes–North America, Europe, and Japan were all growing much more slowly than in the earlier post–World War II period. The synchronization of growth rates had at least two relevant effects for this analysis. First, it meant that demand for credit from U.S. banks was low in the rest of the advanced industrial world as well as at home, so Latin American countries would have better than usual access to loans. Second, it meant that Latin American countries would not have many

[18] Explanations for the synchronization of the growth cycles vary. One is the appearance of floating exchange rates; see Kolm's discussion as summarized in Kindleberger and Laffargue (1982, 3).

alternatives to the United States as far as export markets were concerned and thus would be in special need of loans.

Moving to rates of return for the five periods, shown in Table 13, a contradictory picture emerges. Nominal yields declined by an average of 16 basis points during the 1920s in comparison to an increase during the two light-lending periods.[19] The 1970s, however, had the highest increase of any period (an average of 39 basis points). The evidence thus indicates a different relationship during the two heavy-lending periods with respect to nominal interest rates. Insofar as falling nominal rates in the domestic market stimulate investors to look abroad for more profitable opportunities, interest rates played a role in bringing about the increase in portfolio investment in the 1920s in comparison with the first decades of the twentieth century. This, indeed, is the hypothesis of most contemporary and later analysts of the 1920s (United States 1930a, 28–29; Madden et al. 1937, 13–14; Aldcroft 1977, 250; MacKaman 1977, 157–60; Fishlow 1985, 424). In the 1970s, by contrast, such an argument does not hold since heavy lending occurred together with rising nominal interest rates in the United States. As with growth rates, the 1930s would appear to have been a propitious time for foreign investment, as U.S. interest rates fell, but political and institutional factors were more than sufficient to offset the economic variables.

Yields in constant prices show an even more perverse pattern from the point of view of this hypothesis – the 1920s and 1970s were the only periods when real rates in the U.S. market were *rising* on average. It should be noted, however, that the large 1920s rise is due principally to the jump in real rates between 1920 and 1921. Likewise, the 1970s figures are heavily influ-

---

[19] A basis point is one-hundredth of a percentage point.

TABLE 13

Volume of U.S. Portfolio Investment in Latin America Compared
to Variation in Yield on U.S. Domestic Bonds: 1900–80

Period	Portfolio Investment	Change in Yield[a]	
		Nominal Yield	Real Yield[b]
1900–19	Low	11	−37
1920–30	High	−16	194
1931–53	None	−6	−36
1954–69	Low	28	−4
1970–80	High	39	8

SOURCE: Appendix II.

NOTE: U.S. yield is yield on Moody AAA corporate bond index.
[a] Average change in basis points (1 basis point=0.01 percentage point).
[b] Deflated by GNP deflator.

enced by the increase in real interest rates in 1979 and 1980.[20]
Other than these two pairs of years, real rates were falling during
the two decades although not in a smooth pattern.

Taking a slightly broader view, banks' prospects for profits in
the home market in the two heavy-lending decades were not
bright. In the 1920s two problems clouded the outlook. On the
one hand, firms began to move away from bank credit toward
internal savings and equity issues. On the other hand, the new
Federal Reserve banks were taking over the big-city banks' traditional role of holding smaller banks' reserve balances (de Cecco
1985, 57; Cleveland and Huertas 1985, 127–30). In the 1970s

[20] Real yield went from −7.9 percent in 1920 to 22.9 percent in
1921 for a rise of 3,080 basis points. By 1923 it was back in the 3 to 6
percent range, where it stayed until 1930 when it rose to 13.6 percent.
In the 1970s real interest rates in the United States averaged about 1.5
percent through 1978. In 1979 the rate rose to 4.5 percent, and in
1980 it increased further to 7.6 percent. All figures are calculated from
Appendix II.

some quantitative data are available. Of the ten largest banks, four actually had falling earnings in the U.S. market between 1970 and 1976, while the other six had average earnings of around 5 percent (Hanley 1976). The latter did not even keep up with inflation, which averaged 6.4 percent (Appendix II). Thus, in both decades, dim prospects at home made more profitable foreign lending look especially attractive.

The Bankers' Response

The final hypothesis from Chapter 1 takes us from aggregate characteristics of the U.S. economy, which might be expected to stimulate or discourage capital export, to the behavior of the principal actors. That is, we switch from a macro to a micro level of analysis to see how bankers responded to the political, institutional, and economic factors that confronted them. The hypothesis suggests that heightened expectations and competition among bankers would greatly expand lending until confidence eroded or an outside shock brought the process to a halt.

Several analysts have recently discussed the 1920s and 1970s along the lines of this final hypothesis. The basic idea is summarized by Darity (1985), who says that the banks became "loan pushers." Citing Winkler (1933), Lewis (1938), and others who wrote in the aftermath of the 1930s defaults, Darity suggests that bond salesmen in the 1920s induced borrowers to accept more money than they wanted or needed. A similar phenomenon is alleged to have occurred in the 1970s. For the later decade, Darity can rely on such an authoritative source as Andrew Brimmer (1973, 17), former member of the Board of Governors of the Federal Reserve, who said that "the Eurocurrency banks (especially in London) began to push loans to the developing countries with considerable vigor." Likewise cited is former banker S. C. Gwynne's (1983) exposé on the way he and his bank pushed loans to the Philippines.

The explanations offered for such behavior are vague: surplus funds or creation of a market for U.S. exporters are suggested. A more coherent explanation, which Darity mentions but does not highlight, is competition. Competition, together with the high profits available, is the factor stressed by most writers on the 1920s. With commissions much higher than those available on domestic issues, American investment bankers engaged in aggressive struggles among themselves in order to obtain a continuous flow of new securities. This competition led to tactics ranging from the use of overseas agents and finders' fees to direct bribes of officials of borrowing governments and deceptive prospectuses (Winkler 1933, chap. 1; Madden et al. 1937, 221–26; RIIA 1937, 170–72; Lewis 1938, chap. 18; Lary 1943, 96; MacKaman 1977, chap. 3; Fishlow 1985, 423–24; Felix 1987).[21] De Cecco (1985, 58–59) sums up the point by saying: "The U.S. banks were behaving as if they were concerned with purely domestic operations and were pushed to excesses by the competitive structure of the banking industry of the 1920s. . . . Had the large banks colluded, they definitely would not have been able to build up such a huge operation in such a short time." The investment banks, of course, could afford to be careless about their offerings because they did not hold the bonds in their own portfolios but sold them to individual investors. Thus, if defaults occurred, it would be the individual bondholders who would bear the loss.

The institutional changes between the 1920s and 1970s – from the flotation of bonds by investment banks to the lending of deposits by commercial banks – created the need for a different set of mechanisms to explain competitive behavior. Darity

[21] All of these authors rely heavily on the testimony in the 1930s Senate hearings (United States 1932).

cites the institutional and macroeconomic factors discussed earlier in this chapter: the Eurobanks without alternative clients and with OPEC surpluses to recycle.

Devlin (1987) provides the micro-level foundations for such an argument. Rather than passive arms-length investors, he says, modern commercial banks act like firms which produce and aggressively market their products. In this case, the product is money. During the 1950s and 1960s, the banking industry on the international level was even more oligopolistic than in most domestic markets. Furthermore, there were no legal barriers to collusion on the international level, leading to price stability as sellers avoided price competition in order to share monopoly rents. The 1970s, by contrast, brought a quite different situation. Thanks to the various institutional developments discussed earlier in the chapter, barriers to entry fell considerably, thus leading to a much larger number of banks participating in international lending. The result was manifested in cutthroat price competition for market share.

Devlin shares the view, summarized in Figure 6, that supply of funds for Latin American borrowers exceeded demand. He goes even further, however, and portrays a supply curve that was flat, and shifting downward, until a point when credit rationing was introduced. In other words, the increased competition drove prices down even as volume increased. Although falling prices shaved profit margins coming from interest payments, front-end fees kept Third World loans lucrative for those who were organizing syndicates.[22] The risks of default were ignored

---

[22] Some idea about why smaller banks joined syndicates, despite lack of access to front-end fees, is revealed in an interview in the *Wall Street Journal* (3/25/83). The senior vice president of a bank in South Carolina explained that the big loans were in international syndications, and "it takes loans on the books to make money for the [bank]." Another incentive was future opportunities to finance South Carolina's

by a new generation of bankers who knew the 1930s only
through musty history books.

Summary

An examination of the data on U.S. portfolio investment in the
twentieth century provides support for all five hypotheses presented in Chapter 1, insofar as explanations for long-term trends
are concerned. At particular times – the 1920s and 1970s – the
five factors have come together and reinforced each other, thus
leading to high-lending periods.

In the 1920s the U.S. government eliminated its own wartime lending program, and a series of institutional changes
occurred in the financial market that enabled U.S. investment
banks to replace both their own government and the London
market as the main source of capital export. Shifts in U.S.
domestic income distribution toward high savers provided the
savings necessary to make a high volume of foreign loans. The
decline in domestic interest rates, and the relative drop in U.S.
growth rates with respect to the early part of the century,
prompted foreign lending as an alternative to acquiring domestic
assets. Bankers responded in a competitive way to capture the
available profits, thus building a high volume of debt in a very
short time.

By the 1970s the international economy had become substantially more interdependent. What is intriguing, however, is
that the same general factors remained relevant for explaining
portfolio lending patterns, but they assumed an internationalized form. The institutional changes led to an interna-

---

textile exports. The banker also outlined the problems facing a small
bank in getting information to evaluate a foreign loan.

tionalized capital market in spite of the dominance by U.S. banks. Income distribution was still important, but it was international distribution toward high-saving countries. Growth rates in lending countries remained important, but the synchronization between business cycles in industrial countries became relevant as well. Again bankers competed vigorously to obtain foreign business, and debt was quickly built up.

Demand Factors: Characteristics of Latin American Economies

Although supply-side factors go a long way toward explaining lending patterns, demand must be considered as well. Despite some of the revisionist analysts' discussions of lenders enticing or even "forcing" loans on borrowers (see Kindleberger 1978; Darity 1985; Devlin 1987), a more useful approach tries to understand the relationship between supply and demand. That is, we want to know why borrowers sought foreign capital and how their needs related to trends in lending countries.

In the previous section, I argued that economic trends in the United States can be assumed to be largely independent of what occurs in Latin America. The reverse cannot be assumed since Latin American economies are heavily conditioned by what happens outside their borders and especially in the United States. This conditioning takes two forms that will be labeled structural and process linkages. The former refers to certain structural characteristics of Latin American economies that make them dependent on foreign capital. The latter refers to the growth rate and associated trends in Latin America being heavily influenced by economic conditions in the rest of the world. The two linkages will be examined in turn to see what they imply about Latin America's demand for foreign capital. In addition, the effects of competition from borrowers in other regions will be considered.

Structural Linkage

Demand for foreign capital in underdeveloped countries derives from two basic sources. One source is the underdeveloped nature of the production structure such that many kinds of goods cannot be, or at least are not, produced locally. This situation creates a demand for imports that must be paid for in foreign exchange. The precise kinds of imports vary over time, depending especially on the level of development of the industrial sector in a given country. As is well known, industrialization in Latin America proceeded by an import-substitution path such that consumer goods were the first to be produced locally, followed by intermediate goods (Hirschman 1968; Furtado 1976, chaps. 10–11; Weaver 1980). In the case of the larger countries in the region, a capital goods industry is being developed, but imports nevertheless remain crucial (Leff 1968; Nacional Financiera 1977b; Mitra 1979; Beckel and Lluch 1982). The lack of a full-fledged capital goods industry, together with the need to import inputs, has left the region highly vulnerable to foreign exchange shortages (Diaz-Alejandro 1965).

The second source of demand for external finance derives from the immaturity of domestic capital markets. In theory, local production as well as government deficits could be financed at home through the domestic financial system. In most Latin American countries, however, institutions providing long-term finance do not exist; in others, they are still weak (Basch and Kybal 1970; Wai and Patrick 1973; Wai 1976; OAS 1976; *World Financial Markets*, April–May 1986). In all countries, the principal source of long-term finance is the government itself, usually through state-owned development banks. These banks, in turn, are intermediaries for borrowing in the international capital markets in order to onlend to local firms and government agencies and corporations. Local commercial banks provide mainly short-term loans (United Nations 1970, 1971). In no countries do stock exchanges provide a viable means of corporate finance, although such markets formally exist in nine countries (Basch and Kybal 1970, chap. 3; Wai and Patrick 1973; International Finance Corporation 1981). Only in Mexico since 1955 and Brazil since 1964 has the government begun to develop a market for its own bonds (Ness 1974; OAS 1976, 1115–37; FitzGerald 1977; Baer 1983, chap. 9; Frieden 1985). In most countries, therefore, internal government finance is synonymous with the creation of money. The anticipated inflationary consequences often lead to the search for foreign capital, given the domestic political problems involved in raising taxes.[23]

Both structural linkages imply a *potential* need for foreign capital. The capital goods linkage will *actually* require a foreign capital inflow only if a current account deficit exists. The government finance linkage, however, may require a gross inflow of foreign capital even with a current account surplus since foreign capital is the main source of long term finance. These two sources of demand for external finance can be related to the discussion in Chapter 1, where a set of equations showed the relationship between foreign capital flows, the trade balance,

[23] The choice of methods for financing the government deficit can be part of a general economic strategy. The three Chilean governments between 1958 and 1973 provide an example. Alessandri emphasized foreign loans as a means of holding down inflation; Frei chose a combination of foreign and domestic finance; and Allende purposely financed via emission in order to stimulate the economy (although he was forced to do so to a greater extent than originally planned because of congressional refusal to raise taxes). See Stallings (1978, 184–86).

and domestic balances (public and private). Combining and rearranging the equations to reflect the typical Latin American deficit position, we have the following:

$$(G+I)-(T+S) \equiv (M-X) \equiv (C_I-C_O)+\Delta R$$

where G is government expenditures, I is investment, T is taxes, S is savings, M is imports, X is exports, C_I is capital inflow, C_O is capital outflow, and ΔR is change in reserves. The structural linkages can be located within this framework. They help to produce a surplus of imports over exports $(M>X)$, and they suggest that a substantial part of the domestic deficit $([G+I]>[T+S])$ will be financed externally, thus leading to net capital inflow $(C_I>C_O)$.

These two types of structural linkage between the Latin American and U.S. economies provide the basic reasons for the demand for foreign capital. As long as an advanced industrial sector and domestic capital market are absent, the linkage and therefore the demand for foreign capital will continue. Likewise, the fact that the linkage existed throughout the 1900–80 period implies that Latin American countries needed foreign capital. During most of this period, U.S. capital was virtually the only available source, so the specific form in which the capital was supplied – direct investment, government loans, or portfolio investment – was largely determined by political and institutional developments within the United States.

Process Linkage

The process linkage between Latin America and the United States has had an important influence on short-term fluctuations in the demand for foreign capital. The main way it has operated is through U.S. demand for Latin American merchandise exports. The growth rate of the U.S. economy determines the volume of goods imported. Since a large percentage of Latin American exports go to the United States, U.S. growth rates have a strong effect on Latin American export volume, which, in turn, affects Latin American growth both directly and indirectly. The direct effect comes through production in the export sector, while the indirect effect operates via foreign exchange availability to provide inputs to domestically oriented sectors. This volume of trade mechanism is likely to be reinforced by changes in Latin America's terms of trade as prices for the region's primary exports rise or fall more than their industrial imports (Lewis 1980; Massad 1983).[24]

To see how the process linkage has operated over time and its possible effects on demand for foreign capital, we turn to an examination of certain Latin American economic variables. These include the trade balance, the fiscal balance, growth rates, and the yield premium. After examining the trends in these variables, we shall see whether they are correlated with patterns of heavy and light lending. Even if strong correlations exist, the question remains of how to interpret them. It should be stated at the outset that there is no reason to expect a strong relationship between these variables and the cyclical pattern of portfolio investment, since the latter is only one form of Latin

[24] The Chilean economist Carlos Massad (1983) points to process links based on monetary as well as trade variables. He talks of two traditional and two new monetary links by which a recession in the U.S. economy can be transferred to Latin America. The former include high interest rates in the United States leading to reduced investment in Latin America and bringing about a revaluation of Latin American exchange rates, which are typically pegged to the dollar. The latter include rising interest rates on Latin America's floating rate debt, which sucks money out of the region, and deterioration of U.S. banks' portfolios leading to a decline in lending to Latin America.

TABLE 14

Comparison of Portfolio and Total U.S. Capital Exports to
Latin America: 1910–80
(millions of 1958 dollars, annual averages)

Period	Portfolio Investment	Total Investment	Portfolio/ Latin American Imports	Total/ Latin American Imports
1910–19	$ 37.0	$ 186.5	1.0%	5.1%
1920–30	260.1	483.7	6.0	11.2
1931–53	−54.3	132.3	−1.2	2.9
1954–69	123.7	903.5	1.5	10.6
1970–80	1,669.7	2,740.5	7.9	12.9

SOURCE: Appendixes I and III.

American capital import. Thus, the relationship between the
Latin American variables and total capital import – including
direct investment and government loans as well as portfolio
investment – must also be considered.

Table 14 presents a comparison of trends for portfolio and
total U.S. capital flows to Latin America. The first two columns
show the absolute figures, which indicate a different pattern
between the two. While portfolio investment was high in the
1920s and 1970s and low or negative in the other periods, total
capital export increased monotonically with the exception of
1931–53 when it also fell. When the two variables are calculated
as a percentage of Latin American merchandise imports, in order
to measure the importance of capital flows with respect to the
Latin American economies, the situation changes. Total and
portfolio capital assume the same pattern, although the differences between the periods of heavy and light lending for total
capital are much smaller than they are for portfolio investment.
If non-U.S. capital were included, the basic change would be in
the first period. In fact, if European investment were included,

foreign investment (portfolio and total) would be about 35 percent higher in the first two decades of the twentieth century than during the 1920s.[25] This conclusion for Latin America is consistent with Fishlow's (1985, 390) calculations for total port-folio investment, which he puts at two-thirds the level in 1914–30 as 1900–13.[26] The investment totals for the 1970s would also rise substantially if non-U.S. capital exports were included.

Economic Balances

Data on the Latin American current account are generally avail-able only after World War II, so it is necessary to begin with a discussion of the merchandise balance and, when possible, sup-plement that with information on services. Figure 8 shows the aggregate Latin American merchandise balance since 1910. It indicates that prior to the end of World War II, exports exceeded imports in every year except 1921. During the late 1940s and the 1950s, the balance was frequently negative; after 1967 it was positive only once (1973). The key question, however, is how the merchandise balance related to the current account, which is the counterpart to capital import.

[25] If we were to add European portfolio investment in Latin Amer-ica to that of the United States for the period 1900–19, the total is likely to be around $350 million per year (in 1958 dollars). This estimate is based on the calculation that European capital markets provided Latin American governments with slightly more than $300 million per year between 1900 and 1913 (United Nations 1955, 3–6, and 1965, 7–14). This figure compares to an annual average of $260 million for the 1920s as shown in Table 14. If direct investment is included, then Latin America probably obtained at least twice as much capital from Europe in the 1900–13 period as from the United States in the 1920s (ibid.).

[26] Since the periods discussed here are not the same, no direct comparisons can be made, but the general trend is similar.

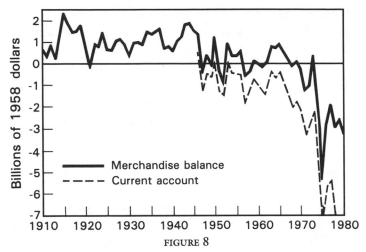

FIGURE 8

Latin American Balance of Payments: 1910–80

SOURCE: Appendix III.

From 1946 that question can be answered directly. Figure 8 demonstrates that the current account for the region as a whole was positive in only three years (1946, 1950, and 1953). In other words, in the post–World War II period, imports of goods and services – including the payment of profits and interest – exceeded exports of goods and services in all but three years. If the situation for individual countries is examined, it turns out that more than 80 percent were in deficit at any given time. Those who were most often in surplus were the smallest countries (in Central America and the Caribbean region) together with oil-exporting Venezuela.[27]

[27] These figures are averages for five-year periods; a higher percentage (about one-third in 1960–80) was in surplus in any individual year. The country distribution was as follows: Argentina was in surplus in two five-year periods out of a possible seven for which data are available; Colombia, in one; Cuba, in two (Cuba was eliminated from the calcula-

What can be said about the pre–World War II years? Specifically, was the positive merchandise balance sufficient to offset the service balance including the outflow of profits and interest? The answer undoubtedly varied over time. The only attempt to estimate the regional balance of payments for the period before the mid-1940s is a United Nations study covering 1925–29 (United Nations 1953, 6). That study indicates that the current account was negative with an average annual deficit of $140 million. The deficit was due mainly to a large outflow for profits and interest. At the same time, the export boom had ended so that export revenue was growing more slowly. In the 1930s, when most debt payments were suspended and profit remittance was limited, a current account surplus probably existed (ibid.).[28]

In the early part of the century, the outcome depends on one's hypothesis about services including profits and interest. Table 15 shows that, if it is assumed that 15 percent of export revenue went for net service payments (the 1946–60 situation), then the region had a current account surplus most of the time between 1910 and 1924. If there was a 30 percent service outflow (the 1925–29 and 1970–80 situation), then there were deficits except during the war. Based on individual country calculations, the latter seems the most reasonable assumption.[29]

tions after 1959); Dominican Republic, in three; El Salvador, in two; Guatemala, in four; Haiti, in two; Paraguay, in one; Peru, in three; Uruguay, in three; and Venezuela, in three. Eight countries (Bolivia, Brazil, Chile, Costa Rica, Ecuador, Mexico, Nicaragua, and Panama) were never in surplus. Calculated from United Nations (1965, annex I, tables D, E, and F) and Interamerican Development Bank (1981).

[28] The United Nations (1965, 28) estimates that *if* all payments had been made, debt service alone (excluding profit remittance and the rest of the service balance) would have absorbed about 20 percent of export revenues in the mid-1930s.

[29] The choice of the 30 percent estimate as more likely is based on

TABLE 15

Estimates of Latin American Current Account: 1910–24
(millions of dollars)

Year	Hypothesis A[a]	Hypothesis B[b]
1910	−$ 8	−$205
1911	−105	−302
1912	24	−214
1913	−160	−384
1914	157	−42
1915	509	260
1916	374	91
1917	332	23
1918	404	42
1919	581	116
1920	24	−498
1921	−354	−658
1922	144	−172
1923	31	−336
1924	320	−116

SOURCE: Appendix III.

[a] 15 percent of export revenue spent on services.
[b] 30 percent of export revenue spent on services.

Turning to the fiscal balance, Figure 9 indicates that, for the region as a whole, a fiscal deficit existed in all but four years between 1900 and 1980; the surplus years were 1903 and

recalculations for two individual countries – Chile and Peru. Mamalakis (1976, 58–64), in his balance of payments estimates for Chile in the 1920s, suggests that payments to foreign capital between 1925 and 1930 absorbed 31 percent of export revenues. Moreover, he mentions another 25 percent for service imports and adds that merchandise imports are likely to be underestimated because of smuggling and underinvoicing. Bertram (1974, 287–91) finds similar results for Peru.

1905–7. Examination of individual country balances reveals that about two-thirds of the countries had deficits in any given period and that percentage increased steadily over time. Thus, around half the countries had deficits through 1910, two-thirds from 1911 through 1960, and seventeen of nineteen countries after 1960.[30] Furthermore, during the 1920s the largest borrowers had the largest deficits. That group included Argentina, Brazil, Chile, and Colombia, which together had deficits averaging 16 percent of expenditures, while the six countries that did not borrow at all had a small surplus. The medium borrowers fell in between. In the 1970s the situation changed somewhat, and the medium borrowers (Argentina, Chile, Peru, and Venezuela) had the largest deficits. This apparent anomaly arose because the largest borrowers (Brazil and Mexico) sought loans mainly to finance state corporations rather than the central government, and the former are not included in the deficit figures used here.

Figure 9, it should be pointed out, gives an overly optimistic picture of government finance since debt service payments are not included in the expenditure category. This fact has two implications. First is the obvious point that the deficits including amortization and interest were larger. Second, and more important for the topic at hand, service payments on the external debt required foreign currency. Foreign currency was also essential for public works and other investment projects since much of the

[30] The figures again refer to a surplus on the average over five-year periods. The same countries that had surpluses on the current account also tended to have them on the fiscal balance: Venezuela and the various Central American and Caribbean nations. Mexico too was generally in fiscal surplus until the mid-1930s. If the data were available, the preferable unit of analysis would be the public-sector balance (which includes public enterprises and decentralized agencies) rather than the fiscal balance (which includes only the central government). The former has also been in massive and growing deficit, as FitzGerald (1979, 214) documents for the 1950–75 period.

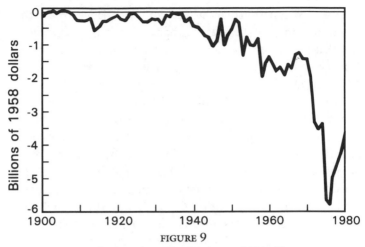

FIGURE 9

Latin American Fiscal Balance: 1900–80

SOURCE: Appendix III.

equipment and raw materials had to be imported. Beyond
providing foreign exchange, foreign borrowing enabled governments to finance rising expenditures without increasing taxes, a
habit that was left over from the nineteenth century (Jenks
1927, chap. 9; Cottrell 1975, 45).

Data on long-term trends in the balance of payments and the
fiscal balance are summarized for the five subperiods in Table 16.
Both balances show increasing deficits over the course of the
eighty years. With the fiscal balance, this relationship is monotonic throughout the five subperiods – that is, each period shows
a larger average deficit than the previous period when measured
in constant dollars. With the current account, the same monotonic change occurs with the single exception of the 1931–53
period. This kind of monotonic pattern clearly provides little
help in accounting for the lending cycles, where the 1920s and
1970s are the periods of heavy portfolio investment.

TABLE 16

Volume of U.S. Portfolio Investment in Latin America Compared
to Variation in Latin American Economic Balances: 1900–80
(millions of 1958 dollars)

Period	Portfolio Investment	Fiscal Balance (annual average)	Current Account (annual average)
1900–19	Low	−$ 160	−$ 246[a]
1920–30	High	−190	−457
1931–53	None	−474	70
1954–69	Low	−1,426	−1,014
1970–80	High	−3,864	−5,225

SOURCES: Appendix III for fiscal balance and for current account from 1946; current account for 1910–45 from Table 15 (1910–24), United Nations 1953, 6 (1925–29), and author's estimates (1930–45).

[a] Period is 1910–19.

For total capital import, however, a relationship does exist. Since Table 16 measures the two balances in absolute amounts, the proper figures from Table 14 are also the absolute amounts. In all cases—leaving aside 1931–53—there is a continuous increase in the deficits and a continuous increase in foreign capital. The question, however, concerns the interpretation. One interpretation is that foreign capital was sought because deficits occurred. This interpretation follows the literature on the "two-gap" model (Chenery and Strout 1966; Vanek 1967, 105–24), where foreign capital is seen as filling either the savings or the foreign exchange gap (or both) in Third World countries, with foreign capital supplementing domestic resources.

Critics of this theory have suggested an alternative interpretation. Griffin (1970), Weisskopf (1972), and others have provided evidence that foreign capital actually substitutes for, rather than supplements, domestic resources. That is, domestic savings—government and private—may decline as a result of foreign capital inflow. The fall in savings can arise, for example, if governments expend less effort on tax collection, if foreign investors preempt the most profitable investment projects, or if consumption of imported goods increases. Via this interpretation, deficits (fiscal and balance of payments) may exist because foreign capital is available. Most of the evidence is for the 1960s, so more research would be needed for earlier and later periods before any firm conclusions could be reached. Some data to begin examining the causal mechanisms, focusing on relationships within heavy-lending periods, are presented in the following chapter.

Growth Patterns

Although data are scarce and it is hard to generalize across countries, evidence seems to indicate that the periods of high growth in twentieth-century Latin America have been the pre–World War I years and the period 1960–74. Part of the difficulty in making such a statement is that regional data on gross domestic product (GDP) are available only from 1940, so it is necessary to rely on proxy variables and individual country studies for the earlier years. Two possible proxies are imports (under the assumption that domestic growth stimulates demand for imports) and exports (under the assumption that high export levels stimulate domestic growth).[31]

Table 17 shows growth rates of imports, exports, and total trade (imports plus exports) for the Latin American region during the five subperiods introduced earlier to measure peak-

[31] Both of these measures have a fairly close relationship to GDP, and to each other, in the period (1946–80) when all are available. Although the trends are similar, GDP growth is less volatile (both on the upward and downward sides) than trade.

to-peak rates.[32] The table indicates that the 1920s represented a fall in *value* of trade in comparison with the first two decades of the twentieth century, while the 1970s witnessed a very large increase with respect to the 1954–69 period. Although data on trade *volume* are difficult to find for the early part of the century, they appear to move in the same direction as the value figures, although the trends are somewhat damped (United Nations 1953, 1–4; *Monthly Bulletin of Statistics,* various issues).[33] Thus, the trade data present a mixed picture when correlated with portfolio lending trends. One of the heavy-lending periods is associated with very low growth rates, while the other is associated with the highest growth of the century. If non-U.S. investment is included, however, there is an association between trade flows and foreign investment – the pre–World War I years and the 1970s are both the periods of highest trade growth and highest investment flows. This pattern would support the hypothesis discussed in Chapter 1 about the correlation between export value in borrowing countries and investment flows. The suggested link was that rising exports give lenders confidence that their loans can be serviced.

[32] For the reasons given in the discussion on U.S. growth rates, a redefinition of the periods is needed. The U.S. periods are used here to facilitate comparison. Based on the trade figures, the Latin American cycle appears to be slightly different (no detailed studies exist on the Latin American business cycle), but the basic conclusions are not altered by choice of starting and ending dates.

[33] The United Nations study (1953, 3) gives a volume index for Latin American trade for 1901–5, 1913, and 1928. Combining the export and import indices, we get an increase of 75.5 percent between 1901–5 and 1913 compared with 22.6 percent between 1913 and 1928. Based on the League of Nations data (*Monthly Bulletin of Statistics,* various issues), it appears that volume in 1913 and 1919 were probably at fairly similar levels. Likewise, there does not seem to have been much increase between 1928 and 1929.

TABLE 17

Volume of U.S. Portfolio Investment in Latin America Compared
to Variation in Latin American Trade and GDP: 1903–79
(1958 dollars)

Period	Portfolio Investment	Rates of Growth			
		Exports	Imports	Trade[a]	GDP
1903–19	Low	5.15%	7.51%	6.33%	n.a.
1919–29	High	1.75	4.04	2.90	n.a.
1929–53	None	3.13	4.68	3.91	4.74[b]
1953–69	Low	0.68	1.05	0.87	5.42
1969–79	High	11.35	13.20	12.28	5.93

SOURCES: Appendix III and United Nations (1953, 3).

[a] Exports plus imports.
[b] Period is 1941–53.

Table 17 also presents data on regional GDP growth for the
years when such data are available. These figures indicate that the
1970s had the highest growth rates, but in this case the difference between that decade and the others is not nearly as large as
with the trade data. The increase is only 0.5 of 1 percent with
respect to 1954–69. The 1941–54 growth rate is lower than the
other two and would presumably be lower still if the 1930s were
included.

Clearly, the largest countries in the region – which have also
been the most frequent borrowers – had a very strong effect on
the regional totals. Thus, it is important to single out the long-
term growth patterns of Argentina (Diaz-Alejandro 1970a),
Brazil (Villela and Suzigan 1977; Baer 1965, 1983), Chile (Ballesteros and Davis 1963; Mamalakis 1976), Mexico (Reynolds
1970; Solis 1979), and Peru (Thorp and Bertram 1978). The
varying types of data used by these authors indicate that all five
countries grew rapidly in the first years of the century, based

mostly on rapid increase in primary exports. The 1920s generally saw a slowdown with the end of the export boom, but more diversity was apparent than in previous decades.

Among the three largest countries, postrevolutionary Mexico was facing domestic economic problems as well as a diplomatic confrontation with the U.S. government, which had imposed an economic boycott. Mexico was the only country of the five that was not involved in the borrowing spree of the 1920s (Turlington 1930, chaps. 7–8; Smith 1972). Argentina suffered a drop in growth rates in comparison to earlier years (Diaz-Alejandro 1970a, 18–24), as did Brazil, although high levels of capital formation occurred in Brazil (Baer 1983, 39–43). As for the two medium-sized countries, Peru's government maintained demand through high levels of expenditure based on foreign borrowing (Thorp and Bertram 1978, chaps. 4–6), while Chile had a mixed performance in the first half of the decade but strong growth from 1925 to 1929 (Ballesteros and Davis 1963; Mamalakis 1976, chap. 1). The 1930s again saw the region's economies moving in tandem, in a depressed state like most of the rest of the world. Some, especially Chile, were hit more heavily than others (González-Casanova 1977; Thorp 1984).

The post–World War II period also presented a picture of divergent economic paths within Latin America – in large part due to an increased government role in the economy and different development strategies across countries and across time. Chile had especially wide swings in this sense (Cavarozzi 1976; Stallings 1978), while postwar economic history in Argentina was marked by secular decline as well as cyclical fluctuations (Diaz-Alejandro 1970a). The strongest continuous growth performance was maintained by Mexico (Reynolds 1970; Solis 1979) and by smaller Peru (Thorp and Bertram 1978; FitzGerald 1979). Brazil also had generally high growth rates, but its performance was less consistent than that of Mexico or Peru (Baer 1983). All but Mexico and Chile suffered some slowdown in the latter half of the 1970s, but the reasons were varied.

When compared with lending volume for the individual countries, these growth patterns again lead to the conclusion that there is little basis for believing that high growth in Latin America stimulated U.S. portfolio lending. Low growth rates in Mexico went together with low lending in the 1920s, but U.S. foreign policy appears to be the primary link. With the possible exception of Chile in the latter half of the decade, the high lending of the 1920s was not accompanied by historically high growth rates. In the 1970s high growth in Brazil and Mexico did accompany high lending but, for the other countries, political and institutional factors seem to provide better explanations for lending patterns. Including European capital, however, again brings about a better fit between lending and growth.

Yield Premium

A final long-term trend of potential relevance to investment patterns is the yield premium. This variable may serve as an indication of demand, and it may also be a mechanism for attracting foreign capital. As would surely be expected, a premium has continually existed for Latin American loans with respect to loans in the United States itself; that is, the yield on the former has exceeded that on the latter. The main reason for this premium is that investors consider Latin American loans to be riskier than loans at home. Whether this is actually true may be debated, but such is the perception.[34] In an equilibrium situation, this premium would exactly offset the perceived additional risk. In less-than-perfect capital markets, however, the premium may exceed perceived risk and thus serve as a source of attraction for investors to move money abroad.

There is not one yield premium but many, depending on which yields or interest rates are being considered. Two have been selected for use here. One (PREM1) is the difference between the average yield on Latin American bonds and the yield on prime U.S. securities, in this case the Moody index of AAA corporate bonds. This premium is available for the entire century. For the 1970s a second premium (PREM2) is added. It is the difference between the average interest rate charged on Latin American Euroloans (LIBOR plus spread) and that on U.S. domestic business loans.[35]

Using PREM1 as an example, since it is the only premium that exists for the entire period (except 1931–54 when no Latin American issues were floated), Table 18 shows the variation for the four remaining periods. It includes the level of the premium itself and the premium as a percentage of total U.S. yield. The latter is important since the size of the premium had a different significance depending on the total U.S. yield. The premium on Eurocredits is also shown, although any strict comparison with earlier periods is impossible since this premium only exists during the 1970s. Nevertheless, the similarity between the size,

[34] Data on the relative incidence of default for foreign versus domestic loans by U.S. banks in the 1970s indicate a *lower* default rate for foreign loans; see the banks' annual reports. Edelstein (1982, chap. 4) found similar results for the nineteenth century.

[35] The business loan rate is very closely related to the U.S. prime rate, but the former is preferable in that it represents the rate at which loans were actually made rather than a theoretical benchmark.

TABLE 18

Volume of U.S. Portfolio Investment in Latin America Compared
to Variation in Premium Between U.S. and Latin American Bond
Yields: 1900–80

Period	Portfolio Investment	Premium[a]	Premium/ U.S. Yield[b]
1900–19	Low	1.29%	31.0%
1920–30	High	1.90	37.7
1955–69	Low	1.72	37.6
1970–80	Low (High)[c]	0.86 (0.63)[c]	10.0 (6.8)[c]

SOURCE: Appendixes II and III.

[a] Premium is defined as the difference between the average yield on Latin American bonds
floated by U.S. banks and yield on Moody's AAA corporate bond index.
[b] U.S. yield is yield on Moody's AAA corporate bond index.
[c] Euroloan volume and premium with respect to U.S. business loan interest rate.

absolute and relative, of the premium on bonds and credits in
1970–80 supports the idea of a significant drop in the size of the
premium.

Two interpretations can be made of the data in Table 18. On
the one hand, like other factors discussed in this section, the
premium provides little basis for distinguishing between heavy-
and light-lending periods. Although there is some increase in
the absolute and relative size of the premium in the 1920s
compared to the two earlier decades, there is little difference
between the 1920s and 1955–69. Certainly, the low premium
for the 1970s is not useful in accounting for the heavy portfolio
investment of that decade. For the components of total capital
flow other than portfolio investment, the premium is not relevant since direct investment and government loans are not
closely related to interest rates.

On the other hand, Table 18 is useful in trying to analyze the
shifts of the supply and demand curves that were discussed at the

beginning of the chapter (Figure 6) and again in the section on bankers' response. The latter discussion raises the possibility that both the 1920s and 1970s represented periods of "loan pushing." Because of surplus funds, profits, and competition, investment banks in the 1920s and commercial banks in the 1970s are said to have persuaded borrowers to accept more money than they needed. A good deal of evidence exists to support this view. Nevertheless, the data on loan premiums in Table 18 suggest that a distinction needs to be made between the two decades. The decline in the premium in the 1970s indeed supports the notion of loan pushing or, to use more neutral terminology, an increase in supply of funds that exceeded the increase in demand. For the 1920s, by contrast, the premium *increased* in comparison with 1900–19. Both the premium and the standardized premium (premium/U.S. yield) went up. The rise could be partially attributable to greater inelasticity of supply as the new lenders required a greater increase in the premium to provide the much larger amounts of money during the 1920s, but it also suggests that demand for foreign capital was more important than the loan-pushing hypothesis implies.

Some further insights can be obtained by looking at Devlin's (1987) list of criteria for supply-led growth of lending: (1) proportion of loans to risky borrowers increases, (2) price varies substantially and tends to fall, (3) finance is provided for nontraditional purposes such as consumption or refinancing, (4) loans are oversubscribed, and (5) collateral is not required. All five of these criteria were met during the 1970s as Devlin himself demonstrates and as has been shown earlier in this book. In the 1920s, however, at least two of the criteria did not hold. The spread varied little and actually tended to increase, and collateral was usually required. These trends provide further indication that, while some loan pushing may have existed in the 1920s, the phenomenon was more restrained than in the 1970s. As stated earlier, the volume of total finance actually fell with respect to the earlier period, both for Latin America and elsewhere. The increase in the 1970s, by contrast, was without precedent. Similar relationships between loan volume and the premium within the two heavy-lending decades will be found in the next chapter.

Competition from Non–Latin American Borrowers

A few of the writers on British capital export, such as Hall (1963) and Fishlow (1985), paid special attention to competition among borrowing countries and regions in explaining the pattern of nineteenth-century capital flows. That topic is also potentially relevant for a discussion of U.S. capital export to Latin America in the twentieth century. In particular, it could be hypothesized that Latin American demand for U.S. capital would be satisfied only if demand were slack in advanced industrial countries that were preferred borrowers. This, of course, is merely an extension of the idea that capital export occurs in slack periods of the U.S. economy itself, as discussed earlier in the chapter.

Insofar as long-term trends in U.S. portfolio investment are concerned, there is some evidence for the notion of Latin America as a residual borrower. Table 19 presents data on portfolio investment in Latin America and the advanced industrial countries. Because the periods constructed for Latin America are not very useful for other regions, the data are grouped into five-year periods. An initial way to analyze the table is to focus on the Latin American percentage of total loans. In general, the five-year percentage figures are substantially above or below the overall average of 29 percent.

In those periods when Latin America had a particularly small share of loans, there is historical evidence to suggest that the

TABLE 19
Volume of U.S. Portfolio Investment in Latin America
and Advanced Industrial Countries: 1900–79
(millions of 1958 dollars, annual averages)

Period	Latin America	Advanced Industrial Countries[a]	Total[b]	Latin American Percentage
1900–04	$ 25	$ 140	$ 165	15.2%
1905–09	88	12	100	88.0
1910–14	15	54	69	21.7
1915–19	20	1,512	1,532	1.3
1920–24	152	779	931	16.3
1925–29	374	606	980	38.2
1930–34	−16	−300	−316	5.1
1935–39	−105	−235	−340	30.9
1940–44	−53	128	75	−
1945–49	−40	153	113	−
1950–54	8	172	180	4.4
1955–59	123	516	639	19.2
1960–64	166	700	866	19.2
1965–69	85	343	428	19.9
1970–74	710	1,403	2,113	33.6
1975–79	2,268	3,295	5,563	40.8
AVERAGE	239	580	819	29.2

SOURCES: Appendixes I and V; *Survey of Current Business* (June issues).

a Residual for total U.S. portfolio investment in all regions minus Latin America (mainly Europe and Canada) for 1900–59; Europe and Canada only for 1960–79.
b Total of first two columns.

region was being crowded out of the market. The most obvious case was the World War I years when U.S. attention was almost completely focused on aiding the combatants in Europe.[36] Ad-

36 After the United States entered the war, finance came from the government. Prior to that time, it was provided by the private market. During World War II, by contrast, the private market never played an important role. See Appendix I.

ditional funds went to Canada, which began to borrow in the
United States because the London market was closed during the
war. Thus, very little was left over for Latin America. Likewise,
during World War II and the following decade the Latin American share was either negative or very small as the war and
reconstruction absorbed the foreign credits that the U.S. market
was willing to provide. The first half of the 1920s, as well as the
remainder of the period before the 1970s, also found Latin
America at least 10 points below the overall average. The former
has already been identified as a period of concentration on
Europe. The latter is a bit more difficult to interpret. Whether
the low level of Latin American borrowing was due to the
lingering influence of the defaults, or to Europe and the United
States itself absorbing the available savings, is hard to determine.
In the two early instances when Latin America had a higher than
average share of loans (1905–9 and 1925–29), the absolute
volume of portfolio investment fell for the advanced industrial
countries, presumably indicating lack of demand. The two other
periods of stronger than average Latin American share were the
1970s, when a large supply of funds made crowding out less
likely.

Overall, then, there does seem to be some indication that
Latin American borrowers had best access to U.S. credit markets
when European and Canadian demand was weak. Likewise,
dramatic events involving Europe, such as war and reconstruction, could severely limit Latin American access. Further discussion in Chapter 5 of a possible regional trade-off during the
1920s and the 1970s leads to similar conclusions.

Summary

Several indicators of long-term demand patterns in Latin America have been examined in this chapter. These include the fiscal

balance, the merchandise balance (supplemented when available by the current account), and growth rates (GDP or proxies). The yield premium has also been considered. In no case did these patterns show a clear relationship with the alternating light- and heavy-lending periods that have been seen to characterize U.S. portfolio investment. Not surprisingly, a better fit was found with total capital export and with portfolio investment if non-U.S. flows are also included since – from the borrower's point of view – the total volume of capital is more relevant than the individual components. Moreover, some evidence of Latin American demand being crowded out by preferred borrowers was discovered.

Conclusions

Having considered in some detail the factors that stimulated U.S. loans to Latin America during the twentieth century, we are now in a position to put forward an argument to tie together the various component parts. The first point to stress is the cyclical pattern of lending. Although there have been only two lending booms in the U.S.–Latin American case – and it is hard to argue that two peaks constitute a cyclical pattern – nevertheless those booms should be seen as part of a longer process that goes back at least as far as the early nineteenth century. Although it seems clear that the U.S. pattern is not a continuation of the well-behaved cycles described by Cairncross for British lending between 1870 and 1914, with their integrated trade/migration/lending dynamic, it does seem to fall within the boundaries of the Kindleberger–Minsky cyclical analysis. The latter is somewhat less regular and more reliant on exogenous events. Such cycles have occurred in Latin America in the 1820s, 1860s, 1880s, 1920s, and 1970s. As Kindleberger says (1985, 193), "bankers were camping on doors of Latin American finance ministers" during these periods.

Even though the Kindleberger–Minsky model provides a useful starting place for analyzing U.S. lending to Latin America, the evidence in this chapter suggests several ways in which that model needs to be modified. One problem is the heavy reliance on a random outside shock to start the process. Such an approach is insufficient since a series of preconditions – political, institutional, and economic – are required for large-scale private lending to occur. Furthermore, the political, institutional, and economic factors appear to be linked together in a process of cumulative causation. Given these preconditions, an external shock may play a role. A closely related point concerns the emphasis on psychological factors in the Kindleberger–Minsky model. The heart of the model is the sudden buildup of "euphoria," later followed by "distress" and even "loan revulsion" when things go bad. Indeed, psychological factors probably are important; it seems clear that they are much more important in the financial sphere than in the "real" economy. Nevertheless, concrete nonpsychological factors are at least as relevant.

Finally, the emphasis on the supply side needs to be tempered by an analysis of the role of demand and the relationship between supply and demand. Again, this chapter has provided the basis for discussing this topic. On the one hand, the evidence indicates that demand for foreign capital existed in Latin America because of certain structural deficiencies – lack of an advanced industrial sector and domestic capital markets. On the other hand, the evidence appears to show that trends in demand had little effect on patterns of lending. It is the latter point that needs more consideration. While it is not surprising to discover that there is little relationship between Latin American variables and U.S. portfolio investment trends, since portfolio investment is only one type of capital import, a reexamination of the data reveals a more complex set of relationships.

We begin by juxtaposing some of the U.S. and Latin American data discussed above for the two heavy-lending periods. The 1920s were characterized by a decline in growth rates in the United States in comparison with the two previous decades. Acting through the trade link, this decline could be expected to lead to lower growth in Latin America as was indeed the case. Declining U.S. growth, combined with changes in institutions and income distribution, led to capital export from the United States which was attracted to Latin America by the relatively high interest rates available there. Latin America, in turn, used the capital to finance current account and government deficits. As European sources dried up, the supply of U.S. capital increased to replace them. This was the major change during the 1920s. Competition among U.S. bankers helped to fuel the increase, but the U.S. supply was smaller than that provided by the Europeans before 1920. Thus, supply of U.S. capital probably shifted less than demand for it, leaving supply as the constraint on loan volume.

The pattern in the 1970s was quite different. The latter decade also saw a decline in U.S. growth rates, but growth in Latin America remained high. The main reason was a deliberate decision by many Latin American governments to finance their burgeoning current account and budget deficits, rather than cutting growth rates. Financing the deficits was possible because of new changes in institutions and distribution during the 1960s and 1970s that led to enormous increases in the amount of capital available through the Eurocurrency market. The attraction for foreign capital in the 1970s was not high interest premiums but high growth rates that made Latin America appear as an attractive investment location. Consequently, both supply and demand increased substantially. Since the former increased even more rapidly than the latter—again stimulated by competition among lenders trying to increase their profits and market share—demand became the constraint determining the actual amount of money borrowed. Thus, the failure to find a common relationship between Latin American variables and portfolio lending patterns in the 1920s and 1970s does not mean that demand was never important. Rather, it means that demand interacted with supply in different ways in the two periods.

5

Short-Term Fluctuations in U.S. Portfolio Investment

In comparison to the dramatic nature of long cycles, short-term economic fluctuations often appear mundane. Yet study of short-term change is important in theoretical terms because it provides the opportunity to examine the effects of variables that could be washed out by structural shifts. Also, of course, from the point of view of bankers and policymakers, what happens from year to year is much more important than what happens from decade to decade.

In this spirit, we now turn from long- to short-term changes in U.S. portfolio investment in Latin America. The goal of this chapter is to explore some hypotheses about lending relationships within the periods of heavy lending—the 1920s and the 1970s. In these two decades, portfolio investment constituted the majority of capital exported from the United States and, likewise, a majority of the foreign capital going to Latin America. Consequently, an analysis that focuses on this type of capital flow should be able to capture the major relationships on both sides. Within these shorter periods, political and institutional factors can be considered constant, thus providing the opportunity to concentrate on relations among the economic variables.[1]

Three general questions are posed in the chapter. First, we want to know if the same economic variables that were useful in explaining long-term trends are also relevant in the short run. Thus, we shall examine relationships between portfolio investment flows and income distribution, growth rates, and yield on U.S. securities. Latin American variables of interest are growth rates and the government and foreign balances. As a way of examining the interrelationship between U.S. and Latin American variables, an analysis is made of the yield premium, which is the difference between U.S. yields and those obtained on Latin American loans.[2] The second question focuses on a comparison of short-term patterns during the 1920s and the 1970s. There we ask how short-term relationships changed over the intervening fifty years. Third, we look back at the literature on financial crises and the behavior of bankers to determine whether the lending process during the two decades offers support for the mechanisms said to produce financial crises.

[1] The idea of holding political and institutional factors constant does not mean that no changes took place. It simply refers to the fact that all U.S. administrations during the 1920s and 1970s followed a policy of letting the banks operate in a fairly unrestricted fashion and that a set of financial institutions had been established that provided the basis for lending in each of the two decades.

[2] Other ways of studying supply and demand relationships include constructing a simultaneous-equation model or using a reduced-form model with beta weights. The problem with the former is finding Latin American (demand) variables that are independent of U.S. (supply) variables. It is extremely difficult to discover such variables. Problems with a reduced-form model have similar roots: multicollinearity is very strong. Moreover, the small number of observations makes elaborate statistical analysis of dubious value.

Links Between U.S. and Latin American Economies

Before beginning a detailed analysis of individual relationships within the two decades, it will be useful to present an overall model showing the major links between the U.S. and Latin American variables being considered. The model, shown in Figure 10, includes three levels of relationships. Those indicated by heavy solid lines are the focus of the chapter. The lighter solid lines are linkages that will be discussed but only briefly. The broken lines represent relationships that are not of immediate concern in this book but will be dealt with in future research. The direction of the relationships, and their positive or negative expected values, are taken from the long-term discussion in Chapter 4. The long-term patterns thus constitute the hypotheses for the short-term analysis.

These hypotheses suggest that three U.S. variables are major determinants of portfolio investment in Latin America. The U.S. growth rate and U.S. interest rates are negatively related to capital export in the model, while income share to high savers is positively linked to capital export. The three Latin American variables, by contrast, involve greater uncertainty. The two economic balances are shown as reciprocal relationships because the direction of causation could not be determined from the long-term evidence. Was portfolio investment sought to offset the fiscal and foreign deficits, or did the deficits exist because foreign capital was available? Likewise, the sign on the relationship between portfolio investment and growth in Latin America is indeterminate because these variables were related in different ways in different periods. In the short-term analysis, clarification will again be sought on these questions. Demand for loans from preferred borrowers in advanced industrial countries is expected to be negatively related to Latin American portfolio investment.

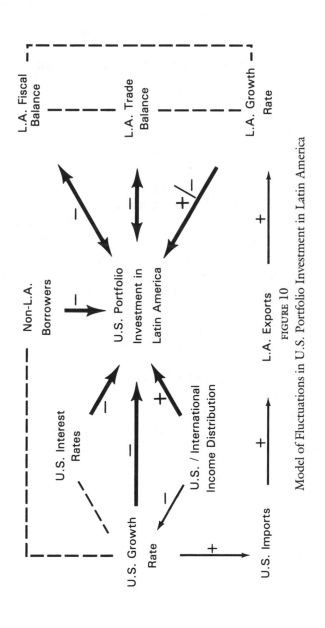

FIGURE 10

Model of Fluctuations in U.S. Portfolio Investment in Latin America

Apart from the major hypotheses, other characteristics of the model require brief comment. First, the model incorporates the "process linkage" discussed in Chapter 4 whereby growth patterns in the United States are transmitted to Latin America through volume and terms of trade. These trade linkages can be seen as the counterpart of the financial relationships with which we are primarily concerned. Second, there are important relationships among the Latin American variables themselves – the growth rate, the fiscal balance, and the trade balance. A complete understanding of the lending process would need to incorporate an analysis of the Latin American relationships, but it goes beyond the scope of this book except for a few brief observations that will be made later in the chapter.[3] Likewise, a complete analysis would also have to deal with the relationship beween the U.S. economy and the demand for loans from non–Latin American borrowers. Finally, note that the price of the loans themselves, as opposed to the price of competing assets, is not included in the model. That price – and specifically the loan premium – is discussed separately as a way of trying to distinguish between supply and demand pressures.

The complexity of the model, in contrast to the limited number of data points available during the two eleven-year periods, means that the model as a whole cannot be estimated. It is presented as a heuristic device to facilitate comprehension of the overall picture. Similarly, because of statistical problems in identifying the equations referring to the *ex ante* role of supply and demand factors, no definitive determination of their respective roles (the push/pull controversy in the literature on Britain) is attempted. The main goal is a more modest one of examining

---

[3] The interrelationship among these variables in a specific Latin American country will be discussed extensively in my forthcoming book on Peru's experience with the international capital markets.

plausible hypotheses on both sides, although the lending premium can provide a few clues about the relative importance of supply and demand.

The 1920s

In analyzing U.S. portfolio investment in Latin America during the 1920s, we first examine economic variables in the United States as the lending economy. Then we focus attention on Latin America, where borrowing took place. Finally, as a way of studying the role of supply (U.S.) and demand (Latin American) factors, we look at some data on the yield premium and how it related to volume of loans.

U.S. Economic Trends

The 1920s were a period when people in the United States—government officials, corporate directors, and individual investors—were adjusting to a new role in the international economy. No longer was the United States a net capital importer, nor was it one of several second-tier countries behind a dominant Great Britain. As a result of World War I, it had suddenly been transformed into the major international economic power. One manifestation of the change was the substantial rise in exports, resulting in trade and current account surpluses on the balance of payments. Public and private leaders alike believed that exports were crucially related to the health of the domestic economy, providing a way to utilize the newly created capacity in U.S. factories. In turn, merchandise exports were thought to require capital export to provide a means of finance since high levels of protectionism were maintained (MacKaman 1977, chaps. 2–3). The implications of such a pattern of trade and finance on the ability of other countries to service the resulting debt were either ignored or discounted (Fishlow 1985).

The U.S. government's decision not to continue its wartime loans in the postwar period opened the necessary space for private banks to expand their own lending. As noted in Chapter 4, institutional developments – including the redeployment of the sales force from the Liberty Bond campaign – enabled U.S. investment banks to replace their British counterparts in issuing foreign bonds after the war. Large-scale U.S. private lending thus began in the decade of the 1920s, which can be divided into several subperiods according to volume of foreign bonds issued in the United States. The first period ran from 1920 to 1923 and was characterized by a fairly low volume of loans. The second, representing the boom years of foreign lending, occurred between 1924 and 1928. The final two years of the decade, 1929–30, witnessed a sharp decline. Loans to Latin America generally followed these overall trends although – as we shall see – they were especially heavily concentrated in the latter half of the decade. The initial question of interest is whether these portfolio investment trends are related to trends in U.S. economic variables.

An important conclusion of the long-term analysis was that the development of international financial institutions must be accompanied by an income distribution that provides adequate funds for those institutions if large-scale lending is to take place. In Chapter 4 we established that the 1920s represented the only period during the twentieth century when a substantial redistribution toward high-income individuals occurred. Now we want to test the hypothesis that income distribution and investment flows were also positively correlated within the decade. Figure 11 suggests that such an intradecade relationship did exist. It compares volume of portfolio investment to Latin America (in constant dollars) with the share of income going to the top 1 percent of the U.S. population, the 1.2 million people who were the principal purchasers of foreign bonds.[4]

Both variables show two cycles. The first was similar for the two variables, centering around a 1921–22 peak. The second involved a slightly more complex relationship. Income share and loan volume both began to increase in 1923, but the lending peak occurred in 1926–28, whereas the income peak was in 1928–29. Thus, the principal divergence was in 1929 when income concentration remained high but lending fell off sharply. That divergence, of course, was explained by the upsurge of U.S. stock market activity in 1929 that displaced foreign lending.

In statistical terms, the income/lending relationship is significant at the 95 percent confidence level,[5] but we must go beyond statistical analysis to decipher its economic meaning. Clearly, the correlation provides support for the notion that regressive re-

[4] For a discussion of the purchasers of bonds in the 1920s, see Chapter 4 (especially footnote 11).

[5] In general, the regression model used in this chapter is a multiplicative one—that is, the variables are the natural logarithms of the absolute values, indicated in the equations by "ln." This procedure is convenient because the resulting coefficients are elasticities. Nevertheless, in a few cases—those relating growth rates and portfolio investment—problems of autocorrelation mean that a preferable form is rates of change of the variables. In addition to the equations themselves, t statistics are given in parentheses under the coefficients, and R^2 and Durbin–Watson (DW) statistics are provided. For eleven observations and a two-tailed test, a t statistic greater than 2.23 is significant at the 95 percent confidence level. For the Durbin–Watson statistic, in an equation with one independent variable and fifteen or fewer observations, the null hypothesis of no autocorrelation can be accepted with 95 percent confidence between 1.36 and 2.64. The inconclusive zone is between 1.08 and 1.36 or 2.64 and 2.92.

The equation underlying Figure 11 is the following:

ln PORT = −9.48 + 5.37 ln INCOME $R^2 = 0.42$; DW = 2.07
        (1.65) (2.56)

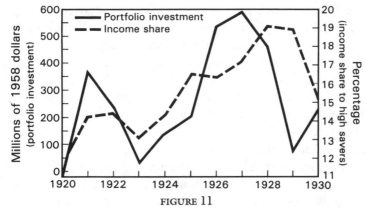

FIGURE 11

U.S. Income Distribution and Portfolio Investment: 1920–30

SOURCE: Appendix I; Kuznets (1953, 637).

distribution facilitates foreign lending, which is not surprising given the well-known positive relationship between high income and savings. Indeed, savings did increase substantially during the decade – for example, time deposits doubled from $17.4 billion in 1920 to $35.2 billion in 1930 (United States 1976, X689) – and the absolute volume of savings of the upper-income group increased as did their savings propensity.[6] The investment banks were able to direct some of those savings toward foreign bonds through extensive "educational" campaigns, in addition to more dubious sales tactics that we shall discuss shortly.

We can gain a more thorough understanding of the relationship between distribution and lending patterns by examining the behavior of two other U.S. economic variables during

[6] Kuznets (1953, table 47) provides some estimates of savings by income category for this period. His data indicate that the top 1 percent of the population increased its savings/income ratio from 42 to 43 percent between 1920 and 1929, and its savings as a percentage of total national income rose from 5.7 to 7.4 percent over the same period.

the 1920s—growth rates and yield. Whether foreign lending would take place on any large scale should depend on the state of the U.S. economy. If growth and yields were high in the United States itself, the attractions of foreign lending, with its higher perceived risk, would be less appealing than if the U.S. economy were relatively depressed. Furthermore, even if large-scale international lending did occur, Latin America's share would probably depend on demand for loans from more familiar borrowers such as Europe and Canada.

The decade of the 1920s was characterized by strong cycles in the U.S. economy, more pronounced than would be found in the post–World War II period because of lack of government policies to counter them. As can be seen in Figure 12, three cycles occurred during the decade. The first ran from 1921 to 1924 with a peak growth rate of 16 percent. The second, between 1924 and 1927, had a peak of 8 percent. The third, between 1928 and 1930, had a peak of 7 percent. Thus, the cycles had declining amplitudes and, in the case of the third, a declining time period as well.

We can obtain an initial notion about the relationship between the U.S. growth rate and portfolio investment in Latin America from Figure 12, which displays both variables. The graph suggests a negative relationship between the two; in statistical terms, it is significant at the 95 percent confidence level.[7] Though far from exact, troughs in growth rates tend to be associated with peaks in capital export and vice versa. In the early part of the decade, the depressed year 1921 was associated with

[7] The equation for Figure 12 is

$$\dot{PORT} = 385.19 - 65.19\,\dot{GNP} \qquad R^2 = 0.66; \; DW = 1.47$$
$$\;\;\;\;\;\;(2.34)\;\;\;(4.20)$$

As explained in footnote 5 above, this equation uses rates of change (indicated by dots over various symbols) to deal with problems of autocorrelation.

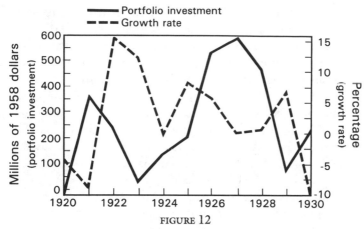

FIGURE 12

U.S. Growth Rate and Portfolio Investment: 1920–30

SOURCE: Appendixes I and II.

high loan volume in contrast to 1923 when loans fell off sharply but economic growth was strong. In 1925 opposing trends again emerged as growth rates began to decelerate, while lending moved toward its highest volume. The end of the decade also saw an inverse pattern. The 1929 growth upswing contrasted with a sharp drop in lending; the following year saw lending briefly pick up as growth rates began their decline into depression.

Latin American lending was not alone in its countercyclical characteristics. Two earlier studies have examined quarterly data for U.S. portfolio investment to all regions during the 1920s, and both find a strong countercyclical relationship with a one-quarter lag (Lary 1943; Mintz 1951). As the National Bureau of Economic Research study reports: "Loan cycles move counter to business cycles with almost perfect synchronism" (Mintz 1951, 11). Nevertheless, Latin American loans do appear to have played a particularly important role: while the peaks in U.S. growth rates declined over the decade, capital export to Latin

America rose. The mechanism posited here is that as demand for loans decreased in the United States during troughs in the business cycle, then capital export increased. The Latin American role relates to the pattern of income distribution. The shift in income toward high savers during the 1920s probably contributed to the decline in U.S. growth peaks over the decade. Much of the additional savings were exported, and they went disproportionately to Latin America during the last half of the decade. The export of savings prevented growth rates from falling even further since they were the counterpart to demand for U.S. goods.

As growth rates declined over the decade, so did the yield on financial assets that would be alternative investments for those purchasing Latin American bonds. Most economists writing on the 1920s have placed primary emphasis on this factor as an explanation of U.S. portfolio investment in Latin America and other countries as well (United States 1930a, 28–39; Madden et al. 1937, 13–14; Aldcroft 1977, 250; Fishlow 1985, 424). They believed that the low and falling yields on domestic assets prompted investors to look abroad where a higher return was available. In an equilibrium model, of course, this hypothesis would not make sense. The difference in yield would simply represent the difference in risk between U.S. and Latin American investment. In a real-world situation, however, with less than perfect capital markets, such a hypothesis cannot be ruled out a priori.

Figure 13 displays the relationship between volume of portfolio investment and the yield on top-quality U.S. corporate bonds rated AAA by Moody's Investor Service. It supports the hypothesis of a statistically significant negative relationship between the two variables on a year-to-year basis in addition to the general fall in yields over the decade as a whole.[8] The main exception to the negative correlation occurred in 1921, the last

[8] The equation for Figure 13 is
$$\ln PORT = 17.11 - 7.39 \ln YIELD \qquad R^2 = 0.37; DW = 2.13$$
$$\quad\;\; (3.29) \quad (2.30)$$

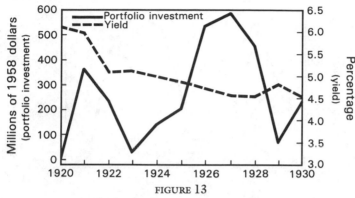

FIGURE 13
U.S. Yield and Portfolio Investment: 1920–30

SOURCE: Appendixes I and II.

year of high interest rates. That year nevertheless saw very high lending to Latin America, mainly due to a fall in demand for loans in Europe and Canada during the economic downturn.

The question of loan demand in other parts of the world raises another issue that was relevant in explaining long-term lending patterns. As discussed in Chapter 4, Latin America's access to U.S. funds during the twentieth century – public as well as private – often appeared to depend on lack of demand from preferred borrowers such as Europe and Canada. Figure 14 suggests that a similar tendency also existed at certain points within the decade. From 1920 to 1922, loans to Latin America moved in sharp opposition to loans to other regions (mainly Europe and Canada). In 1924 the Dawes Loan stimulated an enormous surge of lending to Europe,[9] but Latin American loans increased only slightly from their 1923 trough. Not until demand elsewhere dropped off in 1926 did Latin American

[9] The Dawes Loan was a bond issue of 800 million reichsmarks, sold in the United States and various European markets, to help finance German reparation payments. It resulted from the recommendations of

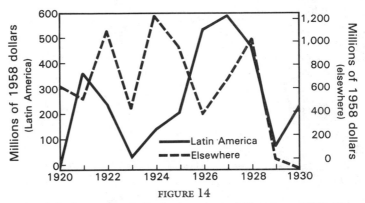

FIGURE 14

Portfolio Investment in Latin America and Elsewhere: 1920–30

SOURCE: Appendix I.

loans increase substantially. The brief upsurge of Latin American loans in 1930 can also be partly attributed to the net negative lending to Europe. Only in 1923 and 1929 did lending drop simultaneously for all regions.[10]

In general, Latin America's share of total loans was fairly low during the first half of the decade, when demand was high in Europe for reconstruction purposes and currency reforms. As these sources of demand dissipated, loans to Latin America became increasingly important (Brown 1940, 583–87). Latin America's weighted average share of total loans between 1920 and 1925 was 16.6 percent, while between 1926 and 1930 it

---

an official committee of experts, under the chairmanship of Chicago banker Charles G. Dawes, appointed to consider solutions to Germany's inability to meet its payments. The U.S. portion of the loan, about half of the total (some $110 million), was oversubscribed eleven times. See Kindleberger (1984, 302–4).

[10] These two simultaneous falls, together with the otherwise negative pattern, completely eliminate any statistical correlation.

$$\ln \text{PORT}^{LA} = 5.06 + 0.02 \ln \text{PORT}^{OTHER} \qquad R^2 = 0.00; \text{DW} = 1.45$$
$$(2.82) \quad (0.08)$$

rose to 48.8 percent. Thus a "crowding out" hypothesis does appear to have some validity during the 1920s.

Latin American Economic Trends

Like the United States, Latin American economies in the 1920s were in a period of transition. The era of export-led growth based on primary products, which began in the last decades of the nineteenth century, was coming to an end. The slowdown was due largely to price declines as an oversupply of primary commodities appeared. At the same time, the international economic context in which Latin America had operated since independence was changing in fundamental ways as the United States displaced Britain and other European countries in both trade and finance. Finally, in a few countries, the more active governments that would appear everywhere after World War II had begun to emerge (Thorp 1984, chap. 1). As we shall see in Chapter 6, the Leguía regime in Peru was trying to reverse that country's laissez-faire economy. Postrevolutionary Mexico was initiating a policy of government-sponsored industrialization as were the Alessandri and successor governments in Chile. Brazil and Argentina lagged behind these three but were far ahead of Central America, where governments maintained their traditional passive stance (Thorp 1984, chaps. 3, 7–8, 10–11).

The U.S. influence in Latin America can be seen in various ways. One is the correlation between growth rates in the two regions. As we can observe by comparing Figures 12 and 17, growth rates in Latin America followed those in the United States with a one- or two-year lag.[11] Thus, two cycles occurred in

[11] The lags—and particularly their varying length—make statistical analysis of the relationship between portfolio investment flows and Latin American variables more complex than analysis of U.S. variables.

Latin America during the 1920s.[12] The first was from 1921 to 1925; the second lasted from 1925 to 1930. The brief U.S. peak in 1929 was not repeated. To review the mechanisms discussed in the previous chapter, the main ways in which U.S. growth cycles were transferred to Latin America involved international trade patterns. Since a large percentage of Latin American exports went to the United States, and U.S. imports showed a strong positive correlation with growth rates, high U.S. growth rates resulted in high exports from Latin America. High Latin American exports, in turn, stimulated high growth in that region and led to the positive (lagged) relationship between U.S. and Latin American trends. The terms of trade played a reinforcing role.

To understand the effect that Latin American exports would have on Latin American GDP also requires consideration of imports. That is, higher growth rates would be expected to pull in additional imports which might exceed the increment in exports. In such a case, automatic or induced effects in response to a trade or current account deficit might cut the growth rate. To arrive at the overall result, we need to compare the trade balance with growth rates. Doing so reveals a fairly strong positive relationship, meaning that an export surplus was associated with higher growth.[13]

Nevertheless, the lags can sometimes provide valuable clues to the causal process under way. Moreover, a lagged relationship may have a different meaning than the nonlagged form. A good example, as we shall see, is the relationship between Latin American growth rates and portfolio investment.

[12] As indicated earlier, GDP figures for most Latin American countries were not calculated until after World War II. Data for Argentina and Brazil–the two largest countries and the two largest borrowers in the 1920s–are available. These data are used in Figure 17.

[13] The correlation coefficient between the Latin American trade balance and growth rates for the entire decade of the 1920s was 0.69.

Of course, Latin American growth trends were not entirely determined by the external sector and thus U.S. economic performance. Domestic economic policies in Latin America were also important, although not nearly as important as they would become after World War II when more active governments came into existence throughout the region. One way of examining domestic economic policies is to focus on the fiscal deficit. As it happens, growth rates and the fiscal balance were related in different ways during the two halves of the decade. Before 1925 they were positively correlated; after that time a negative relationship existed, although there is no indication that demand management policies were being consciously followed.[14]

More directly relevant to the subject of this study is the relationship between the two balances and portfolio investment flows to the region. Figure 15 displays the trends for portfolio investment and the trade balance. As we would expect, there is a negative correlation, since the current and capital accounts counterbalance each other, and we are examining the basic components of each during this decade. Nevertheless, the relationship is not statistically significant.[15] An important reason is that prior to the 1940s no data are available for the service balance including interest and dividend payments. The esti-

[14] The correlation coefficient between the Latin American fiscal balance and growth rates for the 1920s was a low 0.31 because of the different relationships during different parts of the decade. It should be noted that demand management policies did become more common in the 1930s for some countries in the region. In fact, the degree to which governments became more active is seen by some analysts as explaining part of the differential impact of the Depression on various countries of the region. For a discussion of this point, see Thorp (1984).

[15] The equation for Figure 15 is

$$\ln \text{PORT} = 6.35 - 0.18 \ln \text{TRADE} \qquad R^2 = 0.04; \text{DW} = 1.17$$
$$(3.29) \quad (0.61)$$

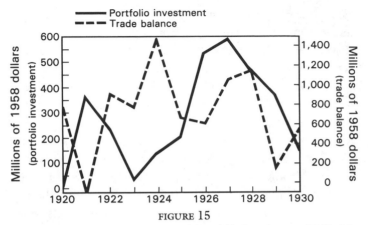

FIGURE 15
Latin American Trade Balance and Portfolio Investment: 1920–30

SOURCE: Appendixes I and III.

mates made in the previous chapter assumed a constant percentage of export earnings going to services during the decade. In reality, of course, that would not be true, and a more adequate measure of the current account would be more highly correlated with portfolio investment flows.

More interesting are the data shown in Figure 16, which indicate a close relationship between portfolio investment and the fiscal balance. What is most significant about this graph is the lag between capital inflows and the fiscal balance: there was a strong relationship between capital inflows and the fiscal balance of the following year.[16] With a one-year lag on the fiscal balance, peaks and troughs of the two variables coincided exactly: the lending peaks of 1921 and 1926–27 were immediately followed

[16] The lagged equation for Figure 16, after eliminating the 1920 outlier, is

$$\ln PORT = 2.40 - 0.62 \ln FISCAL_{-1} \qquad R^2 = 0.59; \ DW = 1.52$$
$$(2.44) \quad (3.20)$$

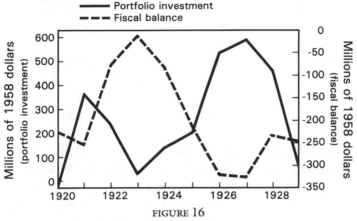

FIGURE 16
Latin American Fiscal Balance (Lagged)
and Portfolio Investment: 1920–29

SOURCE: Appendixes I and III.

by the largest fiscal deficits of the decade in 1922 and 1927–28. If we look at the two largest borrowers, Argentina and Brazil, this same pattern generally appeared. In Argentina, the negative lagged relationship appeared throughout the decade, while in the case of Brazil it was present until 1927 (calculated from Appendix IV).

This lagged pattern is important because it provides a few clues about the causal relationship between portfolio investment and the deficits. Governments were spending according to what they could borrow the previous year, indicating that the availability of foreign capital made the deficits possible rather than governments running deficits and then seeking capital to balance the budget. Such behavior is consistent with the notion of relatively passive governments in the region before the Depression.

Latin American growth rates also show a significant relationship to portfolio investment flows. As will be recalled from Chapter 4, the long-term data suggest that the high level of portfolio investment in the 1920s was associated with growth rates that were low when compared with the early part of the twentieth century. The export boom had petered out, and no alternative growth stimulus had taken its place. Inspection of Figure 17 suggests that the short-term pattern was similar in some ways to the long-term trend. The first part of the decade was characterized by close inverse movements. From 1920 through 1925, the two variables moved in opposite directions each year. The two growth peaks, 1920 and 1923, matched the two investment troughs. After 1925 the correlation is less clear, although, for the decade as a whole, the relationship is statistically significant.[17] Quarterly data for Argentina and Brazil, as reported in the NBER study mentioned earlier, reinforce the conclusion that Latin American governments were borrowing primarily during downswings in the business cycle. Thus, Mintz (1951, 15–20) reports that while European countries tended to borrow during periods of prosperity, the two Latin American countries borrowed when their economies were "relatively depressed."

Although not of direct relevance to this study–which is mainly concerned with *why* lending took place–the data in Figure 17 also provide some insights into the effects of loans. With a one- or two-year lag on growth, the two curves reveal a moderately strong positive relationship. That is, a year or two after large portfolio investment inflows, growth picked up and vice versa. Although the lag was longer in the first part of the

[17] The equation for Figure 17, which again uses rates of change rather than logs of absolute values, is

$$\dot{\mathrm{PORT}} = 496.27 - 63.09\,\mathrm{LA\dot{G}NP} \qquad R^2 = 0.48;\ \mathrm{DW} = 1.51$$
$$\quad\ \ (2.33)\quad (2.89)$$

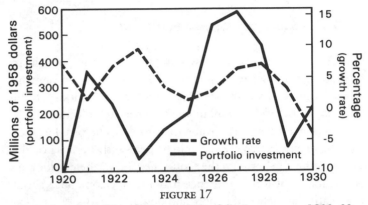

FIGURE 17

Latin American Growth Rate and Portfolio Investment: 1920–30

SOURCE: Appendixes I and III.

decade than the second, the overall relationship is significant at the 90 percent confidence level.[18] It seems, therefore, that the governments borrowed when growth was low. The loan proceeds then enabled spending to increase which, in turn, stimulated growth. As stated previously, there is no indication that a Keynesian fiscal policy was being consciously carried out in this period, but the effects were similar. In principle, a Latin American upturn, which pulled in more imports, would stimulate growth in the United States. The low weight of exports in the U.S. economy, however, plus the low percentage of U.S. exports going to Latin America, meant that this effect was probably quite small.[19]

[18] The lagged equation for Figure 17, using growth rate for Latin American output and absolute value of portfolio investment, is

$$PORT = 138.82 + 32.19 \ \dot{L}AGNP_{-1} \qquad R^2 = 0.33; \ DW = 0.70$$
$$\quad\;\;(1.61) \quad\;\;(1.98)$$

The Durbin–Watson statistic is very low.

[19] Only 5.7 percent of U.S. gross national product went abroad as

Yield Premium and Portfolio Investment

In this kind of interrelated system, how far is it possible to
separate the influences of supply (U.S. variables) and demand
(Latin American variables)? One approach is to look at the
behavior of the yield premium with respect to volume of U.S.
portfolio investment. The statistical problems involved in such
an analysis are extremely difficult to deal with because of the
interrelationship between the economies. Nevertheless, looking
at qualitative historical evidence may provide some idea about
the relative influence of supply and demand factors.[20]

To analyze the premium, we start with the two nominal yields
from which the premium is calculated.[21] On the U.S. side, the
yield used is that for the most highly rated domestic bond
issues – those classified AAA by Moody's Investor Service. Other
long-term yields closely paralleled that on AAA bonds. That
yield, as can be seen in Figure 18, gradually declined over the
decade. The exception was a small increase in 1929, reflecting
the high domestic demand for capital to finance stock purchases
during the speculative binge of that year.

The other curve in Figure 18 is the yield actually earned on
Latin American bonds floated in New York. That curve is weakly

---

exports during the 1920s and, of that amount, only 17.2 percent was
sold in Latin America. Multiplying the two figures together comes to
around 1 percent – an idea of the small influence of Latin American
growth rates on the United States in that period. A related discussion is
found in Fleisig (1972), who tries to quantify feedback on the U.S.
economy in the 1930s from Third World countries in general.

[20] A similar analysis has been carried out for the 1970s by Fleming
and Howson (1980) and Fleming (1981).

[21] Nominal yields are used for the 1920s and real yields for the 1970s
on the assumption that only in the period of sustained high inflation in
the 1970s did money illusion disappear.

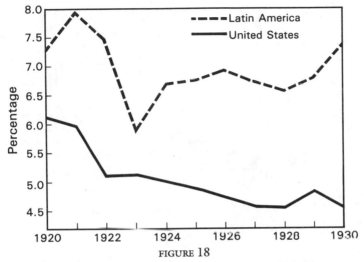

FIGURE 18

Yield on U.S. and Latin American Bonds: 1920–30

SOURCE: Appendixes II and III.

related to the U.S. yield, although with a lag at the beginning of
the decade, but there were two important exceptions and a less
important one. The significant exceptions included increases in
1926 and 1930. The 1926 increase represented the first year of
the period when Latin American issues dominated U.S. foreign
lending and a year when total foreign lending fell. The 1930
increase clearly reflected the need to overcome the negative
effects of the chaotic conditions in the financial markets and the
incipient Latin American defaults. The dip in the Latin American yield in 1923, by contrast, does not seem to have reflected
any basic trend but rather the fact that the few Latin American
issues floated that year came from countries (mainly Cuba) with
exceptionally close relationships with the United States and
therefore relatively low yields.

If we then calculate the premium that Latin American issues

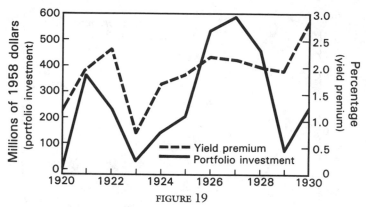

FIGURE 19

Yield Premium and Portfolio Investment: 1920–30

SOURCE: Appendixes I, II, and III.

brought over the top-grade U.S. issues, we note in Figure 19 that the premium increased from 1920 to 1922, from 1923 to 1926, and 1929 to 1930, stabilizing or even falling in the periods in between. This pattern roughly follows the movements in volume shown in Figure 19, although the premium did not rise as much as might have been expected during the high-lending period from 1926 to 1928. This deviation from expectations is probably related to the following discussion on competition among bankers. In statistical terms, the relationship is significant at the 95 percent confidence level.[22]

Insofar as the evidence indicates a positive relationship between loan volume and the premium, the question is how to interpret this evidence. A high premium is likely to result from one of two situations. On the one hand, demand could exceed supply at a given yield in which case the yield (including the

[22] The equation for Figure 19 is

$$\ln \text{PORT} = 3.73 + 2.48 \ln \text{PREMIUM} \qquad R^2 = 0.52; \, DW = 1.49$$
$$\quad\;\; (6.85) \quad (3.11)$$

premium) would be expected to rise. On the other hand, lenders' perceptions of the existence of a particularly high risk could also lead to a high premium. (Here we are assuming a less than perfect capital market such that the premium more than offsets perceived risk, thus acting as a source of attraction for foreign investment.) It may well be that both reasons were important during the 1920s. A significant clue comes from the fact, as indicated in Chapter 4, that total foreign capital supplied to Latin American governments in the first two decades of the twentieth century was about 35 percent above the average annual amount supplied by the United States during the 1920s. Since the United States was the only significant source of foreign capital in the 1920s, it is not unlikely that some demand pressure was present during the decade.[23]

Three years stand out in this sense. First, there is a sharp increase in the premium between 1920 and 1921 when Latin America undertook its first heavy borrowing operations in the U.S. markets. The premium rose even higher in 1922 when Latin American lending fell in net, although not in gross, terms. Second, there was an increase in 1926 when Latin America moved into its three heaviest borrowing years in the decade. Finally, there was the increase in 1930 when a high premium had to be paid to overcome the disorder in the U.S. capital markets and fear of defaults abroad. The first two cases represented substantial increases in Latin American borrowing in the U.S. markets and thus could be seen as involving increased risk as well

[23] The only other country providing any significant amount of capital to Latin America during the 1920s was Great Britain. A comparison of the gross volume of securities issued between 1920 and 1931 is $2 billion in New York and $232 million in London (Fishlow 1985, 419). The original figure of £51 million for Britain was converted at the average exchange rate for the 1920–31 period.

as pressure on supply. The last instance presumably centered on risk considerations.

In either case – increased perception of risk or increased demand in terms of given supply – supply factors acted as a constraint on loan volume. This conclusion is reinforced by the lagged relationship between portfolio investment and the Latin American fiscal balance as governments spent what they could borrow the previous year. The Peruvian case study in Chapter 6 points in the same direction, although additional country analyses would be helpful for gaining a better understanding of the processes involved.

It might appear that these conclusions contradict the literature discussed earlier on financial crises and the related "loan pusher" hypothesis. Those applying this approach to the 1920s (such as Kindleberger 1978, 1985; Darity 1985) have concentrated on the period 1924–28. The Dawes Loan in 1924 is identified as the exogenous factor that set off a new lending surge because it increased investor confidence in the economic capacity and stability of foreign governments. This initial stimulus is then said to have led to euphoric expectations among investors which resulted in prices being bid up on bond issues. Bankers played an important role as competition among banking houses in the search for profits led them to pursue borrowers in an aggressive fashion. This boom came to an abrupt halt in 1929, as investors turned from bonds to stocks, although the slowdown had begun the previous year as interest rates rose in the United States. The resulting lack of funds for borrowers triggered a chain of defaults which, in turn, disillusioned investors and limited borrowing possibilities for four decades.

Several comments are in order about this line of analysis. Most important, it does seem to capture an essential component of what was happening in the capital markets during the period. This is especially true with respect to the behavior of the bankers. The 1930s Senate hearings make fascinating reading as they reveal the means that some banking houses used to make profits. Encouraging borrowing for useless projects, withholding information on the state of borrowers' economies, disregarding warnings from bank economists as well as government officials in borrowing countries, paying bribes – all were described as common practices brought about by the pressures of competition and the lure of higher profits than could be gained at home (United States 1932).

Nonetheless, some reservations must be expressed about the story just told. First, the focus on the Dawes Loan as the single determinant of the lending surge is a massive oversimplification. As noted in the previous chapter, a variety of political, institutional, and economic factors had to come together before a single factor could set off a lending boom. Second, insofar as we are interested in the Latin American lending pattern, it must be pointed out that loans did not really pick up for two years after the Dawes Loan. That is, Latin American borrowing must be seen in the context of lending to more favored borrowers. Third, despite the competition among bankers, unethical behavior, and senseless loans, there were nevertheless limits on lending possibilities due to the institutional arrangements in place at the time. Banks were reliant on funds from an investing public that was still quite small in the 1920s. Total U.S. capital export in all forms in the 1920s amounted to only 8 percent of total U.S. investment – of which portfolio investment was 5 percent – in comparison to 45 percent in Great Britain before World War I (Appendixes I and II; Cairncross 1953, 169, 180). Moreover, the fact that the ultimate purchasers of foreign bonds were not the banks themselves meant that they were at the mercy of investors' changing preferences for alternative assets. These shifting preferences not only had the potential to disrupt profitable opportunities for the banks, but the fact that the banks were not

the ultimate investors also had implications for the crisis and
default stages outlined in the crisis literature. The importance of
these limits can be seen by comparison with events and processes
in the 1970s, to which we now turn.

The 1970s

In examining the situation of the 1970s, the same organization
used earlier will be followed. Thus, we first look at trends in the
U.S. economy and some international relationships as well,
since the U.S. and international spheres have become increasingly interconnected in the last two decades. Then we look
at trends in Latin American economies. Finally, we again look at
the interest premium to help interpret the role of supply and
demand factors.

U.S. and International Economic Trends

During the 1970s portfolio investment reemerged as the main
source of capital transfer from the United States to Latin America as the Alliance for Progress was phased out and the resulting
drop in cheap government loans again opened up space for more
expensive private-sector credits. The institutional context in
which this transfer took place, however, had changed substantially in comparison with the 1920s. As explained in Chapter 4,
commercial banks had replaced investment banks as the principal financial intermediaries, so that portfolio investment in the
1970s took place via direct loans from the commercial banks.
Funds came from their own individual domestic depositors or,
more often, from deposits purchased from other banks in the
Eurocurrency market. The interbank market thus eliminated
any constraints on loanable funds in the domestic markets. In

the case of the United States, these constraints had become serious by the mid-1960s as banks lost deposits to nonbank financial institutions and their supply of government securities had been run down.[24] These conditions, of course, changed substantially after the oil price rises in 1973–74 and 1979 when bankers began to talk of "excess liquidity."

The first banks to become involved in Latin American and other Third World lending were the large money-center banks with headquarters in New York and San Francisco but operating out of London or other financial centers. These loans began when the banks' traditional clients faded from the market with the simultaneous recession in the advanced industrial countries during 1970 and 1971. Interest on the new Third World loans was only one source of profit for the banks; more lucrative were front-end management fees. Thus the money-center banks began to popularize the concept of "syndicated" loans, whereby the bank that arranged a loan would keep only part of its own books and sell the rest to other banks (Mathis 1975, chap. 9; Mendelsohn 1980, chaps. 11–20). Some purchasers were other money-center banks, but an increasing share went to smaller U.S. institutions, often referred to as regional banks. The regional banks wanted to participate in the profits and prestige involved with Third World loans, but they did not have the reputation or the expertise to manage loans themselves.[25] Bring-

[24] This development was reflected in the switch from asset to liability management on the part of U.S. banks as they began actively to seek deposits to satisfy demand for loans at home. One of the instruments of liability management was Eurodollar deposits. See Goodhart (1984, chap. 5) and Winningham (1978, chap. 3).

[25] I asked a number of bankers why they decided to participate in loan syndicates that they did not organize themselves. For small banks, the answer is obvious—they had no other way to take part since they did not have the capacity to organize syndicates. For larger banks, the reason often seemed to be that they owed the managing bank a favor or

ing these banks into the lending process was, in many ways, analogous to "educating" the investing public in the 1920s. In addition to the U.S. regional banks, European and Japanese banks also began to participate, but they assumed management roles as well as taking shares of loans.

Beyond the differences in institutional framework – and perhaps not unrelated, as we shall see – the pattern of portfolio investment also differed from the 1920s. Rather than flowing in cycles, Latin American lending in the 1970s increased steadily from 1970 to 1976 and then leveled off. The pattern for non–Latin American loans was similar, although the peak occurred in 1978 (see Figure 22). In the discussion of the 1920s, several hypotheses about relationships between the portfolio investment pattern and the U.S. economy were tested. An initial question for the 1970s is whether these same relationships were repeated.

In the discussion of long-term lending trends, the argument was made that financial institutions had to have access to a large volume of savings for heavy lending to occur. During the 1920s these savings came from individuals, especially wealthy individuals, in the United States. Earlier in this chapter, a positive relationship was found between the share of income to those high-saving individuals and the volume of portfolio investment. In the 1970s the internationalization of the capital markets, including the major source of deposits, leads to a focus on *countries* that were high savers, specifically OPEC countries. As oil prices were raised, the surpluses were largely deposited in the Eurocurrency market, thus providing an additional influx of

---

wished to remain on good terms for future deals. Profits were not a determining factor since syndicated loans were not highly profitable unless management fees were included. Another important reason was to maintain good relations with the borrower in order to obtain other, more lucrative business.

funds to lending banks. The nearest analog to the percentage of U.S. income to high savers in the 1920s is the balance of payments (current account) position of the OPEC countries.

Figure 20 displays the relationship between portfolio investment and the OPEC current account representing the international distribution of income. Although statistically significant at the 95 percent confidence level,[26] the graph indicates that the positive relationship was not a smooth one. Lending increased faster than the OPEC surpluses between 1970 and 1973, whereas the surpluses rose sharply with the oil price increases between 1973 and 1974. The most dramatic and interesting deviation occurred in 1978 when the OPEC surpluses had largely disappeared, yet lending remained high.

It is instructional to compare 1978 with 1929 when the principal source of funds for bond purchases also disappeared as money was diverted from foreign bonds to the stock market. In the 1920s, lending dried up as well, whereas in the 1970s institutional arrangements meant that lending continued regardless of the decline in OPEC surpluses. Alternative sources of funds existed through interbank purchases of deposits, and foreign loans were too important for bank profits to let them cease. Another reason for continued lending in the 1970s, even with the disappearance of the OPEC deposits, was the need to safeguard loans already made. A cutoff of lending would have produced balance of payments crises in borrowing countries (as indeed happened after 1982) that would endanger service of previous loans. This, in turn, would cause serious problems for the banks since—unlike the situation of the 1920s—they themselves were still holding large amounts of Latin American debt in their own portfolios.

[26] The equation for Figure 20 is
$$\ln PORT = 6.19 + 0.45 \ln OPEC \qquad R^2 = 0.61; \ DW = 1.45$$
$$(20.82) \quad (3.77)$$

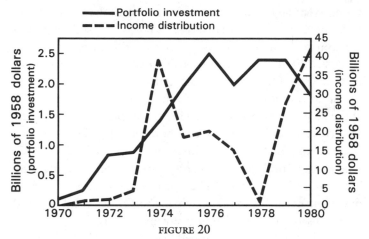

FIGURE 20

International Income Distribution and Portfolio Investment:
1970–80

SOURCE: Appendix I; IMF, *Annual Report* (1981, 18).

In addition to income distribution, portfolio investment in
the 1920s was also related to growth rates and domestic yields in
the United States. Both of the latter relationships were negative.
The results with respect to these two variables are a major
difference between the two heavy-lending decades. In the 1970s
neither U.S. growth rates nor U.S. yields were related to lending
patterns in a statistically significant way. Both showed negative
correlations but they were very weak.[27] The OPEC surpluses
appear to have been the single most important variable in this

[27] The equations for portfolio investment with U.S. gross national
product and yield are

$$\text{P\.ORT} = 126.21 - 14.15 \ \text{G\.NP} \qquad R^2 = 0.07; \ DW = 0.84$$
$$\qquad (1.88) \quad (0.85)$$
$$\ln \text{PORT} = 7.26 - 0.21 \ \ln \text{YIELD} \qquad R^2 = 0.04; \ DW = 0.30$$
$$\qquad (14.30) \quad (0.57)$$

cluster. The strongest relationship was between the OPEC surpluses and portfolio investment itself, as already discussed, but a weak linkage also existed between OPEC and U.S. growth rates. That correlation was negative, as was the still weaker one between OPEC and yield on U.S. assets.[28]

Figure 21 shows the OPEC surpluses and the U.S. growth rate whose relationship was mediated by U.S. economic policy focused on combating inflation. Similar patterns appeared in other advanced industrial countries where, in addition to inflation, the balance of payments was also an important consideration. In the U.S. case, policy trends were especially clear in terms of the money supply. In both 1974 and 1975, the money supply fell, and in 1978–80 it slowed significantly from its normal path (Appendix II). Fiscal policy moved in similar directions as the deficit decreased in both 1974 and 1979 (*Statistical Abstract of the United States* 1984, 135).

As seen in Figure 21, two cycles occurred in U.S. gross national product during the decade. The first preceded the oil price rises and was weakening before OPEC acted in late 1973. The price rises thus added to the factors already depressing the economy. The second cycle began as oil prices fell in real terms from 1975 through 1978. The second set of price increases again exacerbated an already weakening economy. Interest rates generally followed the growth pattern although with divergences at the beginning and end of the decade.

The overall picture, then, reflected the much more internationalized world economy in the 1970s. The international cap-

---

[28] The equations for OPEC surpluses with U.S. gross national product and yield are

$$\text{GNP} = 4.17 - 0.09 \text{ OPEC} \qquad R^2 = 0.20; \text{DW} = 1.53$$
$$(3.37) \quad (1.51)$$
$$\ln \text{YIELD} = 1.46 - 0.20 \ln \text{OPEC} \qquad R^2 = 0.15; \text{DW} = 1.66$$
$$(3.75) \quad (1.27)$$

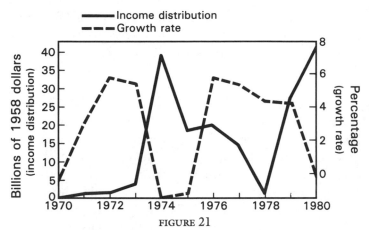

FIGURE 21

International Income Distribution and U.S. Growth Rate: 1970–80

SOURCE: Appendix II; IMF, *Annual Report* (1981, 18).

ital market was dominated by the international distribution of income which directly determined portfolio investment rather than being linked via U.S. domestic variables. On the contrary, those U.S. variables themselves were strongly influenced by the international context in contrast to the 1920s when all of the major trends ramified out from the U.S. economy. These changes require some reconsideration of the model presented in Figure 10. The causal relationship indicated there between portfolio investment and U.S. growth and interest rates becomes much less important for the 1970s, while international income distribution carries the main burden of causation with respect to portfolio investment. Moreover, the relationship between income distribution and U.S. growth rates is more significant than it was in the 1920s.

Another indicator of the increased internationalization of the world economy was the greater synchronization of borrowing from the international capital market. In the 1920s there was an

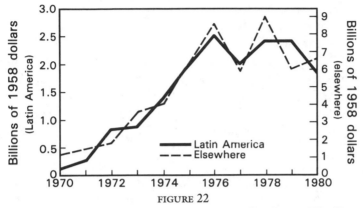

FIGURE 22

Portfolio Investment in Latin America and Elsewhere: 1970–80

SOURCE: Appendix I.

alternation between Latin American and other (mainly European) borrowing which disappeared in the 1970s. For both Latin America and the other borrowing countries, lending built up from a low base during the early 1970s. Then, spurred by the increased availability of funds after 1973, it continued to rise for several more years before leveling off. The close coincidence of Latin American and non–Latin American borrowing is clearly demonstrated in Figure 22. The only remaining trace of alternating borrowing periods is in rates of growth rather than absolute levels of borrowing.[29]

The periods of highest growth in loans to Latin America took place when loans to non–Latin American borrowers slowed somewhat. In particular, Latin American borrowing grew faster at the beginning of the decade (1970–72) and in the period following the oil price increases (1973–76). Moreover, it fell

[29] The equation for Figure 22 is
$$\ln PORT^{LA} = -3.88 + 1.31 \ln PORT^{OTHER} \qquad R^2 = 0.88; \ DW = 2.04$$
$$(2.89) \quad (8.15)$$

more slowly in the last two years of the decade (1978–80). This pattern is due mainly to changes in borrowing among the advanced industrial countries that increased most rapidly in 1972–74 and 1975–78; other Third World borrowing was similar to that of Latin America (calculated from Appendix V). Thus, the "crowding out" hypothesis seems less relevant in the 1970s than in the 1920s, a finding consistent with the much greater availability of funds in the 1970s.

Latin American Economic Trends

Latin American economies in the 1970s were substantially different than in the 1920s. Two of these changes are potentially relevant to this discussion. On the one hand, Latin American countries had become much more industrialized. No longer were they mere exporters of primary goods that imported the majority of needed industrial products. In general, however, the industrialization process had not progressed to the point of self-sufficiency in capital equipment. Some of the larger countries had begun to establish capital goods industries, but even they remained heavily dependent on imports of this type together with technology (Beckel and Lluch 1982). On the other hand, governments in Latin America, like those in the advanced industrial world, had become much more active. This greater activity involved many areas—from regulation to subsidies to direct ownership via public corporations. Governments also emerged as major employers and purchasers of goods and services. The perceived need for rapid growth led to ever-increasing expenditures, both current and capital. Since it was difficult for taxes to keep up with expenditures, what FitzGerald (1978), following O'Connor, calls a "fiscal crisis of the state" became widespread. These fiscal crises—or budget deficits—became closely connected

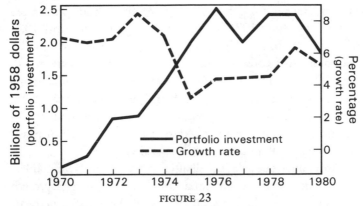

FIGURE 23

Latin American Growth Rate and Portfolio Investment: 1970–80

SOURCE: Appendixes I and III.

to foreign borrowing since domestic capital markets remained poorly developed.[30]

What did not change was the close relationship between U.S. and Latin American growth patterns. As a comparison between Figures 21 and 23 indicates, Latin American growth during the 1970s generally reflected that of the United States with a one-year lag. Thus, Latin America also had two cycles during the decade. One ran from 1970 to 1975, while the other went from 1975 to 1981, with negative growth continuing through 1983. Although the growth *patterns* were very similar in the two regions, growth *rates* were not. Typically, growth rates in Latin America were almost twice as high as U.S. rates; only in 1976 and 1977 were the former below the latter.

As we can observe in Figure 23, the years of highest growth rates in Latin America were at the beginning of the decade when

[30] For an extended discussion of Latin American economic developments between the 1920s and 1970s, see Chapter 4.

Euroloans were just getting started. As these loans accelerated between 1973 and 1976, Latin American growth fell until 1975 when it began to increase again. At that point, the loan flow had leveled off. As a consequence, the relationship between growth rates and portfolio investment is negative.[31] The complete picture, however, is more complex than Figure 23 alone can show. Only by going back to the comparison between growth rates in Latin America and the advanced industrial countries is it possible to see the full impact of the loans after 1973.

Latin American growth fell after that year but by much less than the decline in the industrial countries. The average growth rate in Latin America between 1974 and 1980 was 5.1 percent, while the average OECD rate was only 2.6 percent (Appendix III and IMF Annual Report 1981). The difference was made possible by loans from the Euromarket as most Latin American governments decided to finance their vastly increased current account deficits resulting from the oil price increase. The alternative would have been to reduce the deficits by cutting growth rates. Behind this policy choice was the assumption that the international recession would be short-lived and trade would pick up before debt reached unmanageable levels. When the second oil shock occurred in 1979, however, it was clear that the gamble had been lost and recession became inevitable. Brazil was the most prominent example of this strategy (Bacha and Malan 1987), but it was not alone (Enders and Mattione 1984).

We can gain a further understanding of the process just described by looking at the fiscal balance and the current account in Latin America. Both showed strong negative rela-

[31] The best form of the equation behind Figure 23, in terms of autocorrelation problems, is growth rate for Latin American output and absolute level of portfolio investment.

$$PORT = 3,764.25 - 382.41 \; L\dot{A}GNP \qquad R^2 = 0.47; \; DW = 1.11$$
$$\quad\;\; (4.59) \quad\;\; (2.82)$$

tionships with portfolio flows such that the larger the deficits, the larger the capital inflows to finance them. In Chapter 4 and earlier in this chapter, we noted that it is difficult to determine whether the deficits induced the capital inflows or the availability of foreign capital led to the deficits. Based on the discussion in the previous paragraphs, it seems clear that the latter interpretation is more accurate for the 1970s. If it had not been for the capital available to Latin American governments through the Eurocurrency market, they would have been forced to cut spending and imports and to accept the resulting recession. It was the availability of foreign capital that made the deficits possible. The most compelling evidence is the reduction in deficits after foreign capital was cut off in 1982 (United Nations 1985a).

As can be seen in Figures 24 and 25, both of the deficits increased over the decade. The relationship between the current account and portfolio inflows was generally negative, but there were some interesting exceptions.[32] The slight improvement in the current account in 1973 was not reflected in decreased borrowing because the two biggest borrowers (Brazil and Mexico) had increased deficits. Likewise, the stronger improvement in the current account in 1976 coincided with the heaviest borrowing of the decade. The country composition of borrowing again offers some explanation. This time Brazil and Mexico did have slightly lower deficits and their borrowing fell accordingly, but two other governments (Venezuela and Argentina) entered the market despite current account surpluses. Like some other OPEC countries, Venezuela had started borrowing as its oil surpluses fell in real terms and spending outran even its

[32] The equation for Figure 24 is

$$\ln PORT = -4.49 - 1.36 \ln CURRENT \qquad R^2 = 0.64; \ DW = 0.84$$
$$(1.57) \quad (4.04)$$

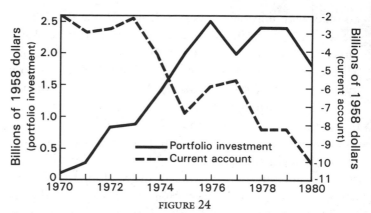

FIGURE 24
Latin American Current Account and Portfolio Investment:
1970–80

SOURCE: Appendixes I and III.

vastly increased revenues (Karl 1983). Argentina's behavior is attributable to the return of the military to power in 1976, which created the business confidence that finally allowed the country to join the lending boom (Stallings 1982). The third time that current account balances and lending diverged was the last two years of the decade, when the deficits increased while borrowing from U.S. banks leveled off. The larger deficits were financed by the new inflow of portfolio funds from Europe and Japan that began at this time.

As was the case in the 1920s, the fiscal balance (Figure 25) was more closely related to capital inflows than was the balance of payments.[33] This closer relationship is perhaps predictable, since the vast majority of loans went to the public sector. Unlike the 1920s, however, no lag was involved in the relationship;

[33] The equation for Figure 25 is
   ln PORT = −8.31 − 1.88 ln FISCAL $R^2 = 0.77$; DW = 1.95
              (2.98)   (5.51)

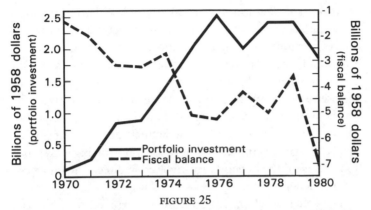

FIGURE 25

Latin American Fiscal Balance and Portfolio Investment: 1970–80

SOURCE: Appendixes I and III.

peaks and troughs generally coincided. Three years (1974, 1979, and 1980) stand out as outliers in Figure 25. In both 1974 and 1979, portfolio investment was higher than would have been predicted from the improved fiscal balance. In both cases, the difference was largely accounted for by Venezuela. Venezuela's government budget relies very heavily on oil revenues and thus went into large surplus after the oil price increases. After the first price increase, Venezuela's own borrowing was low; the increased borrowing came from other nations, especially Brazil and Mexico. In 1979, by contrast, Venezuela itself was a heavy borrower despite its budget surplus. In 1980 U.S. lending fell as the fiscal balance went into its biggest deficit of the decade. As with the current account, this disjunction was made possible by the increased importance of non-U.S. lending.

Although oil played a significant role in both these relationships in the post-1973 period—both the current account and the fiscal deficits (via subsidies and government purchases) were inflated by the oil price increases—it was not the only force at work. The development strategies of the Latin American governments were also very important in determining the volume of portfolio investment and the fiscal and foreign balances. Two broad types of development strategy can be identified. One was exemplified by Brazil and Mexico, where the governments themselves borrowed large quantities of money in order to build up the industrial sector. Large-scale projects in capital goods, energy, infrastructure, and manufactured exports were developed through government corporations. Borrowing was seen as a way to avoid the dependency involved in direct foreign investment (Frieden 1985).

The other development strategy was typified by Chile and Argentina in the late 1970s, where neoconservative governments tried to reduce the traditionally heavy state role in the economy. In the latter cases, most of the foreign borrowing was done by the private sector, partially in response to high interest rates in the domestic markets. Often the private borrowers were local banks that then lent the funds to local individuals or companies. Some was used for investment, but most went for speculative purposes or the import of luxury consumer goods. In fact, "deindustrialization" characterized both economies during the late 1970s and early 1980s (Foxley 1983).[34]

Interest Premium and Portfolio Investment

The relative importance of supply and demand in the 1970s is at least as difficult to untangle as it was in the 1920s, but again the premium can offer some help in interpretation. Because of the different structures in place, the premium for the 1970s was

[34] For a comparison of debt outcomes under the two development strategies, see Stallings (1983b).

constructed from different rates of return than for the earlier period, but the basic idea remains the same. The U.S. rate in the 1970s is the real interest rate on short-term U.S. business loans that would have been the main alternative to international loans for the banks.[35] As can be seen in Figure 26, this rate had little trend until 1979–80 when it moved up sharply. From 1970 to 1978, it averaged 1.5 percent, whereas the average for 1979 and 1980 was 6.0 percent. The other curve in Figure 26 is the real interest rate on Latin American Euroloans, which is composed of the LIBOR plus the average spread paid by Latin American borrowers. The Latin American rate, which is only available since 1971, followed a path that was very similar to its U.S. counterpart.

The premium is then calculated by subtracting the U.S. from the Latin American rate.[36] As shown in Figure 27, the premium generally declined throughout the decade. Three subperiods can be identified: 1971–73 with a premium near or above 1 percent, 1974–78 with a premium near or below 0.5 percent, and 1979–80 with a negative premium. Figure 27 also shows the volume of portfolio investment, and we can see that a negative relationship prevailed between the two variables. It is statistically significant at the 95 percent confidence level.[37] A high premium

[35] See Chapter 4 (footnote 35) for a discussion of the relationship between the business loan rate and the prime rate and reason for using the former.

[36] The premium discussed in this chapter is *not* the same as what is usually called the "spread" on a loan. The spread is the markup over a bank's cost of funds (that is, the rate it pays for deposits, usually the LIBOR). The premium is the difference between the total interest rate (cost of funds plus markup) in two different markets. There is no reason why the spread and the premium should behave in a similar way.

[37] The equation for Figure 27 is

ln PORT = 8.24 − 1.11 ln PREMIUM $\quad R^2 = 0.45$; DW = 1.78
$\qquad$ (19.55) $\quad$ (2.57)

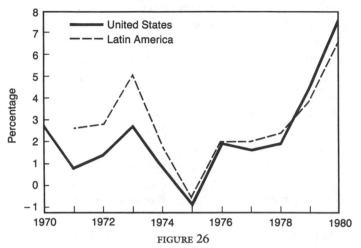

FIGURE 26

Real Interest Rate on U.S. and Latin American Loans: 1970–80

SOURCE: Appendixes II and III.

accompanied the low lending levels at the beginning of the decade, and then it went down as lending increased through 1976. During the 1977–80 period, lending leveled off while the premium rose and then fell, eventually reaching negative levels in 1979–80. Not surprisingly, U.S. banks accounted for a substantially smaller proportion of Latin American lending in 1979–80 than they did during the rest of the decade.

How should we interpret this negative relationship? Why should smaller premiums call forth more lending and larger premiums less? The results are certainly counterintuitive and the opposite to those found in the 1920s. The 1970s context, however, was also quite different from the 1920s and helps to explain the different results. In the earlier decade, the amount of money available to the Latin American governments decreased in comparison to the years prior to 1920. In the 1970s, by contrast, there was an enormous increase in total funds avail-

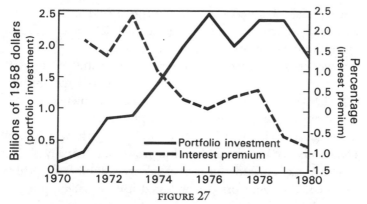

FIGURE 27

Interest Premium and Portfolio Investment: 1970–80

SOURCE: Appendixes I, II, and III.

able. Despite the simultaneous increase in demand for foreign capital in Latin America, whether for government-sponsored development projects or private-sector uses, the supply of capital appears to have exceeded the needs.

It is this somewhat anomalous situation that takes us back to the financial crisis literature and the "loan pushing" hypothesis discussed earlier. Although some support was found for such a hypothesis in the 1920s, there were clearly institutional limits on the banks' ability to increase loans. In the 1970s any reasonable notion of limits disappeared when the Eurocurrency market replaced individual investors as the primary source of funds. After 1973 OPEC deposits dramatically increased the supply of capital available to the largest banks, and the interbank market further multiplied those funds and also provided them to banks not favored by OPEC. Simultaneously, the market for loans in the advanced industrial countries shrank as the recession hit. These circumstances set the stage for a scramble among banks to make loans to the only enthusiastic borrowers—Third World, and especially Latin American, governments that wanted to finance their increased balance of payments deficits in addition to continuing their other spending priorities.

Competition among banks rose enormously in the course of the decade. In the early 1970s, only a handful of large, mainly U.S., banking firms were making loans to Latin America. By the end of the decade, there were at least eight hundred banks from all the advanced industrial countries and some others as well.[38] The number of U.S. banks had also grown substantially as the smaller banks entered the market. As the number of banks increased, the competition manifested itself in falling profits, arising through lower markups on the banks' cost of funds and through longer maturities. Syndicates of banks bid against each other to obtain loan contracts, especially for the highly publicized "jumbo" deals. In the extreme, the banks tried to get business by encouraging borrowers to refinance their old loans at better terms. Refinancing meant lower interest rates, but it also meant additional fees for managing banks, and the fees were more lucrative than interest income. Syndications tended to be oversubscribed, and borrowers were often persuaded to accept more money than they had originally sought (Devlin 1987).

Although some observers began to warn of potential problems, the "euphoria" that Kindleberger (1978) has described was well entrenched by mid-decade. Profits from Third World lending enabled the banks to avoid the recession plaguing their

[38] The figure of eight hundred is surely an underestimate. It is based on the number of banks from all countries that participated in the renegotiation of the Mexican debt in 1982–83; see Kraft (1984, 21). The *Country Exposure Lending Survey*, which tracks the activities of U.S. banks engaged in international lending, includes some two hundred institutions from this country alone. A far higher estimate is that of Treasury Secretary Donald Regan, who stated in 1983 that 1,500 U.S. banks had lent to Latin America (*Wall Street Journal*, 3/25/83).

industrial counterparts, and prominent bankers denied any problems in the offing. Citicorp's Walter Wriston was famous for his determined optimism, but most others shared the position in a more restrained way (Sampson 1982, 123, 259; Moffitt 1983, 225–26; Makin 1984, 150). The only major setback came in 1974–75, when two international banks failed and calls briefly went out for cooperation between the banks and public-sector agencies, especially the International Monetary Fund (Spero 1979). Lending dipped as a consequence of the bank failures, and a two-tier market resulted for a time. The Peruvian debt crisis in 1976–78 – to be discussed in the next chapter – might have provided an early warning, but by 1979 it was resolved and the lending went forward again. In fact, the Peruvian finance minister, Manuel Ulloa, is reported to have been a prime target of bankers wanting to contract loans at the World Bank/IMF annual meeting in September 1980 (Makin 1984, 5). Not until the Mexican crisis of August 1982 did Kindleberger's "distress" period begin, although U.S. banks had already begun to pull back as profits fell in the late 1970s.

In comparison to the 1920s, then, the 1970s seem to be much more accurately described by the loan-pushing hypothesis and the crisis sequence. Rather than following the traditional "arms-length" lending model that Friedman (1977) describes, bankers as salesmen out pushing a product seems a more satisfactory model (Delamaide 1984; Makin 1984; Darity 1985; Devlin 1987). The results presented in Figure 27 – falling premium accompanied by rising loan volume – provide further evidence for this conclusion.

Even in the 1970s, however, it would be misleading to see lending as exclusively a supply-determined process. Latin American borrowers were not simple, unwitting victims of rapacious bankers. They made decisions to borrow – both to pay for increased oil imports and for other purposes. Borrowing exceeded the swollen oil bills by substantial amounts; total net capital inflow exceeded even the current account deficits as reserves were built up. The availability of loans was welcomed both by the governments that borrowed to finance their own activities and by those that promoted borrowing by the private sector.

Nevertheless, it was ultimately a demand constraint that set the limits on portfolio investment flows as the large increase in funds exceeded the absorptive capacity of Latin American borrowers. For the case of the two largest borrowers—Brazil and Mexico—this conclusion has been verified through interviews with bankers, economists, and government officials. All agree that the two countries could have borrowed more during the 1970s on similar terms but chose not to do so. Brazil put up various barriers to foreign borrowing in the latter half of the decade, while Mexico is said to have borrowed to finance certain projects and then stopped in spite of continuing offers of funds (Interviews 2754, 3155, 4156). With the exception of the 1976–78 crisis period, the Peruvian case, which is discussed in detail in Chapter 6, points in the same direction.

Conclusions

To conclude, we return to the questions mentioned in the introduction to this chapter. Were the same variables involved in short- as in long-term relationships? Did the pattern of relationships in the 1970s differ from that in the 1920s? Did the crisis sequence accurately describe the lending process within the two decades?

In the long-term analysis in Chapter 4, a number of variables on both the U.S. (supply) and Latin American (demand) side were found to be correlated with portfolio investment flows. On the supply side, these variables included political context, institutions, income distribution, growth, and yield. Considering political stance and institutions constant in the short-term analysis, and looking at year-on-year relationships for income distribution, growth, and yield, all three factors were found to be statistically significant in the 1920s. In the 1970s, by contrast, only the distribution variable was statistically significant, and it was a very different form of income distribution than in the 1920s.

On the demand side, several long-term variables were analyzed, including Latin American growth rates and the fiscal and foreign balances. These same variables were found to be related to portfolio investment patterns in the short-term analysis but in different ways in the two heavy-lending periods. In the 1920s only the growth rate and the fiscal balance were statistically significant. In the 1970s all of the demand variables were significant. In both cases, a problem arose in how to interpret the relationship between the balances and lending volume.

We can answer the first two questions in the following way: many of the economic variables appear to be relevant in both the long and short run, but there were differences in which of the long-term variables were significant in the short-term analysis in the 1920s compared to the 1970s. These short-term differences, in turn, reinforce the differences that were found in the long-term analysis with respect to supply and demand influences. Specifically, the high correlation between supply variables and portfolio investment trends in the 1920s, together with a weak relationship between the latter and demand variables, reinforce the notion of a supply-dominated process. Latin American governments probably wanted more foreign capital than they received (in line with the fact that they were getting less than they had been accustomed to from European sources), but they had to settle for what they could get. The lagged relationship with the fiscal balance also points to a passive government stance. The big changes came on the part of the United States, where foreign investment suddenly burgeoned. The stronger correlation between portfolio investment and Latin American variables in the 1970s is consistent with the generally stronger government role in the later period. The falling premium nevertheless suggests that even more money was available than Latin Americans could or would borrow, so that demand came to be the constraint on volume of investment.

In Chapter 4, we noted that Latin American borrowing from both British and U.S. lenders had followed a long-term boom/bust pattern that would be predicted by the literature on financial crises. Surges of lending were followed by defaults that severely limited further loans for several decades. In this chapter, additional support for this literature was found in terms of the process within the two heavy-lending decades. Euphoric expectations led to intense competition among lenders to the point that profits fell. In some cases, borrowers may have been persuaded to take more money than they needed. Nevertheless some cautions were suggested for both decades. In the 1920s institutional limits existed to brake the volume of loans that could be made. In the 1970s the Latin Americans' own desire to borrow matched the desire of the bankers to lend. In both instances, it is the interrelationship of supply and demand pressures that needs to be emphasized and understood.

6

The Lending Process

A Case Study of Peru

PERU STOOD on the verge of default on its foreign debt in 1976. The country's military government had borrowed heavily from the Euromarket to finance its state enterprises, counting on the newly discovered oil wealth and the increased revenues from new mining ventures to cover the debt service. Through a combination of bad planning and bad luck, however, a major foreign exchange crisis developed. Not since the early 1930s had such a specter confronted U.S. bankers. How they managed it would be important for the banks' future as well as Peru's.

This chapter looks at the lending history of Peru as a complement to the focus of the rest of the book on the Latin American region as a whole. The aggregate approach has given us an understanding of the prerequisites for lending, the behavior of lenders, the reasons borrowing might occur, and some conclusions about the relative importance of supply and demand in determining the pattern of lending. Nevertheless, it is clear that an aggregate regional approach has its limitations. Some of the limitations can be addressed through a case study of a single country which can provide a detailed look at the interrelationship between lenders and borrowers.

Although Peru is not a "typical" Latin American country—since no country is typical—it does represent a median in several senses. In population and area, it is a medium-sized country within the region. In terms of aggregate and per capita GDP, it falls near the center of the Latin American spectrum. The development of productive forces, especially industry, also finds Peru somewhere between the advanced level of Brazil, Mexico, or Argentina and the smaller Central American and Caribbean countries. Further, Peru is more than just a case study since its crisis in the late 1970s provided a kind of rehearsal for the more serious problems of the next decade.[1]

The chapter is organized in chronological fashion, but five questions underlie the presentation: Who were the major actors in the lending process? Did the Peruvian government want to borrow and, if so, why? Where did the initiative come from? Why did lending cease? How were the resulting problems dealt with? In the concluding section, we shall return to these questions to see how the answers from one case can advance the analysis of the general process.

The Beginning of U.S. Domination in Peru

Like the rest of the Latin American region, Peru's most important nineteenth-century economic relationships were with

---

[1] Practical reasons also exist for the choice of Peru as a case study. There is more information available on foreign loans over time in Peru than for other Latin American countries; see footnotes 9 and 23 below.

Great Britain. As late as the 1890s, some 46 percent of Peru's exports were sent to Britain and 37 percent of its imports came from there. Other major trading partners were Chile (for exports) and Chile and Germany (for imports). Only in 1899 did the United States exceed the importance of the latter two countries, while remaining far behind Britain (Bonilla 1977, app. 3).

Peru's principal source of foreign investment was also Great Britain; this investment generally took the form of bonds floated on the London market. Two loan cycles occurred in the nineteenth century. The first began with two bond issues, in 1822 and 1825, while the war with Spain was still in progress. They were spent mainly on munitions and quickly fell into default as the newly independent country faced a shortage of foreign exchange. Not until the late 1840s, after the beginning of the guano bonanza, was an agreement made with the bondholders so that Peru regained its access to the London capital market (Wynne 1951, 109–11).

The second loan cycle occurred during the guano era itself, which ran from 1840 to 1879.[2] As would happen in the twentieth century, the government spent even more than its vastly increased revenues and looked to the international capital market to cover the difference. The earliest loans in this cycle were floated in the 1850s, but the big increase in foreign debt came between 1869 and 1872 when the total amount rose from £8.6 to £35 million. The new debt was mainly for the proposed construction of an extensive network of railroads which was never completed (McQueen 1926). Since the guano boom was

[2] Peru's guano (fertilizer) resource, which accounted for 60 to 70 percent of total exports between 1840 and 1879, was managed differently than export production in other Latin American countries. The government owned the guano deposits and received some 60 percent of the revenues from their exploitation. See Hunt (1973), Bonilla (1974), and Mathew (1977) for discussion of the guano period.

petering out, the new loans proved to be unsustainable, and the government was forced to declare bankruptcy for a second time in 1876. Settlement of this second default, not reached until 1889, involved a unique procedure. The bondholders were converted into stockholders of the newly established Peruvian Corporation. To cancel the debt, the corporation was ceded control of all railroads in the country for a period of sixty-six years in addition to the remaining guano resources, a franchise to operate steamers on Lake Titicaca, and about 5,000 acres of land (Wynne 1951, 120–81; Bonilla 1977, 30–32).

Although Britain was not heavily involved in direct investment in Peru, an exception was in banking. The London Bank of Mexico and South America established a branch in Lima in 1863. As the only foreign bank in the city, it quickly became one of the most important. Over time, however, the bank ran into problems and, near the end of the century, the decision was made to convert it into a joint venture with Peruvian capital. In June 1897, the Banco del Perú y Londres opened with the British firm as minority shareholder. The new bank was the dominant financial institution in Peru until its bankruptcy in 1931 (Joslin 1963, 87–88, 91–94, 211; Quiroz 1986).

When Peru's international economic relations began to be reconstructed after its defeat by Chile in the War of the Pacific, they no longer revolved around Britain; rather the United States began to emerge as the dominant power. The change in trade relations can be seen in Table 20. U.S. importance increased from the 1890s on, but it was not until World War I that the United States finally displaced Britain as Peru's main trade partner. Foreign investment also began a slow process of change in nationality, with U.S. investments overtaking those of Britain at approximately the same time that the shift in trade relations occurred. Of equal importance was the change in form of foreign investment in this period. Rather than issuing bonds, U.S. companies engaged in direct investment in Peru. The most

TABLE 20

Peru: U.S. Share in Trade and Direct Foreign Investment, 1900–29

Year	Imports	Exports	Direct Investment[a]
1900	12%	21%	10%
1905	16	9	23
1910	18	28	36
1914	32	34	40
1919	62	46	69
1924	32	22	74
1929	34	22	71

SOURCES: Bonilla (1980, 82–83) for trade; Bertram (1974, 43) for investment.

[a] U.S. share of U.S. plus British investment only.

important were the Cerro de Pasco Corporation (copper), the International Petroleum Corporation (oil), and W. R. Grace and Co. (textiles, commerce, agriculture, and finance).

The direct investment of particular interest to this study was the arrival of U.S. banks. In 1919 Mercantile Bank of the Americas (MBA) opened its first Latin American branch in Lima. As explained in Chapter 2, MBA was a consortium formed to finance U.S. trade with Latin America; the principal owners were Brown Brothers, J. and W. Seligman, and Guaranty Trust. Arriving in Peru during the war, it quickly grew at the expense of both local and foreign (British and German) banks. In 1920 another U.S. bank, National City Bank of New York, opened a branch in Lima.[3] Apparently, National City's competi-

[3] Bollinger (1971, 245) suggests that an agreement originally existed whereby Mercantile Bank of the Americas and National City Bank would not compete in the same country, but the latter's success in Brazil and Argentina persuaded it to expand. Whether an agreement existed or not, the U.S. government clearly disapproved of competition between U.S. banks. As the head of the Bureau of Foreign and Domestic

tion had an adverse effect on MBA since the latter's business rapidly declined, and the bank was sold to the Royal Bank of Canada in 1925 (Phelps 1927; Mayer 1968; Bollinger 1971, 234–53). There were also some initial attempts to renew Peru's foreign borrowing in this period. Several small loans were floated in London, and President Manuel Pardo is said to have been bargaining with National City Bank (with the help of the International Petroleum Corporation) for a $15 million loan in 1915–16. Opposition within Peru itself, together with pressure from the Peruvian Corporation, temporarily ended the dealings (Bertram 1974, 228–29), although they would reappear on a large scale in the 1920s.

The First Loan Cycle: The Leguía Government, 1919–30

From the end of the nineteenth century, Peru had been governed by the Civilista party that was dominated by the country's so-called oligarchy. Despite strong frictions within the party, between what are often called "bourgeois" and "señorial" groups, the period did have some cohesive characteristics. First, political participation was limited to a very small percentage of the population, principally the well-to-do in the major cities near the coast, while the vast majority, the Indians of the highlands, were excluded. Second, the state fashioned by the Civilistas was a weak one with its activities limited by the small

---

Commerce said: "There was no excuse for the National City Bank to establish an office in Lima in competition with the office of MBA. . . . On the other hand, it was a mistake for MBA to open up in Brazil and Argentina in competition with the National City. . . . Competition among American banks in new fields or in fields that are pretty well developed by existing local or foreign banks should be discouraged" (Jones 1924).

amount of taxes it was willing (or able) to collect. Third, although some structural change was being thrust upon the country by both political and economic forces,[4] the main tendency of the Civilistas was to let things evolve rather than actively to seek change (Basadre 1964, vol. 8; Pike 1967, chap. 7; Quijano 1973; Cotler 1978, chap. 3). By 1919 this gradualist and elitist approach had produced a significant buildup of tension which was exacerbated by an economic downturn as the war ended. Large-scale political mobilizations took place in the cities under anarchist leadership, and a general strike was called. The frightened Civilistas could come up with no solution but to call out the army and massacre four hundred persons (Cotler 1978, 180–82).

Political-Economic Background

These conditions witnessed the return to Lima of Augusto B. Leguía. Leguía had been president of Peru on the Civilista ticket from 1908 to 1912 but was nevertheless somewhat of an outsider. Educated in Chile, he married into the Peruvian oligarchy but followed a business-oriented career with strong foreign connections (Pike 1967, 195). In the 1919 elections, he ran against the Civilista candidate and was backed by a coalition of groups excluded from power during the previous years. Although Leguía is generally believed to have won the election, he engineered a coup in order to call for new congressional elections in which his supporters gained a majority (Cotler 1978, 182–83). This was the beginning of eleven years (the *"oncenio"*) of authoritarian rule.

[4] The process of industrialization in this period has been especially noted; see Thorp and Bertram (1976).

Since Leguía offered no detailed political-economic program, his goals must be inferred. Fortunately, there is a considerable consensus on this issue among both Peruvian and foreign authors.[5] These observers indicate that Leguía's main aim was to "modernize" the country or to "promote capitalism." In order to achieve this overall goal, a number of interrelated tasks were necessary: incorporate a larger share of the population into political and economic participation to prevent further radicalization of the opposition; create a strong state to undertake a large share of capital accumulation, particularly the provision of infrastructure; bring in foreign capital as allies, since the oligarchy had proved itself incapable of developing national capitalism; and build up the armed forces as a guarantee of stability if all else failed.

Attracting foreign capital was the key point because it would provide the additional resources necessary to achieve the other goals. This context also specified a certain type of foreign capital—portfolio investment—as most desirable, since it would increase government revenues; direct investment would also be useful, but loans were crucial. Data on use of the loans indicate that they indeed went to finance a growing government deficit. Deficits occurred in every year of the *oncenio*, reaching a peak in 1928 when the deficit represented 53 percent of expenditures

[5] Most of the major socioeconomic histories of Peru adhere to the interpretation of the Leguía regime described here. See, for example, Basadre (1964, vol. 9, chap. 180); Pike (1967, chap. 8); Quijano (1973, 67–136); Caravedo (1977); Cotler (1978, chaps. 3–4); and Burga and Flores-Galindo (1979, pt. 2, chap. 5). One author who dissents from this interpretation is Bertram (1974, 55–59). Bertram argues that the Leguía years were not a distinct period "in any but a narrow political sense." Going further, he denies that there was a real split in the Peruvian oligarchy between "traditional" and "bourgeois" groups. Although Bertram criticizes others for lack of evidence to support their position, he is not very strong himself in this regard.

(Peru 1935, tables 182–84). The proceeds were used mainly for public works, external debt service, internal funding, and general government expenditures.[6] Increased military expenditures were also prominent within the budget.

There are some indications that the balance of payments was also an important factor in the borrowing process. Although the official figures on the merchandise balance show large surpluses for every year except 1921, two attempts to reconstruct the balance of payments conclude that service transactions probably made the overall balance negative.[7] Pressure on the exchange rate, which was floating in this period, supports the deficit hypothesis for at least half of the decade.[8] In terms of the concepts introduced in Chapter 4, then, the 1920s loans to Peru were associated with both aspects of the structural linkage— budget finance and foreign exchange.

The Lending Process

Lending to the Leguía government divides itself into three distinct periods: 1919–23, 1924–28, and 1929–30. During the

[6] The portion actually going to public works is disputed. Various estimates exist, ranging from $66 to $130 million over the eleven-year period in comparison with $90 million in new loan money (Table 21). Bertram (1974, 47–51) compares four estimates of public works expenditures and also cites Seligman's representative Lawrence Dennis (see footnote 18 below), saying that the works were worth only half of what was paid for them because of graft and inefficiency.

[7] The reconstructions are for the first half of 1922, though they have more general implications. The original estimate was made by the U.S. financial advisor William Cumberland (1922), who concluded that a small deficit probably existed. Bertram (1974, 287–91) later calculated that it was more substantial.

[8] The years when the rate dropped substantially were 1921–22, 1926–27, and 1930; see Peru (1935, table 42).

first period, lending was light; in the second, it was stepped up dramatically, only to fall off again in the third period at the end of the decade. As might be expected, the lending process also varied greatly among the three periods.[9]

1919–23. Table 21 indicates that only about $13 million of foreign credits were received by the Peruvian government between 1919 and 1923, of which three-fourths came from Britain. U.S. banks proved very reluctant to lend to Leguía despite his best efforts to persuade them. Even before taking power, Leguía had begun his drive to secure loans from U.S. banks. On his way back to Peru, he stopped in New York to discuss his plans. Among others, he met with Frank Vanderlip of National City Bank to whom he promised much business (United States 1933, 2104). By January 1920, the date of the Second Pan American Financial Conference, Leguía had already elaborated a vast plan to develop industry and agriculture, to build railroads and public works, and to refinance existing debts. The estimate, as presented at the conference, was that these plans would require $150 million in foreign loans (United States 1921, 154–56). Such amounts would never be forthcoming.

[9] Some excellent primary sources exist for the study of foreign lending in the 1920s. One source is a set of Senate hearings (United States 1927, 1932, 1933) held to investigate lending practices. In thousands of pages of testimony, including numerous documents, major bankers were cross-examined on their loans. A second source is material in the U.S. National Archives, especially Record Groups 59 (State Department) and 151 (Bureau of Foreign and Domestic Commerce). This material is mainly correspondence and documents about the government's role in the lending process. I have examined the Commerce Department documentation but have mainly relied on others, especially Tulchin (1971) and MacKaman (1977), for the State Department files. The exception is the State Department documentation on the Cumberland mission.

TABLE 21
Peru: External Public Debt Outstanding, 1919–30
(millions of dollars and pounds)

Year	Debt in Dollars	Debt in Pounds	Total (dollars)[a]
1919	–	£1.0	$ 4.4
1920	–	1.0	3.7
1921	–	0.9	3.5
1922	$ 2.4	2.7	14.4
1923	2.1	3.4	17.7
1924	8.8	3.3	23.4
1925	13.5	3.2	29.0
1926	30.5	3.1	45.6
1927	66.4[b]	3.0	81.0
1928	90.7	4.9	114.5
1929	89.7	3.6	107.2
1930	88.5	3.5	105.3

SOURCE: Bertram (1974, 43).

[a] Converted at average annual exchange rate in New York (United States 1930b, 173).
[b] Excludes $29 million of bonds in process of redemption.

To obtain the loans he was so anxious for, Leguía tried several methods to influence the banks. One was to declare, ad nauseam, his friendship and admiration for the United States (Carey 1964, chap. 3). A second tactic was to seek allies among nonfinancial corporations. An early example was a contract with the Foundation Company to construct sanitation facilities. Under Foundation Company encouragement, J. P. Morgan and Chase National Bank began negotiations for a $15 million refunding loan (Tulchin 1971, 199). Another method was to threaten to turn to Britain for loans. As an extension, Leguía announced that he would move $12 million of Peruvian gold reserves from National City Bank in New York to the Bank of England. A State Department protest prevented this transfer in the first instance, but Leguía later carried out his threat as his financial situation deteriorated (MacKaman 1977, 584–86).

Although the U.S. government was anxious for the banks to lend to Peru (and other Latin American countries) as a way to stimulate trade and avoid the return of British influence once the war was over, it hesitated to take action despite encouragement by embassy personnel in Lima.[10] By mid-1921, however, with the refunding loan (by now turned over to Guaranty Trust) still not completed, State Department officials agreed to meet with a representative of the Foundation Company and one from Guaranty Trust. The latter indicated that his bank would be willing to make loans but only under two conditions. First, the Leguía government would be required to consult with the State Department "for advice and recommendations in any financial arrangements which it may desire to make in this instance and in the future." Second, Guaranty Trust wanted the State Department to recommend an American citizen who would act as Leguía's financial advisor and administer the customs service (ibid., 541). Surprisingly, given the State Department's hesitancy to get involved, the undersecretary agreed to the plan, provided the initiative came from Peru.[11]

[10] In the State and Commerce Departments in Washington, as well as the U.S. Embassy in Lima, the trade/loans relationship was supported despite some complaints about the negative effects. One such complaint was launched by William Cumberland, the U.S. economic advisor in Lima. He criticized government actions as "a form of propagating the doctrine that our foreign trade, notably exports, should be extended aggressively and that foreign investments constitute the most certain means of stimulating trade. . . . Consuls and commercial attachés, through activities in the field and reports to the home government, try to promote trade and investment whereas in many cases warnings of danger involved in proposed loans or commercial transactions would be more appropriate" (quoted in MacKaman 1977, 701).

[11] The government's foreign loan policy in the 1920s is discussed in

The advisor selected was William Cumberland, the State Department's own foreign trade advisor. Cumberland left for Peru in October 1921 with the broad grant of authority insisted upon by Guaranty Trust. His contract, in addition to guaranteeing him access to the president and any documents related to finance, gave him total control over customs, which represented the majority of government income. He was also to be consulted in advance of any government economic policies and to become a director of any financial agency that was established (Cumberland 1921).

Guaranty Trust immediately began negotiations for a loan by sending a commission to investigate the financial situation in Peru. The commission's negative report gave the bank leverage to make further demands on the government. Leguía was required to establish a central bank (of which Cumberland would be a director), drop plans to transfer gold reserves without U.S. banks' consent, balance the budget, control spending, and obtain foreign rather than domestic credit in the event of a deficit. Moreover, Guaranty Trust was given an option on any future loans guaranteed by the customs revenue, which essentially gave it a monopoly on Peruvian external finance (MacKaman 1977,

---

Chapter 4. A concise summary of this somewhat contradictory policy with special reference to Peru is found in a letter sent by Assistant Secretary of State Dearing to several New York banks: "[The Department] would be interested, of course, in having Peru's finances rehabilitated and having this take place with American assistance.... It [is] desirable for Americans to have as much a hand as possible in the development of Peru and its resources and for [the United States] to play the role in that and in all other South American countries which [its] interest... entitles [it] to play, but... it [is] not the Department's business to be giving guarantees or to be saying anything which would indicate that it intended to apply any force in making South American governments live up to their obligations to the banks" (quoted in Tulchin 1971, 201–2).

604–6). Despite his desire for U.S. funds, Leguía resisted external control of his finances although he did establish a central
bank. Clearly demands for fiscal restraint would undermine all
his plans for modernization.[12]

With State Department prodding, a small $2.5 million loan
was finally signed in July 1922, guaranteed by the petroleum
revenues, but Leguía spent the proceeds in less than a month
and asked for more. He also wanted to bring in another bank,
but Guaranty Trust held future options. The chargé d'affaires in
the Lima embassy urged the State Department to break the
impasse and warned that Leguía would turn to Britain if an
arrangement were not made. This threat was apparently sufficient for the department to violate its general noninterference
policy again.[13] Guaranty Trust was persuaded to give up its
option, and the State Department brought the Wall Street firm
of White Weld into the negotiations (Tulchin 1971, 202–3). By
that time, however, the conditions of the bond market had
changed, and many banks were eager to step in.

1924–28. Peru's fortunes in the U.S. capital markets changed
dramatically in the five years between 1924 and 1928, compared
to the previous five-year period. More than $130 million of
loans were made, ten times the amount in the 1919–23 pe-

[12] For all his currying favor with the United States, Leguía was not
willing to accept U.S. advice that interfered with his own plans. He
complained to the U.S. Embassy in Lima, and he complained to
Washington. See, for example, United States (1927, 84).

[13] The State Department did occasionally place obstacles in the way
of the banks' plans. One such example in Peru was a proposed loan by
Harriman and Co. to pay for destroyers that the Merchant Shipbuild-
ing Corporation was going to construct for the Peruvian government.
The State Department opposed the loan even though the company
threatened to go to Britain to obtain funds (Tulchin 1971, 202–3).

riod.[14] Along with the increase in volume came changes in lending procedures. Leguía no longer had to cajole and threaten the bankers, nor did the State Department have to intervene to encourage the banks to lend. On the contrary, the banks went on the offensive, soliciting loans in attempts to beat out their competition and ignoring warning signs that the loans might not be very good risks.

As soon as the Guaranty Trust option was suspended, Leguía announced his desire for a $50 million refunding loan as well as several specialized loans to further his various development projects (*La Prensa*, 5/6/24). White Weld, the bank introduced into Peru by the State Department, was quick to oblige with a $7 million contract in October 1924. This loan was to be used for refunding and providing sanitary facilities for various cities (*NYSE Listings* A-6536).[15] As the Peruvian economy appeared to improve, the banks' enthusiasm for lending to the country increased and was encouraged by the U.S. government. The director of the Bureau of Foreign and Domestic Commerce, for example, said in 1925 that "Peru is entering a period of stable economic growth likely to surpass that witnessed in the past. . . . Our technological experience and the products of our factories are especially suitable for meeting the conditions and

[14] Only about $90 million of new money actually entered Peru via the dollar loans since a significant amount was for refunding previous dollar loans; see Table 21.

[15] The *New York Stock Exchange Listings* (hereafter *NYSE Listings*) are the documents that a prospective borrower, wanting to list an issue on the exchange, must file. They are short versions of the loan contracts and provide information about the borrower, purpose of the loan, conditions, security, amortization, and interest payments. Many of the actual contracts for the Peruvian loans were either published in United States (1932) or are available in the U.S. National Archives. Some are also published in the annual reports of the Peruvian Ministry of Finance.

problems presented in developing Peruvian resources" (Mc-
Queen 1926, v).

A second White Weld loan, for $7.5 million, followed in
December 1925. This one was secured by the Peruvian petroleum revenues and was used to retire the Guaranty Trust loan
of 1922 plus all other loans with liens on petroleum revenues.
The balance was to finish the Olmos irrigation project and retire
internal floating debt (*NYSE Listings* A-6932). This use of external loans to cancel internal debts has been one of the most
criticized parts of Peruvian borrowing. Since servicing external
debt requires foreign exchange, Peru was thus increasing its
future financial problems rather than lessening them (United
States 1932, 1595; Lewis 1938, 383).

By 1926 competition for Peruvian issues had stepped up
sharply, especially among smaller banking houses desirous of
sharing in the profits being reaped by their larger rivals.[16] The
firm of Frank Lisman sent a representative to Lima in January
1926; others that expressed interest included Ames, Emerick,
and Co. and Alvin H. Frank and Co. The State Department
increased competition by advising banks of Leguía's desire for
credit and telling more inexperienced banking houses that Peru
deserved foreign loans (MacKaman 1977, 653). White Weld
remained the government's principal banker, however, floating
two loans in the latter half of 1926. One was a small $2 million
sanitation loan (*NYSE Listings* A-7430), while the other was a

[16] Information on profits is not easy to find or interpret. One of the
problems is the confusion between gross and net profits. For an idea of
the difference, gross profits on the $100 million of loans floated by
Seligman were $5,475,000 while net profits were $601,000. The former includes profits to all banks in the underwriting and distributing
syndicates; in addition, any expenses not paid by the borrower must be
subtracted (United States 1932, 1278). See Tulchin (1971, 176) for
data comparing gross profits of different banks.

more important one for $16 million. The latter was to repay all the loans of the Peruvian tax collecting agency (the Recaudadora) so that the revenues it collected could be used to secure future foreign loans (*NYSE Listings* A-7431). Although the $16 million loan was meant to open the way for much larger flotations by White Weld, it turned out to be the firm's last.

The latter part of 1926 saw two of the largest U.S. banking houses move into Peruvian finance: J. and W. Seligman and National City Bank. Frank Lisman, deciding that the Peruvian loans his representative had been soliciting were too large for his firm to handle, turned the business over to Seligman. He also turned over what would become one of the most notorious scandals of the 1920s lending spree. In his attempt to gain Peruvian business, the Lisman representative had agreed to pay more than $400,000 to the president's son, Juan Leguía, a debt which Seligman assumed (United States 1932, 1279–80, 1769–70).[17]

This new process of soliciting business, and paying commissions in order to obtain it, was said by bankers to be quite common in Latin America in those years (ibid., 1245–1301). In Seligman's case, it paid off handsomely, as the bank became Peru's chief fiscal agent and floated $100 million of loans during 1927 and 1928. Seligman's main partner in these loans was National City Bank, which finally entered the Peruvian market

[17] Juan Leguía, the president's high-living son, was described by Lisman as "trying to rub up against every foreigner who comes to Peru and tries to do business there, with a view to horning in on any commission or transaction he might get." Stating that "I do not think he had any influence particularly with his father, except a negative one," Lisman said his firm paid Leguía so that he would not block their access to information and people in the government (United States 1932, 1769–71). Juan Leguía and the money paid him was one of the topics of greatest interest to the Senate investigating committees.

after abstaining for eight years. In the aftermath, it turned out that the payments to the president's son were not the only way in which the two banks deviated from traditional banking practices. The 1930s Senate hearings revealed that the banks had gone against their own representatives' advice in making the loans as well as concealing information on various negative aspects of Peru's economic condition in the prospectuses offering the loans to the public (United States 1934, 126–31).[18] Even the president of Peru's Reserve Bank came to New York in 1927 to advise against so much money being lent to his government (United States 1932, 1601).

Three large loans were floated by Seligman and the National City Bank. The first was the Tobacco Loan of March 1927, which provided $15 million, secured by funds from the government's tobacco monopoly, to be used for railroads, irrigation projects, sewage facilities, and refunding (*NYSE Listings* A-7733). The second and third loans were the most controversial ones. In early 1927, the Peruvian Congress decided to seek $100 million–known as the National Loan–of which two-thirds would be used to refund and reorganize Peru's debts. The first part of the loan, for $50 million, was floated in October 1927. The loan was unsecured, however, and no particular revenues were assigned to service it. Rather, an agency (the Caja

[18] One of the bankers' representatives who was particularly vocal and detailed in his criticisms of the Peruvian loans was the Seligman representative Lawrence Dennis. An economist who did an extensive analysis of Peru, Dennis told the Senate committee: "They wanted to convince me, as well as themselves, that the loans were sound. . . . They believed it themselves. It was a matter of difference of opinion, you see. . . . [They] said that I was pessimistic, and that these things would work themselves out. I took the position that in the face of the statistics of commerce, production and trade of the country, the government could not go on borrowing at that rate and remain solvent" (United States 1932, 1586–1610).

de Depósitos) was set up to manage payments, with Seligman naming a representative to its board as well as a member of the board of the Reserve Bank (*NYSE Listings* A-8257). Another $35 million was issued in October 1928 under the same terms as the previous loan (*NYSE Listings* A-8560).

Admitting from the advantage of hindsight that these loans had been ill-advised, the bankers stressed the pressures of competition as the main explanation (United States 1932, 25, 343, 845–47, 1323–24, 1774–76). Far from urging caution, the U.S. government seems to have been encouraging the banks to lend. A former Commerce Department representative in Peru testified that he had been reprimanded for not being "sufficiently optimistic" when he warned against the Peruvian loans (ibid., 1610–17). By late 1928 the bankers finally seemed to realize that they might be in trouble. In large part, their lending had been based on Leguía's promises to reform his spending practices, but he proved unwilling or unable to do so. The banks responded by pulling back, thus aggravating the problems.

1929–31. In 1929 much of the U.S. money that had been going into foreign bonds was diverted to the U.S. stock market as speculation rose to unprecedented heights. The consequent lack of funds, together with increasing doubts as to whether they could control Leguía, led to new conflicts between the Peruvian government and its bankers, reminiscent of the situation in the early years of the decade.

Since an ever larger portion of Leguía's expenditures had come to be financed by foreign loans, he was forced to cut expenditures quite substantially in 1929. As a partial way out, he tried to get Seligman to float the remaining $15 million in the National Loan authorization, but the firm refused unless he met a number of conditions. These included balancing the budget, placing the Budget Office and the Reserve Bank under Seligman control, stabilizing the currency, restricting floating debt, and ceasing public works (MacKaman 1977, 682). Leguía refused, presumably realizing that these actions could lead to his overthrow, and a stalemate reigned for most of a year between 1929 and 1930. Seligman provided two bank credits to help tide the situation over, but it did not float the $15 million bond issue. Since a condition of the previous loans was that Seligman had a monopoly on Peruvian finance, Leguía could not turn to another bank.

The economic situation continued to deteriorate (Portocarrero 1981), and the U.S. chargé d'affaires in Lima warned that political opposition and instability were increasing as a consequence. He wanted to arrange a reconciliation between Leguía and the bankers, but the secretary of state told him that he should not "do or say anything which could be construed as an unsolicited offer of advice or assistance. . . . Such an offer would involve a responsibility that this government cannot assume" (MacKaman 1977, 683). Noninterference continued to be the State Department's position until Leguía was overthrown by mounting domestic opposition on August 22, 1930.

With a new president, Colonel Luis Sánchez Cerro, backed by the Civilistas, the State Department warned against repudiating the debt. Sánchez Cerro responded by promptly paying all back interest due, and, in January 1931, the government invited Edwin Kemmerer, the well-known U.S. financial consultant, to come to Lima to advise on what should be done with the economy (Drake 1986). Kemmerer made a number of recommendations, including return to the gold standard, and again warned against default (Kemmerer 1931). Although his economic recommendations were temporarily adopted, his advice on the debt was not, and a moratorium was declared as of April 1, 1931 (*West Coast Leader,* 3/24/31). This measure put $114

million into default and ended Peru's access to the U.S. capital
market for more than thirty years.

Retreat of the Banks: 1931–68

Throughout Latin America, the private banks withdrew as a
major source of external finance following the defaults of the
early 1930s; they would not return in force until the 1970s. The
Peruvian experience during these four decades is illustrative of
processes going on elsewhere in the region as discussed in Chapter 2. Three topics are of particular interest: the negotiations
concerning the defaults, the entry of public capital following
World War II, and the beginning of a new role for the banks in
the mid and late 1960s. In this third process, Peru was a har-
binger of events to come all over Latin America a few years later.

Negotiations over Bond Defaults

In declaring a moratorium on debt service in the spring of 1931,
the Peruvian government was no different than the majority of
governments in the region. It was different, however, in the
length of time taken to reach an agreement with its bondholders. Most countries concluded negotiations some time before World War II (FBPC, various years), but Peru did not reach
a definitive agreement until 1953. An offer to the bondholders
was made in 1947 at the initiative of the powerful APRA party,
which saw the debt as standing in the way of improved economic
relations with the United States (Peru 1947). The offer proposed to cancel all unpaid interest since 1931, beginning to pay
only from 1947. Interest during the first two years would be at a

rate of 1 percent, rising to 2.5 percent by 1953. The Foreign Bondholders' Protective Council recommended that the offer be rejected because of the low interest rate (the bonds were originally floated at 7 to 7.5 percent) and cancellation of interest arrears (FBPC 1948–49, 313–14).

Despite the council's objections, the Peruvian government made a direct offer to the bondholders and, by the end of 1950, nearly 60 percent of U.S. bonds had been converted under the plan (United Nations 1955, 133). Negotiations with the council continued, and in January 1953 an offer was accepted. It called for new forty-five-year bonds to be issued carrying a 3 percent interest rate from 1953. Moreover, bondholders received certificates representing 10 percent of the amount of accrued interest to be paid in fifteen annual installments (FBPC 1951–52, 203–11).[19] Although this agreement ended diplomatic problems between the Peruvian and U.S. governments (Carey 1964, 119–21), it did not open the way for new Peruvian bond issues. Peru's future participation in the U.S. capital markets would come only via new institutional mechanisms.

Public Loans to Peru

Following World War II, the bankers' withdrawal was compensated by increased U.S. direct investment and by public-sector loans. The latter were more nearly equivalent to the earlier bond issues because they were a source of funds to the government per se. The new lenders included the U.S. Export-Import Bank, the U.S. aid agencies, and various multilateral institutions including

---

[19] The full documentation on the Peruvian negotiations is contained in the annual report of the Foreign Bondholders' Protective Council for the biennia 1951–52 and 1953–54.

the World Bank, the Interamerican Development Bank, and the International Monetary Fund.

There was an important relationship between these public-sector loans and Peru's eventual turn to the private banks. Specifically, the buildup and later stagnation of such funds left the government in severe financial difficulties. In the period between 1950 and 1962, Peru had received more than $200 million in loans from U.S. government and multilateral agencies (*U.S. Overseas Loans and Grants* 1976, 57, 185). For other Latin American countries, such funds increased substantially during the 1960s; for Peru, they fell off after the election of a mildly reformist president, Fernando Belaunde, in 1963. Despite the fact that Belaunde was a strong supporter of the Alliance for Progress, his government fell into bad relations with the United States, resulting in a U.S. credit blockade. The multilateral agencies soon followed suit.

The most important point of disagreement involved the International Petroleum Corporation (IPC), a Standard Oil subsidiary. Negotiations with the company over its legal status and privileges had dragged on for years and, in the campaign, Belaunde promised to resolve the situation. The State Department, in turn, decided to condition aid to Peru on a "satisfactory" arrangement with IPC and thus informally withheld aid funds. Since the U.S. government was the most important source of external finance for Latin America during this period, Peru's only recourse was suppliers' credits and the private banks (Einhorn 1974, 17–20; Kuczynski 1977, 106–25, 152–61).

Reentry of the Private Banks

During and after the war, U.S. commercial banks began to make direct loans to Latin America although on a fairly small scale.

Some individual banks provided limited amounts of credit to governments in the region, and a number of major U.S. banks participated in World Bank and Export-Import Bank loans. Peru, for example, received some $6 million through this channel between 1953 and 1960 (World Bank Annual Report, 1953–60).

With the inauguration of the Belaunde government, the process accelerated for two main reasons. On the one hand, Belaunde reinitiated the idea of an active state with increased expenditures and programs for structural change. Such notions had generally been absent from Peru since the time of Leguía. On the other hand, the informal credit blockade mentioned above put severe limitations on the amounts of external finance that could be obtained through public-sector loans. One possible solution was to use suppliers' credits, but these were tied to specific projects. The need for general budget finance led the government to the banks (Interviews 1102 and 1112). In 1965 four banks–Manufacturers Hanover, Bankers Trust, National City Bank, and Continental Illinois–joined forces to provide a $40 million credit (*Peruvian Times*, 8/4/67). A similar loan was made the following year, and in 1967 a third $40 million loan was provided, this time in connection with a first-tranche loan from the IMF. Conditions were placed on the third loan, as the banks followed the IMF lead in imposing limits on Central Bank borrowing (Devlin 1980, 163–64).

By 1968 the medium-term prospects for the Peruvian balance of payments were acknowledged to be bleak–although the longer-term outlook seemed brighter–and the government decided to refinance the commercial debt. In the words of one participant: "It was clear from the first day of negotiations that no refinancing agreement would be signed, and probably not even discussed, until there was an agreement with the International Monetary Fund" (Kuczynski 1977, 251). Since this was now a second-tranche agreement, conditions were stricter than the previous year, involving budget as well as credit restrictions. The banks again "piggybacked" their refinancing package on the IMF agreement (Devlin 1980, 164–65). Once the IMF letter of intent was signed, the banks followed with $198 million of refinancing credits–$68 million from the banks involved in the three previous loans, $60 million from other U.S. banks, and $70 million from European and Japanese banks and government agencies. The completion of the refinancing was announced on September 30, 1968; a military coup occurred two days later. The plotters are said to have been awaiting the conclusion of the negotiations (Kuczynski 1977, 254).

The Second Lending Cycle:
The Military Government, 1968–78

The failure of the Belaunde government to carry out the structural changes it had promised – particularly the agrarian reform – led to increased discontent in Peru. The most important manifestation was a guerrilla movement in the central highlands. The military were heavily involved in putting down the guerrilla and peasant uprisings and, in the process, became more aware of the poverty and underdevelopment of the country, which came to be seen as a major threat to national security. Despairing of a civilian government and private capital being able to resolve these problems, the military themselves decided to take over the government. They envisioned a long-term rule during which time the economy would be strengthened, the country made more independent, and the incipient political rebellion eliminated (Villanueva 1973, chaps. 12–14; Stepan 1978, 117–57; Philip 1978). Despite the nationalistic stand of General Juan Velasco Alvarado, leader of the October 1968 coup, the military government shared a number of important characteristics and problems with the Leguía regime of fifty years before.[20]

Political-Economic Background

The Velasco government was somewhat more explicit about its political-economic program than Leguía had been.[21] Drawing on the National Development Plan for 1971–75, three main goals can be identified. A first aim was rapid economic growth with special emphasis on industrialization. Given the nature of the Peruvian oligarchy, which had not proved itself capable of promoting a strong industrial sector and an independent economy in general, the goal of economic development was interpreted as requiring a much greater state role in the economy including ownership of key sectors. The second major goal was greater equity, which was to be achieved through the redistribu-

---

[20] Similarities include authoritarian rule; low opinion of the oligarchy's ability to develop the country; belief in the need for a strong state; tolerance of graft, corruption, and waste in spending; dependence on the banks; the failure of both to implement their grandiose plans for transforming the country; and their eventual replacement by the rightist opposition. These similarities, however, should not hide the fact that the Velasco reforms were much more profound and long-lasting than those of Leguía although some may have had negative consequences.

[21] Some critics claim that the military government had no strategy or program at all – that documents purporting to lay out such a program were for publicity purposes only. They say that the government was just struggling along with little idea of what it was doing, other than trying to stay in power; see, for example, Schydlowsky and Wicht (1979). Others, while not necessarily agreeing with the program, do see the military as having had one. See, for example, Stepan's analysis (1978, chap. 4) of the military consensus.

tion of land, higher taxes on the rich, and profit sharing plus higher wages and benefits for workers. Finally, greater national autonomy was sought for Peru. Nationalization of certain firms, greater control over foreign investment, and diversification of trade and capital flows were advocated (Peru 1971, vol. 1, chap. 1). These goals were summed up in the notion of the Peruvian model as a "third way" to development, *ni capitalista ni comunista,* the theme of the Velasco government that lasted from 1968 through mid-1975. The rest of the military period (1975–80) was under the rule of General Francisco Morales Bermúdez and constituted a transition to a more traditional capitalist development strategy.

The role to be played by foreign capital under Velasco was ambiguous. On the one hand, the military did want foreign capital. Velasco unequivocally stated that "Latin American development requires foreign capital" (Hunt 1975, 311–12). On the other hand, the government also wanted to change the rules under which this capital would operate. Specifically, it wanted to decide in what sectors investment would take place, when and with what technology it would occur, and what percentage of profits would be remitted. The attempt to implement the new rules led many U.S. corporations to hesitate to enter the Peruvian market, although European and Japanese firms were more willing (Stallings 1983a). Also implicit in the government's overall program was a preference for a certain type of foreign capital. Since the government itself would become the chief economic actor, loans would be more important than direct investment. As it turned out, the government needed even more loans than originally thought since private investment (domestic as well as foreign) did not occur in the quantities expected.

The various roles played by foreign loans during the military government were not dissimilar from those under Leguía. Again foreign capital was needed to finance deficits in both the government budget and balance of payments. After an initially conservative fiscal policy, the public-sector deficit began to rise until it reached a peak of 12 percent of GDP in 1976–77. Most of the rise was due to increased investment (FitzGerald 1979, 306). The largest project in which bank loans were involved was the construction of a pipeline to carry oil from the jungle to the coast. Others included the copper industry, various manufacturing projects, and the expansion of the telephone and railway system (Devlin 1980, 245–50). A question of great interest is the role played by defense expenditures in the accumulation of foreign debt. Although no precise answer can be given, a general indicator is available. Between 1973 and 1980, about one-fourth of *all* new foreign debt (that is, multilateral, bilateral, and suppliers' credits as well as bank loans) went for arms purchases (Banco Central de Reserva, *Memoria,* 1982, 105).[22] Balance of payments problems were closely connected with the budget insofar as government investment involved imports. The merchandise balance went into deficit in 1974 when the large volume of government imports began and that, together with the growing debt service payments, threw the current account into heavy deficit (ibid., various years). It was this deficit, as we shall see, that triggered the 1976–78 crisis and the negotiations with the banks and the IMF.

Lending Process

As was the case in the 1920s, lending to the military government came in three distinct periods. Little lending took place in the

[22] Although presumably most of the arms purchases were financed by suppliers' credits, it is hard to draw any precise lines since, as bankers themselves say, "money is fungible." The bankers' dismay at learning that the Peruvians were spending an almost equal amount of money for Soviet planes as was being lent for the 1976 refinancing is an example of how one amount of money can be substituted for another (*Financial Times,* 8/1/76).

1968–71 period. Then it increased rapidly between 1972 and 1975, only to fall off again during the crisis years of 1976–78. The nature of the lending process varied as well, as would be expected.[23]

1968–71. The early years of the military government were marked by the initiation of a program of structural change including the agrarian reform and nationalization of certain foreign firms. Several major U.S. corporations were affected; the most important were W. R. Grace, Cerro de Pasco, IPC, and Chase Manhattan. As a consequence of IPC seeking the assistance of the U.S. government, another financial blockade was instituted.

The U.S. government's economic blockade, which lasted from 1968 through early 1974, constitutes the essential context for an analysis of foreign capital in Peru in this period. Although the banks were not formally requested to participate (Interview 1102), the blockade surely contributed to their attitude of caution. Some of the effects were indirect – ranging from a generally hostile attitude with respect to Peru to pressure from the banks' clients who were being affected by the reforms – but there were direct effects as well. Since AID funds to the region in general were declining in the period, the main force of the blockade came via the Export-Import Bank and the multilateral

[23] Sources for the 1970s are not nearly as complete as those for the 1920s because archival materials are not available. Nevertheless, some useful sources do exist. Of special importance is a study carried out by Robert Devlin (1980) for the United Nations Economic Commission for Latin America; Devlin had access to the Ministry of Finance records. Another useful study was done by Felipe Reátegui for the Central Reserve Bank; see Peru (1981c). Oscar Ugarteche (1980, 1986) has also worked on recent bank lending to Peru. A final source is interviews. I have interviewed a large number of bankers in New York and London, government officials in Washington, and economic officials in Lima. For more details on these interviews, see the bibliography.

agencies, where the United States used its influence to block loans. Exim's participation was considered an essential prerequisite for some of the large-scale development projects, especially the Cuajone copper mine (Hunt 1975, 326–31).

Another policy affecting the banks in the early 1970s came from the Peruvian side: the military government's restrictions on foreign bank ownership. Although traditionally open to such participation, the policy had already begun to change in the waning months of the Belaunde government. Banks under majority foreign ownership were ordered to divest to the point where they owned less than one-third of total capital or accept the same limitations placed on foreign branches (that is, inability to accept savings or time deposits). In 1970 the restrictions were extended. Banks already operating branches in the country—Citibank, Bank of America, Lloyds, and Bank of Tokyo—were allowed to remain if they maintained a certain minimal level of capitalization and agreed to provide the government with special lines of credit in foreign currency. Foreign participation in "domestic" banks was further lowered to one-fifth (Heraud-Solari 1974).

As a result of the new requirements, the four branch banks continued to operate, and various changes were made by the four local banks under majority foreign control. The two European banks reduced their control over their local affiliates, but the two U.S. banks decided to sell out to the government although the terms varied substantially between the two. Chemical Bank's shares in Banco Internacional were bought for a low price after acrimonious negotiations that left the bank quite bitter toward the Peruvian government (Interview 1103). Chase Manhattan's 51 percent share in Banco Continental, by contrast, was purchased for five and a half times its stock market value (Hunt 1975, 316–17). Despite suggestions that quid pro quo was involved, whereby Chase would lead the syndicate to finance Cuajone, government negotiators deny any connection (Interview 2227).

In part because of the financial blockade, but also because of uncertainty about the effect of government reforms, almost no new bank loans came into the country in the 1968–71 period. The only transactions involved the refinancing of already existing debt, as can be seen in Table 22. As mentioned earlier, the military were very anxious to have the refinancing of the foreign debt completed before they took power. In reality, they found that the announcement of its completion had been somewhat premature, and negotiations still remained to be carried out. Specifically, the general agreements reached with Europe and Japan in late September 1968 still had to be finalized through negotiations with each individual creditor. According to one inside source, it took a great deal of effort to persuade the Europeans and Japanese to go ahead with the accords, but eventually they were confirmed. The U.S. agreements had already been signed (Kuczynski 1977, 254).

Given that the effect of the 1968 refinancing had been to impose a heavy payment burden in 1970–71, the Peruvian government undertook another refinancing in 1969 which led to an agreement covering 75 percent of the service payments due over the next two years (Devlin 1980, 29; de la Melena 1973, 199–200; de la Melena 1976, 86). The negotiations were apparently quite difficult, especially with reference to the period over which repayments would be made. Despite the suspension of payments and threats of a moratorium, the government could not avoid another bunching of payments that led to yet another refinancing two years later (Kuczynski 1977, 257).

Until mid-1969, the banks were protected by the conditions of the IMF standby agreement subscribed by the Belaunde government and ratified by the military. Although the new government decided not to renew the standby when it expired,

TABLE 22

Peru: External Public Debt Outstanding by Source, 1968–78
(millions of dollars)

Year	Governments[a]	International Organizations	Suppliers	Private Banks	Total
1968	$ 153.1	$139.0	$292.7	$ 152.6	$ 737.4
1969	202.6	150.8	354.2	167.2	874.8
1970	222.9	171.6	394.3	156.6	945.4
1971	252.4	191.3	398.5	154.9	997.2
1972	316.1	211.3	382.8	211.0	1,121.2
1973	421.9	219.5	384.3	464.9	1,490.6
1974	696.5	243.1	374.7	868.0	2,182.3
1975	1,085.0	259.5	399.0	1,322.4	3,065.9
1976	1,351.1	267.9	420.3	1,515.1	3,554.4
1977	1,998.7	329.9	502.0	1,480.7	4,311.3
1978	2,582.8	408.1	616.2	1,527.5	5,134.6

SOURCE: Peru (1981c, 8–9).

[a] Beginning in 1974, socialist governments constituted a significant portion of this category: 1974, 20 percent; 1975, 24 percent; 1976, 27 percent; 1977, 37 percent; 1978, 35 percent.

it went out of its way to maintain cordial relations with the IMF as a prerequisite to further borrowing (Devlin 1980, 29). Since the IMF conditions were no longer in force, however, the banks had to set their own. These took the form of limits on the amount of interest and amortization that could be paid on medium- and long-term debt during 1970–75 as a way of limiting the amount of debt contracted. Short-term debt for the government's agent bank, Banco de la Nación, was also restricted (ibid., 165).

A final refinancing in this period took place in 1971 with terms similar to those of 1969. The limits placed on debt service were between $200 and $220 million annually during the 1972–76 period, which was close to what was already being paid in 1972 (ibid., 165–66). Thus, at this point, the banks were trying to prevent Peru from substantially increasing its foreign debt. Very soon this policy would change.

1972–75. Although the credit blockade remained in force until February 1974, Peru's financial situation changed abruptly in 1972. In an about-face reminiscent of 1924, the private banks began to pour funds into the government's coffers as lending conditions changed. As explained in Chapter 2, the early 1970s witnessed major changes in the structure and operations of the international capital markets. Consequently, the banks began to look for new clients among a select group of Third World countries considered to have good export possibilities. Peru was one of those countries.

Despite the government's nationalistic rhetoric and the reforms being undertaken, Peru appeared to the bankers as an attractive risk. One of the reasons was its diversified export structure. Far from being a monoexporter, Peru had a variety of agricultural (sugar, cotton, coffee) and mineral (copper, lead, silver, and iron) resources. The new fishmeal industry developed during the 1960s was also a significant source of exports, and new mines coming into production were expected to greatly increase copper exports (Kuczynski 1977, 4–10). A factor of major importance was the recent oil discovery in the Amazonian jungle. Although few went as far as the state oil company spokesman who declared when PetroPeru struck oil in 1971 that the country's economic future was assured (*Latin America,* 11/26/71), Peruvian and foreign analysts alike put an increasing emphasis on oil. Moreover, the government had tried to remain on good terms with the financial community as indicated by the deal with Chase Manhattan, a conservative monetary policy, and satisfactory relations with the IMF.

In February 1972 the first large new credit since the military took power was arranged by Manufacturers Hanover, long-time lead bank for Peru. Later in the year, Manufacturers Hanover led another loan, and two European banks (Dresdner and Williams & Glyn) provided several credits. The Williams & Glyn loans were for MineroPeru, a new government corporation established to develop the Cerro Verde copper mine, while Dresdner's loan went to the central government. The largest single loan was a $40 million credit to the government's agent bank, Banco de la Nación, led by Wells Fargo, a California bank that was to play a major role in Peruvian finance. Altogether, loans arranged during 1972 totaled $160 million (Appendix V).

The OPEC deposits and the recession in the industrial countries, discussed in earlier chapters, had the effect of further improving Peru's borrowing possibilities. A first consequence of the new situation was increased loan volume. As Table 22 indicates, an average of $400 million of bank loans were received in each of the four years between 1973 and 1976. These sums were ten times the annual amount of loans in the 1960s and an even larger jump with respect to the 1968–71 period when almost no new money arrived. Another consequence was the end of conditions on loans. The limits that the 1971 refinancing placed on the government's ability to contract debt were canceled when the inflow of funds in 1972 and 1973 enabled it to pay off the conditioned loans and thus escape the debt ceiling (Devlin 1980, 166). A third consequence was an improvement in the terms on the loans as interest rates dropped and maturities lengthened. To some extent, there was a reversal in 1975, but this was an international trend and not one specific to Peru, deriving from fears generated by the failure in 1974 of two banks in the United States and Germany (Spero 1979).

The specific mechanisms that brought about the improvement in Peru's situation, as in 1924–28, were availability of funds and competition. The latter manifested itself in both a general and a specific way. In general terms, because of the availability of funds, many banks that had never been involved in Peruvian finance were suddenly anxious to lend. These included European and Japanese banks as well as U.S. regional banks. The competition for loan management and participation led to conditions being dropped and interest rates coming down, on the part of Peru's traditional lenders (the large U.S. banks) in addition to the new ones. The importance of the new lenders can be seen in the fact that there were 15 so-called minor lenders to Peru in the 1965–70 period and 131 in 1971–76 (Devlin 1980, 226–30).

Equally important was a more specific manifestation of competition. Some banks—Wells Fargo was the prime example—wanted to use Peru as a vehicle to expand their international portfolios. As early as 1967, Wells Fargo had decided to "go international." Latin America was considered an obvious entrée because most U.S. international business was there. Within Latin America, Peru stood out for two reasons. It was not already dominated by U.S. banking giants as were Brazil and Mexico. Also, the hiring of Carlos Rodríguez-Pastor, a Peruvian banker who had held an important position in the Central Bank during the final Belaunde years, gave Wells Fargo an inside track for loans (Interview 1110). In the 1970s Wells Fargo became heavily involved in Peruvian finance. Between December 1972 and April 1976, the bank managed $535 million of loans, almost one-third of the total (Appendix V). Its relative exposure in Peru was much higher than any except the small consortium banks (Devlin 1980, 116–17).

Wells Fargo's importance was not limited to providing large amounts of money. Most of the loans managed by the bank produced new lows in interest rates or new highs in maturities, and other banks were forced to follow suit (Appendix V). Finally, Wells Fargo was important through the syndicates it organized. Most U.S. banks tended to organize syndicates consisting of other U.S. banks with occasional representation of the largest European or Canadian institutions. Wells Fargo, by contrast, led much larger syndicates with very few U.S. banks. Those U.S. banks that did participate were generally smaller regional banks rather than the money-center giants. Moreover, numerous consortium banks were involved as well as European and especially Japanese banks (Devlin 1980, 110–11). Thus, Wells Fargo was responsible for introducing many new lenders into Peru, further increasing competition.

Peru's credit rating got an important boost when its conflict with the U.S. government was finally resolved in early 1974. The resolution itself was connected to the banks since it was negotiated by James Greene, then senior vice president for Manufacturers Hanover and later president of American Express Bank. In a feat of economic diplomacy, he arranged for a lump sum as compensation for all companies nationalized by Peru, with separate lists of recipients to be presented by the United States and Peru. Thus, the main disagreement – whether IPC would or would not be compensated – was overcome (*Latin America Eco-*

nomic Report, 3/1/74). Once the Greene Agreement was signed, the Eximbank made a $55 million loan to get the Cuajone copper project under way, and Chase Manhattan led the syndicate to provide private bank financing.

On the surface, all appeared to be going well. Peru had escaped the U.S. credit blockade and nevertheless managed to institute its most important reforms. Growth was high, inflation low, and no serious balance of payments problems existed through 1973. In 1974, however, inflation began to edge up, and a trade deficit occurred for the first time since the military took power. The following year, both these problems became more acute; in addition, the budget deficit doubled. Emergency stabilization measures were introduced, and the crisis was serious enough to justify a change in political leadership in August 1975 as General Francisco Morales Bermúdez overthrew General Juan Velasco Alvarado.

What had happened? Certainly there was waste, corruption, and ill-advised spending. One of the most oft-voiced criticisms – as mentioned earlier – was military spending and arms purchases. In large part, however, the problems derived from the strategy itself, exacerbated by problems of timing. The industrialization strategy envisioned by the government was highly capital-intensive so that, once the investment stage began in 1974, a large volume of imports would be required. If that surge coincided with an export slump or substantially increased debt service payments, then a crisis could arrive before the new projects had time to come onstream. As we shall see, that was exactly the pattern.

1976–78. The traditional way to resolve the balance of payments crisis would have been to go to the IMF and sign a letter of intent. This step would have given Peru access to certain IMF funds as well as opening the door to bilateral, multilateral, and private banking sources that wanted an IMF "seal of approval" before lending. The problem was that the IMF would demand an austerity program which even the relatively conservative Morales Bermúdez officials could not accept. The results would alienate workers (through wage and employment cuts), industrialists (through a fall in demand and thus profits), and the military (through curbs on the purchase of arms). Given that the regime had never had much popular support, the potential was too explosive: the government might be overthrown.

The Peruvians therefore approached the major U.S. banks in March 1976 and asked for a large balance of payments loan without having signed a prior agreement with the IMF. The bankers ultimately accepted the Peruvian proposal, reasoning that if a crunch came, the left-wing faction of the government might end up on top and lead Peru back toward a radical nationalist position as under Velasco. It seemed safer to support the Morales Bermúdez government, with its new rightist tendencies, than to risk such a leftist outcome. One New York banker put the point very bluntly. He said that the "main reason" for the loan was "to perpetuate Morales Bermúdez in power," since the banks considered this the best bet for getting their money back (*Washington Post*, 3/14/78).

Although they accepted the Peruvian position vis-à-vis the IMF, the banks had to save face and mollify their clients who were being threatened by the Peruvian government. These included Marcona Mining Company (still negotiating compensation for the nationalization of its iron mines in mid-1975) and Southern Peru Copper Corporation (which faced problems over depreciation allowances and tax delinquency at its Cuajone mine). Finally, a way had to be found to make sure that Peru generated sufficient foreign exchange to be able to service its debt without resorting to further international credits in the future (Interviews 1108, 2124, 2228).

The resulting deal between Peru and the banks was a two-part program that dealt with all of the banks' problems. On the one hand, it included an orthodox stabilization program, although of a milder sort than the IMF would have demanded, involving a 44 percent devaluation, price increases, and minor budget cuts. On the other hand, it required more favorable treatment of foreign investment, including reopening the jungle and coastline to private oil companies, compensating Marcona, and agreeing with Southern Peru on payments due.[24]

The most controversial aspect of the program was the provision that the banks were to monitor the Peruvian economy to ensure that the agreed-on inflation, budget, and other targets were met. Not since the 1920s had banks become so involved in the domestic activities of a Latin American government. The loan was divided into two equal parts; the first was released immediately, but the second was withheld for several months. Authorization to draw the second portion was to be contingent on agreement of 75 percent of the lenders that Peru was making satisfactory economic progress.

The package was put together by Citibank's Irving Friedman, with the participation of Bank of America, Chase Manhattan, Manufacturers Hanover, Morgan Guaranty, and Wells Fargo. These six banks composed the "steering committee" for the loan, since no bank was willing to take total responsibility as lead manager.[25] The steering committee banks agreed to provide

[24] Published sources on the 1976 agreement include Belliveau (1976), *Andean Report* (August 1976), *Latin America Economic Report* (7/27/76), and Devlin (1980, 167–72). I have also interviewed bankers and Peruvian officials about the terms (Interviews 2228 and 2233).

[25] In interviews, a number of bankers claim that they did not want to go along with the deal but did so because of the power of Citicorp and the leadership of Irving Friedman, Citicorp's troubleshooter who had previously worked at the IMF. Friedman claimed that the bankers would have no problem in managing the situation (as he did with the even more troublesome negotiations in Zaire). Many bankers' explanation for Friedman's role was that he left the IMF on bad terms and was

$200 million, contingent on a further $200 million being raised from private banks in Western Europe, Canada, and Japan. Above and beyond the special conditions described above, the terms on the loan were stiff. The interest rate was 2.25 percent above LIBOR, and the maturity was only five years (Appendix V).

The Peruvian drama repeated itself in 1977, but there was an important change in the cast of characters. Although the balance of payments was expected to improve, a large trade deficit still threatened, and service payments on the debt remained oppressive. Thus, Peru had to look for foreign financing once more. This time, however, the bankers refused to negotiate without IMF participation. The reasons were many, but all pushed in the same direction.

A first factor was opposition to the new monitoring role, especially among the banks themselves. As Alfred Miossi, executive vice president of Continental Illinois, said: "For a private bank to police the actions of a sovereign government puts it into a difficult position. International agencies have a more neutral role and are better suited for this" (Belliveau 1976, 34). Bankers also expressed doubts that they would have as much clout as the IMF because of their commercial ties to Peru. One critic explained: "The banks have a vested interest in Peru, and they've got to think of their commercial lending relations in the country. What are the Peruvians going to think if they start snooping around and delving into the books?" (ibid.).

A second set of factors involved the advantages of working with the IMF. Not only would it provide a more neutral facade, but the banks would also be able to profit from the IMF's

---

trying to get even by usurping the IMF's traditional role. In any case, it is clear that the IMF strongly disapproved of the bankers' move (Interviews 3146, 2233, 2202).

experience in dealing with Third World countries, its access to data on Peru, and its capacity to set up and implement a monitoring procedure. Closer cooperation with the IMF would also comply with the wishes of the Federal Reserve. Chairman Arthur Burns had been advocating such increased cooperation for some time, pressuring the banks to stop acting independently with respect to the debt problem. In a February 1977 speech, he made this position public, declaring: "We need to develop the rule of law in this field, and the only instrument for this is the IMF. Unless we have the rule of law, we will have chaos" (*Business Week*, 3/21/77).

A final factor behind the reversal of the banks' position was a perceived change in the political climate in Peru. In 1976 the banks had been fearful of bringing the government down; intervening events had made them more confident that the outcome would produce a shift to the right rather than the left. The most important evidence for this belief was the July 1976 ouster of several leftist-leaning cabinet ministers; no public protest resulted (*Andean Report*, August 1976). Bankers drew the conclusion that the Peruvian political climate was not as explosive as they had believed it to be the previous year.

Given the banks' insistence on involving the IMF, the Peruvian government acquiesced, and an IMF mission arrived in Lima in March 1977. It recommended a typical stabilization program including devaluing the currency, ending subsidies, cutting the budget deficit, limiting wage increases, and selling off public enterprises (*Caretas*, 4/5/77). There followed months of acrimonious negotiations which included a general strike and the resignation of several top government officials. In the fall of 1977, an agreement was signed, and the first installment of a $100 million IMF loan was released in December. When the mission returned in February, however, it declared Peru to be in massive violation of the agreement—and to have doctored the books to make the situation appear more favorable (*Latin America Economic Report*, 3/10/78). The banks, upon reading the IMF report, called off a $260 million loan then under negotiation. The U.S. Treasury also refused assistance, meaning that Peru's only debt relief still on line was the Soviet Union's agreement to postpone payments on arms purchases (*Financial Times*, 3/16/78).

Morales Bermúdez appealed directly to President Carter when he went to Washington for the signing of the Panama Canal Treaty. Emphasizing his plan to return the country to civilian rule via elections, he argued that Carter should intervene with the IMF in order to soften its conditions and provide direct government assistance. The IMF program would necessitate greater repression, he said, and that could endanger the elections (*Washington Post*, 11/9/77). Carter seemed favorably disposed, but the State and Treasury Departments opposed greater assistance for Peru. Furthermore, the entire executive branch seemed cowed by congressional pressure against "bailing out the banks." Thus, the only assistance forthcoming was a $100 million credit for food imports, although State Department officials stressed that they would be willing to reconsider if the situation became more serious (Interviews 2122 and 2123).

The dilemma of the Morales Bermúdez government was dramatic. The public-sector foreign debt was $5 billion (see Table 22), and Peru was scheduled to pay more than $1 billion in interest and amortization in 1978 alone. The sum would constitute some 55 percent of export revenues, a figure the government estimated could rise to 70 percent by 1980. The Central Bank had virtually no foreign exchange, and lines of credit were shut off (Silva Ruete 1981, 80–119). In practical terms, this meant that without quick action, Peru's imports would have to be reduced sharply, throwing tens of thousands of people out of work and cutting the food supply.

The banks and the IMF nevertheless insisted on further austerity measures as the *sine qua non* for extending any relief. Although some of the leftist political parties in Peru suggested a moratorium on debt payments rather than further austerity (Asheshov 1977, 38), there is no indication that Morales Bermúdez or any of his top officials seriously considered such an option. Their own inclinations, and the overwhelming power of the banks and the IMF, pushed in the same direction. Thus, on May 15, prices were doubled on fuel, public transportation, and basic foodstuffs as government subsidies were eliminated in order to cut the budget deficit (*Latin America Economic Report,* 5/19/78).

Strikes and demonstrations led to a dozen persons being killed and the declaration of martial law in the country, but the government maintained the program. Within days of the new austerity measures, the banks tentatively agreed to roll over some $200 million in amortization owed them during the rest of the year. Interest was still to be paid, however, and the deal was tied to the signing of a new agreement with the IMF (*Financial Times,* 6/1/78). That agreement, completed in August, paved the way for a complete refinancing of the foreign debt as the Peruvians had requested, thus ending what at many points had been a technical default.

Epilogue: A New Lending Cycle

The military period did not formally end until July 1980 when the government was handed back to the newly elected President Belaunde—ironically the same person the military had overthrown in 1968. Nevertheless, from mid-1978 on, the military were clearly lame ducks. At that time, a Constituent Assembly was elected to write a new constitution to prepare for the transition to civilian rule. Furthermore, the top economic jobs were turned over to two civilian technocrats who, in terms of the policies they followed, had more in common with the civilian government to come than with the military regime of the past. A final reason for ending the previous section in 1978 is that Peru's international economic outlook changed substantially as of 1979. This fact, together with the new economic policies, led the bankers to change their opinion about the country's creditworthiness.

In early 1979 government lenders, meeting in the Club of Paris, agreed to put off 90 percent of the interest and amortization payments owed them by Peru in 1979 and 1980. These were turned into seven-year loans with two-year grace periods, and similar arrangements were made with the private banks (Peru 1981c, 15–19). Like most refinancings, the problem with the arrangement was that it placed a heavy repayment burden on succeeding years.

Meanwhile, also in 1979, there was a major turnaround in the prices of Peru's principal exports including oil, silver, and copper. In a display of the continuing crucial role played by external factors (this time in a positive direction), Peru was suddenly catapulted into a $1.5 billion balance of payments surplus as the external manifestations of the crisis abruptly ended.[26] At the end of the year, then, the civilian economic team decided to cancel part of the refinancing, increasing the 1980 payments burden but substantially lightening that for 1981–82 (Ortiz de Zevallos 1980, 19).

As this favorable turn of events developed, the bankers were not long in noticing. The lead role was taken by Libra Bank, a

[26] The relative importance of the rise in export prices and the new economic policies in bringing about Peru's recovery is disputed. Ortiz de Zevallos (1980), for example, attributes major responsibility to the former while Kuczynski (1981) focuses on the latter.

consortium bank operating out of London that specialized in Latin American finance. One of the top officers in this bank was Carlos Santistevan, the former president of the Peruvian Central Bank who had resigned in 1977 in protest over both IMF and military policies. Santistevan convinced his colleagues that Peru was again creditworthy, and Libra provided a $20 million credit in June 1979 (Interview 2233). Other banks were not far behind; in total, more than $600 million of new loans had been contracted by the time the Belaunde government took office in July 1980 (Appendix V).

Although Belaunde had advocated a strong state role in the economy during his previous term as president, his position had changed substantially by 1980.[27] Thus the second Belaunde government wanted to sell off many of the state enterprises established under the military and to rely more heavily on direct foreign investment. With respect to borrowing, the government called for slower growth of the foreign debt in general and less reliance on the private banks in particular (Peru 1981b, 46). In terms of actual results, little change was seen in comparison to the military period. The foreign debt continued to increase rapidly. The long-term foreign debt of the public sector rose from $6.0 billion in December 1980 to $9.8 billion in December 1984, shortly before Belaunde's successor took office. Furthermore, the banks became even more important than before as the government sought foreign loans to finance its large budget deficits (Banco Central de Reserva, *Memoria*, 1984, 153–59).

In order to gain the confidence of the international financial community, President Belaunde appointed Carlos Rodríguez-Pastor as finance minister. A Central Bank official in the first

[27] Presumably the change in Belaunde's position was due to the changes brought about by the military between his two periods as president.

Belaunde administration, Rodríguez-Pastor was the person hired by Wells Fargo to help build up their Peruvian portfolio in the 1970s. He rose to the position of head of the international division at the bank before returning to Peru in January 1982. Unlike most other Latin American governments with major debt problems, the Peruvians claimed that their top priority was to pay what they owed. Thus, Rodríguez-Pastor initiated policies designed to squeeze the economy to obtain foreign exchange for debt payments. These policies, together with various natural disasters, produced one of the most spectacular recessions in Latin American history—a 12 percent drop in GDP in 1983—and an inflation rate of 125 percent (ibid., 117–20, 126).

Despite the austerity policies, high international interest rates and falling export revenues led the country back into a financial crisis. The situation was exacerbated because the banks, frightened by Mexico's near default, ended virtually all loans to Latin America. Thus, from mid-1983 on, Peru was almost continually involved in refinancings, and continually in technical default, as the latest lending cycle ended.[28]

Conclusions

Having looked at the history of Peru's participation in the international capital markets, we conclude by returning to the questions posed in the introduction to the chapter to see how this case study can further our understanding of the lending

[28] Belaunde's successor, Alan García, has established a controversial policy with respect to Peru's foreign debt. The official position is that debt service will be limited to 10 percent of export revenues. Clearly the creditors are not pleased with this arrangement, but they have not taken any drastic steps as García insists that he still wishes to negotiate. See *Andean Report* (various issues) for current information.

process and especially the interrelationship between lenders and borrowers.

Consideration of the main actors in the Peruvian case provides additional insights into the supply side in both the 1920s and the 1970s. First, some important divisions become apparent among the lenders. In both decades, there were traditional lenders who behaved fairly conservatively, and there were banks wanting to break into the market that violated conservative norms and greatly increased lending volume and competition. The actions of Seligman in the 1920s and Wells Fargo in the 1970s show how relations among the banks affected lending.

Second, the case demonstrates some ways in which other U.S. actors influenced the bankers' behavior. In the 1920s bank loans were encouraged by U.S. firms that carried out Leguía's infrastructure projects. The best known was the Foundation Company, which built most of the sanitation works. IPC also helped to negotiate some loans. In the 1970s IPC was highly influential in a negative way since its protest was responsible for the U.S. government's boycott against Peru that led the latter to turn to the banks as its primary source of foreign capital. Bank negotiations with the Peruvian government were also constrained by the situation of some of their multinational customers.

Third, the case clarifies the relationship between public-sector actors and the banks. We can see how the U.S. government, and later the International Monetary Fund, provided a favorable context for private lending. In the early 1920s, before the U.S. banks became enthusiastic lenders in Latin America, the U.S. government occasionally encouraged them to provide funds. More important in both periods, however, the government played a permissive role after the heavy lending began, declining to restrict loan volume despite officials' doubts. Finally, both the U.S. government (in the 1920s) and the IMF (in the

1970s) pressured the Peruvian government to undertake policies desired by the banks, with the implicit promise that loans would follow.

On the borrowing side, the case study makes it clear that, quite apart from the banks' desire to lend, the Peruvian governments did indeed want to borrow. At least in the Peruvian case, the idea of passive governments being "forced" to accept loans so that the banks could make profits is quite misleading. In both the 1920s and 1970s, Peruvian governments wanted to borrow for political as well as economic reasons. They wanted funds to increase their capacity to spend without raising taxes concomitantly. Public expenditures could buy political support as well as strengthen the economy. Investment projects, whether infrastructure in the 1920s or productive facilities in the 1970s, were generally financed by foreign loans. Some current consumption, and increasingly debt service, were also paid for in this way. The balance of payments position was closely related to budgetary reasons for borrowing since much of the equipment for government investment came from abroad. Thus, the Peruvian case reinforces the validity of the structural linkage discussed in Chapter 4.

The initiative for loans in Peru generally seems to have come from the borrowers. Whether money was forthcoming and in what quantities, however, depended on the lenders. This relationship is clearer in the 1920s; in the 1970s, some do say that Peru received unsolicited loan offers (*Business Week*, 9/5/77; Interviews 2232 and 2233). Even if it is true that much of the money was spent unwisely, this does not imply that the government did not want it. Although there is a substantial element of truth in the "loan pusher" hypothesis discussed in Chapters 4 and 5, the Peruvian case suggests some caution about it. A more fruitful approach is to investigate how banks and government borrowers saw their interests as coinciding–and the limits of such mutual interests.

Nevertheless, during both decades, the relationship between borrowers and lenders clearly underwent qualitative changes arising from the lending side. After several years of minimal lending despite the borrowers' desire for loans, conditions in the capital markets changed and banks suddenly had access to greater amounts of money. These new conditions brought vastly increased competition. After 1924 a larger number of investment banks sought to float bond issues to finance Leguía's projects as U.S. investors became more interested in purchasing foreign bonds. The rising competition in the 1970s was even more intense as OPEC deposits increased the banks' liquidity.

Both decades also saw a second change in the banks' behavior, this time toward a virtual cessation of lending. In 1929 and 1977 the banks decided that their Peruvian clients were not the good risks they had appeared to be and, despite the Peruvians' evident desire to borrow, loans were cut off. Seligman refused to float the remainder of the National Loan already authorized by the Peruvian congress. In an analogous way, all of the international banks pulled out of the Peruvian market after negotiations broke down with the IMF in 1977. Serious political as well as economic problems resulted from the cutoff of loans. Both governments were eventually replaced as a result of the ensuing financial crises.

Despite the similarities, however, the outcomes of the two debt crises were very different. In early 1931 Peru became one of the first Latin American countries to declare a default; it would not fully recover its access to the international capital markets for forty years. In the 1970s the Peruvian government was not left to default on its loans but was "aided" in one way or another by the banks themselves and public agencies–the IMF and, to a much lesser extent, the U.S. government. By 1979, loans were again on the rise. With respect to the second crisis, Peru was more than simply a case study. It was the first country in Latin America to suffer a debt crisis in the recent era of loans by commercial banks, and the resulting experience was influential in determining possible solutions once the larger-scale crisis erupted the following decade.

In summary, then, the Peruvian case provides two kinds of data for the general analysis. On the one hand, it helps clarify the relationship between supply and demand, which is difficult to analyze on an aggregate level. On the other hand, its unique experience with an early debt crisis provides the basis for a projection of bank behavior in the 1980s. We shall have more to say about such a projection in the final chapter.

7

The Future in
Historical Perspective

UNDERSTANDING THE debt crisis of the
1980s requires an analysis of the lending process of the 1970s
that led to the debt accumulation. Before intelligent decisions
can be made about how to deal with the problems that have
resulted, it is necessary to know why U.S. banks lent to foreign
borrowers in the first place. Furthermore, an understanding of
present circumstances is greatly facilitated by an even longer
historical perspective. The lending boom of the 1970s was not
the first time that private banks have been the main source of
external finance for the Third World. As we have seen, U.S.
banks were also the main intermediaries in the 1920s as were
British banks in the previous century. Taking a historical approach also facilitates use of the body of theoretical literature
purporting to explain why earlier investors were willing to send
their money abroad. These theories, based on a previous epoch,
need to be modified to take account of twentieth-century condi-

tions, but they are a useful starting point for trying to understand the present.

The main goal of this final chapter is to draw on the various kinds of data and analysis presented earlier in the book in order to interpret U.S. private bank lending to Latin America during the twentieth century. By extension, the Latin American case should also be relevant for understanding the experiences of other Third World areas. The conclusions about U.S. lending are then briefly compared to previous theories of capital export. Finally, the debt crisis of the 1980s is discussed to show how the results of the study–which ends with 1980–are useful for understanding the recent period of international financial turmoil.

U.S. Lending in the 1920s and 1970s

U.S. private bank lending to Latin America in the twentieth century occurred in a cyclical pattern that can be seen as an extension of British loan cycles in the nineteenth century. More than 90 percent of all U.S. private loans to Latin America between 1900 and 1980 were made in the 1920s or the 1970s. The question of primary interest in previous chapters is why this pattern occurred. What factors need to be taken into account to explain the two lending booms in a century where the private banks were otherwise uninterested in Third World finance?

Evidence from the twentieth century suggests three necessary and two sufficient conditions on the supply side. Obviously demand was also a necessary condition, but we shall discuss it separately. The necessary factors were a propitious political climate, an adequate institutional framework, and an income distribution pattern that made a large volume of savings available to the lending institutions. The sufficient factors were those which made acquisition of domestic assets relatively less attractive than investment abroad. They included low growth rates and low rates of return in the investors' home economy.

The first necessary condition for large-scale lending was an appropriate political stance on the part of the U.S. government. Although some analysts have portrayed private loans as an extension of U.S. foreign policy, or a government strategy to incorporate Latin America into the American sphere of influence, there is little evidence for this interpretation. Banks made foreign loans because it was profitable to do so, and it was precisely in periods of *least* government involvement that private lending flourished. *Lack* of regulation and the *absence* of public-sector lending that could crowd out demand for more expensive private loans were essential.

During World War I, for example, most of the international lending was carried out by the U.S. government. If this trend had been continued into the postwar period, the volume of private lending in the 1920s would certainly have been much lower. As it was, the government decided to end its loans and turn over the lending operation to the private sector. Private banks then provided several billions of dollars to foreign borrowers including Latin America. A similar phenomenon occurred in the 1970s when the Alliance for Progress had petered out and U.S. "foreign aid" flows fell off sharply. It was then that private lending again became the dominant source of international finance.

In addition to government lending, government regulations—or the absence thereof—were crucial in determining private banks' loan volume. Both in the 1920s and the 1970s, officials had doubts about the quality of some loans that were being made. Restrictive regulations could have limited lending volume, but a laissez-faire stance prevailed and enabled loans (and therefore debt) to mount rapidly. After the defaults of the 1930s, by contrast, a number of legal restrictions did discourage foreign lending. These measures included the Securities Act, which established more stringent rules for issuing bonds, and the Banking (Glass–Steagall) Act, which divorced investment from commercial banking and thus limited the funds available to investment banks which had been the main channel for foreign loans.

A final important factor in discussing the political context of foreign lending–although one on which information is lacking–was investors' perceptions of their government's support if problems arose. Insofar as U.S. investors in the 1920s were informed about British lending in the past, they would have known that the British government had not been willing to collect payments for its bondholders, and they might have anticipated similar treatment. Possession of such information cannot be assumed, however, and no direct evidence exists about *ex ante* views. *Ex post,* it is clear that the U.S. government did not support its bondholders any more than the British government had. In the 1970s evidence suggests that the largest commercial banks did assume that the U.S. government and the International Monetary Fund would have to back them if debt problems arose, since they were crucial to the operation of the U.S. and world economy. Thus, an institutional difference, to which we now turn, probably affected the political context.

The creation of an institutional framework was another necessary condition for large-scale U.S. lending because, prior to 1913, the country had been a capital importer with little need for an infrastructure to support international finance. In fact, even the domestic banking structure was underdeveloped, especially as seen through the lack of a central bank, and nationally chartered banks were prohibited from establishing branches abroad. Consequently, the initial institutional step was the passage of the Federal Reserve Act of 1913, which the large New York banks had been advocating for some time. The new legislation established a central bank that could conduct monetary policy and discount bank acceptances, and it eliminated the prohibition against foreign branches which led immediately to a major branching movement between 1914 and 1920.

In addition to the branches, which increased the banks' knowledge of Latin America and hence their willingness to make loans there, domestic institutional developments were also required. In particular, methods for selling a large volume of bonds had to be established. These took the form of securities affiliates which either had their own retail outlets or made arrangements with brokerage firms for bond distribution. These "bond salesmen," some of whom had been engaged previously in the sale of war bonds, were necessary since the U.S. investing public had little knowledge of foreign securities.

A second set of institutional developments preceded the 1970s lending boom. These involved the formation of the Eurocurrency market. In order to escape regulations and credit controls at home, U.S. banks began to set up branches in London which would lend dollars to multinational corporations. Complementary innovations increased the attractiveness of the new market to bankers. These measures included syndicated loans, whereby banks joined to provide funds and share risk and profits; floating interest rates, which transferred risk of rising rates from lenders to borrowers; and cross-default clauses, which made it impossible for a borrower to play off one lender against another.

The new market eliminated problems with supply of funds, since they could now be purchased through interbank channels, and the absence of regulations enabled the market to grow very rapidly. When movements of the business cycle in the early 1970s sidelined many of the Eurobanks' traditional clients, Latin American governments began to be seen as attractive alternatives. Without this new institutional development, the large-scale lending of the 1970s would not have been possible. The U.S. bond market had never regained its interest in Latin American issues after the debacle of the 1930s, and domestic offices of the commercial banks could not have generated the volume of savings that the Euromarket made available.

The third necessary condition for lending was an income distribution pattern that provided substantial savings to the banking institutions. In the 1920s, these savings derived from a redistribution of personal income within the United States that provided an increasing share to the wealthiest individuals who were also the high savers. Between 1919 and 1928, the share of national income to the top 1 percent of the income scale rose from 12 to 19 percent, while the top 5 percent increased from 24 to 34 percent. After the 1920s the share of both groups fell, reaching 7 and 18 percent respectively by 1946; they have stayed relatively constant since then.

In the 1970s, by contrast, international distribution was the key in order to provide savings to the internationalized Eurocurrency market. This time the savings were generated through a redistribution of income to high-saving countries – the small-population, low-industrialized subgroup within OPEC. Between 1973 and 1974, the current account surplus of OPEC countries rose from $7 billion to $68 billion while the rest of the world incurred corresponding deficits. The newly wealthy OPEC governments wanted to keep their expanded export revenues in a highly liquid form, so a large percentage was deposited with the Eurobanks. This policy gave the banks access to an even larger supply of money to lend in the 1970s than did the redistribution of income within the United States in the 1920s.

A propitious political context, an institutional infrastructure, and substantial liquidity, however, did not mean that banks would lend abroad or especially that they would lend to Third World countries. As long as there was a high level of demand for funds in the United States itself, and as long as the rate of return was acceptable, there was no reason to look abroad with its higher perceived risk. Thus the sufficient condition for foreign lending was a sluggish U.S. economy which, all else being equal, would limit demand for loans and put downward pressure on interest rates. For lending to occur in Third World countries, a further precondition was that demand for loans also be slack in the other advanced industrial countries which were preferred borrowers from the point of view of U.S. bankers.

In both the 1920s and 1970s, growth in the United States fell when compared to the preceding periods, and this fall was indeed accompanied by increased foreign lending. The relationship between U.S. growth and lending *within* the two decades was more uneven. During the 1920s foreign loans in general followed a countercyclical pattern, and Latin American loans assumed importance at the end of the decade when European loan demand fell off. Lending in the 1970s, by contrast, did not show a clear year-on-year relationship with U.S. domestic growth rates, and the vastly increased volume of available funds meant that demand in all countries could be satisfied simultaneously.

Domestic interest rates in the United States behaved in a way that was consistent with growth patterns. Nominal interest rates in the 1920s (which were the rates generally cited in the contemporary literature) declined throughout the decade. Most observers and analysts pointed to this factor as the primary reason for the large-scale foreign investment that took place. The relationship within the decade between lending and interest rates was also inversely correlated. By the 1970s, attention had turned to real interest rates. They declined and then returned to the level at the beginning of the decade, showing no trend until 1979–80, when they rose dramatically. Not surprisingly, U.S.

foreign loans increased until the final years of the decade when they leveled off.

Given this set of necessary and sufficient conditions, it is then possible to consider the lenders' response. That response was based on the banks' search for profits which, at those times when the prerequisites were in place, led them abroad. Once a single important bank went abroad, whether to establish branch offices or make loans to foreign customers, then its major rivals quickly followed. Competition thus became a crucial element in fueling the lending process and reached intense levels in both the 1920s and 1970s. U.S. investment bankers rushed to make loans to Latin American countries in the 1920s, taking advantage of the investing public's desire to purchase foreign bonds. In the 1970s a similar phenomenon occurred as commercial bankers offered their OPEC deposits to the governments of Latin America's fast-growing nations.

The preceding analysis assumes that demand for loans existed abroad. In the case of Latin America, the discussion in Chapter 4 of the structural linkages between the U.S. and Latin American economies justifies such an assumption. As long as the capital goods industry and domestic capital markets are not well developed, foreign capital will be required both to supplement domestic savings (for the government and the private sector) and to provide foreign exchange for imports. Moreover, foreign capital may be needed to change the maturity structure of local savings since insufficient long-term funds are available from local banks. The government budget deficit and the trade deficit are reflections of the structural linkages, but they cannot be taken as indicators of loan demand per se since the deficits may exist because of the availability of foreign capital rather than vice versa.

Latin America had continually increasing deficits for both the government budget and the current account during the twentieth century. The one exception was the current account in the 1930s when the region was receiving virtually no capital inflow but was partially servicing its debt and thus exporting capital. On a year-to-year basis, a close relationship has existed between capital inflows and the two deficits–especially the government deficit–although again the causal relationship is difficult to interpret. Turning to the issue of causation, the question is whether supply or demand factors were more important in explaining the lending pattern in the 1920s and 1970s. The question is not an easy one to answer, especially for economies as interrelated as those of the United States and Latin America. At least two problems are involved. On the one hand, the nature of the interrelationship needs to be spelled out. What precisely were the links that joined the lending and borrowing economies? On the other hand, the relative weight of the two sets of factors at any given time must be determined. It is useful to note here that we should not expect either a demand- or supply-led model always to predominate; different circumstances may bring forth one or the other.

Two types of linkages are posited in the preceding chapters of the book. One is the structural linkage just referred to whereby the lack of certain production and financial capabilities lead to a general need for foreign capital over the long run. The other is the process linkage which deals with the short-term relationship between capital flows and economic processes in Latin America. The heart of the process linkage focuses on the trade relationship between the United States and Latin America and shows how trade is related to long-term external finance as well as the more traditional links with short-term bankers' acceptances. Because of the changes in productive structure (increased industrialization) and government role in the economy (increased functions of various types) in the 1970s compared to the 1920s, the nature of the process linkage varied somewhat in detail although the basic parameters remained the same.

In both periods, low GNP growth in the United States brought about a stagnation in the volume of imports which meant a slowdown in Latin American exports compared to what would otherwise have been the case. The slower growth of exports, in turn, put a damper on GNP growth in the Latin American countries themselves. In the early part of the century, when exports were a more important component of Latin American output than they would be later, the effect on output of a fall in trade was relatively direct on that portion of the economy which was closely linked to the market. In the post–World War II period, by contrast, exports became more important as a source of inputs for the industrial sector than as a priority per se. Thus, a slow growth of exports, which created foreign exchange bottlenecks, had its main effect on industry and then spread to related services. As discussed above, however, the same slowdown in the U.S. economy that had a negative impact on Latin America via the trade effect also tended to make capital export to the region more likely since it lowered demand for loans in the United States and perhaps led to lower rates of return as well.

In the case of the government budget in Latin America, there was again a difference between the 1920s and 1970s–in this instance because of the difference in the government role in the economy. Before World War II and the Keynesian revolution, governments in Latin America tended to be fairly passive. This passive stance was reflected in a lagged relationship between capital inflows and government deficits. Deficits were correlated with capital inflows of the preceding year, which implies that spending was determined by the finance that could be obtained. In the 1970s the government role in welfare programs as well as public enterprises meant that expenditures increased and revenues fell as a consequence of a decline in growth. The resulting deficit was again offset by increased foreign capital inflow, but there was no lag involved as governments planned the volume of funds they would seek in terms of projected needs.

Despite the problems involved in sorting out the interrelationship between supply of foreign loans and demand, there is some evidence—both at the aggregate regional level and in individual country studies—that can be of help. This evidence suggests that change in supply dominated change in lending in the sense that an increase in the supply of loanable funds, for reasons independent of events in Latin America, made large-scale lending possible in the 1920s and 1970s. In the 1920s Latin American governments probably wanted more foreign capital than was made available to them (which was reflected in a rise in the interest premium). This was a likely situation, since the Latin Americans had been accustomed to larger amounts of portfolio investment from Europe in the first two decades of the twentieth century than they received from the United States in the 1920s. Thus, supply became the constraint on lending. In the 1970s a different situation occurred. On the one hand, Latin American governments assumed a more active role in their respective economies, which led to the demand for large amounts of foreign capital. On the other hand, the liquidity of the Eurocurrency market was so great and competition made the bankers' desire to lend so intense that available capital exceeded even what the newly active Latin American governments wished to borrow (which brought about a drop in the interest premium). Consequently, demand became a brake on lending.

U.S. Lending and Theories of Capital Export

How do these conclusions about U.S. private bank lending to Latin America in the twentieth century relate to previous theories of capital export based on the British experience? Although many specific points could be discussed, this book makes four general contributions to the theoretical debate.

A first contribution is to reinforce the previously held view that lending occurs in cycles. At least two types of cycles are discussed in the literature. On the one hand, there are the endogenously generated, regularly timed cycles that Cairncross discovered for the 1870–1914 period. Those twenty-year cycles worked through trade and migration of labor. As capital was borrowed abroad, immigrants went to help with the projects that were being financed, attracted by high wages made possible by favorable terms of trade. Their departure produced a depression in the construction industry and other sectors at home, thus leading investors to prefer foreign rather than domestic bonds. A change in the terms of trade to favor Britain led to a cessation of foreign investment followed by a reversal of the process just described.

On the other hand, there are the more irregular, exogenously triggered cycles found by Kindleberger that occur as far back as 1720. This second type of cycle is conceptualized primarily in psychological terms. An exogenous event aroused investor expectations, which quickly turned to "euphoria." This euphoric atmosphere led to the bidding up of the price of loans through speculative excesses. Another exogenous event eventually soured expectations, leading to disillusion, or "financial distress." If a lender of last resort did not step in, a crisis could result, and the losses could produce "financial revulsion," as investors became unwilling to provide additional funds to defaulting borrowers. A new generation of lenders often had to emerge before another cycle got under way.

Although the analysis in this book indicates that foreign lending has retained its boom/bust pattern in the twentieth century, the characteristics of the two cycles in U.S. lending are not adequately described by either Cairncross or Kindleberger. Some elements of each theory are relevant, but the overall cyclical process needs to be reformulated in ways explored in the following discussion. Furthermore, the question is still open as to whether the current cycle will end in default, as did most of its predecessors. The latter question is dealt with in the final section of this chapter.

The second theoretical contribution of this book focuses on explanations of loan cycles. With respect to the literature on Britain, the analysis presented here reaffirms the importance of some factors, while eliminating or modifying others. Variables that were important in both Britain and the United States include growth rates and rates of return. In the British case, growth patterns—reflected in investment trends rather than GNP—have been identified as the central factor in understanding British overseas lending. Investment trends were closely connected to rates of return, although a difference of opinion exists about whether the crucial factor was an absolute fall in profit rates at home or the existence of relatively more attractive rates abroad. The connection was illustrated most clearly by Edelstein for the period 1870–1914. He compared rates of return in Britain and borrowing countries and concluded that there was a secular decline in both but also a pattern of alternating dominance of home and foreign returns. The timing was very similar to the investment cycles that Cairncross described. These same variables were found to be related to U.S. lending, when growth rates fell in the United States during the periods of heavy lending as compared to preceding years. Likewise, domestic yield and the yield premium emerged as important determinants of U.S. loan volume.

Not all variables, however, were of equal importance in the two cases. Early on, it was argued that migration and trade should be discarded as explanations of U.S. lending. Migratory patterns in the twentieth century were in an opposite direction from that of a hundred years earlier: net migration was to the United States, not to the borrowing countries. Trade is a more complex issue, but the nature of trade/lending patterns in the twentieth century also suggests that this relationship has had little relevance. On the one hand, trade as a percentage of GNP in the United States has been only one-third to one-fourth the ratio in Britain. On the other hand, the close link between the two variables has disappeared. The British period constituted an integrated process of trade and capital flows that served to bring new primary products to the world market. In the 1920s trade was only related in indirect and contradictory ways. In any case, overproduction of primary products rather than scarcity had become the problem. In the 1970s trade patterns were internationalized so that loans from the United States were financing OPEC's trade as much as U.S. trade. Of course, the very lack of a trade/lending relationship in the twentieth century has been important in bringing about debt crises, but that is a separate issue.

This book also reconceptualizes certain variables and challenges previous views about their importance. For example, Fishlow makes a convincing case that British lending derived from economic causes. Rebutting the well-known interpretation of Feis, Fishlow argues that politics may have constituted the basis for continental lending but that profits were the sufficient motivating force in England. Furthermore, the capital market functioned with virtually no official interference, and, in general, the government refused to intervene to help collect debts. Economic motives also appear to have been dominant in U.S. lending, but politics must be defined more broadly than Fishlow allows. A propitious political context, where the government neither competes with private banks nor tries to regulate their activities, is itself clearly a policy choice. Furthermore, expectations of government assistance may have been important in persuading U.S. investors to assume risks.

Institutions were of interest in explaining capital export in Britain, but the debate centered not on institutional change but on whether existing institutions were biased in favor of foreign rather than domestic lending. This emphasis occurred because the necessary financial infrastructure was already in place before the initiation of the period of large-scale international lending from 1870 to 1914. In the U.S. case, by contrast, change and development were the main focus of the institutional argument. The development of adequate institutions early in the twentieth century was a necessary condition for the United States to become the major capital exporting nation. Likewise, the emergence of the Eurocurrency market after World War II was a necessary prerequisite for the second lending boom of the century.

Change in income distribution also appears to have been unnecessary in order to stimulate British lending. Edelstein's analysis of distribution and lending patterns in Britain, for example, revealed only weak links at turning points in loan cycles. The distribution of wealth and income in Britian was already highly concentrated, and although some decline may actually have occurred in the share going to the wealthiest groups, concentration remained much higher than in the United States. Change in distribution was thus more important in the U.S. case, and a reconceptualization of the income variable was required for the later period. Redistribution of income toward high-saving individuals in the United States was a prerequisite in the 1920s so that large-scale lending would be possible. In the 1970s the required redistribution was toward high-saving countries (OPEC) as the internationalized Euromarket displaced the U.S. market.

This book's third contribution to theories of capital export is that it combines the relevant factors in a different way than had been done previously. Many authors writing on British capital export have concentrated on a single variable to explain lending trends; rates of return have been the most common choice. Other books have included several variables but with little attempt to discern the relationship among them. It has been argued here that such an approach is inadequate. A number of variables – political and institutional as well as economic – must be combined into an overall model. At least two analysts have taken a similar approach. One is Cairncross, who focuses on trade, migration, and price changes to explain lending patterns. The other is Kindleberger, whose approach relies primarily on exogenous shocks, expectations, and institutional factors in the form of a central bank or other lender of last resort.

Although these more complex structural models are far superior to single-variable analysis, both have significant drawbacks. The Cairncross model fails in the U.S. case because the model is geared to a specific set of relationships that no longer existed after World War I. The Kindleberger model is more general and therefore of current potential relevance. The problem is that the model is incomplete. For Kindleberger's variables to become relevant, a number of prerequisites must be in place. In particular, this book suggests a cumulative causation model on the supply side, where components include political context, institutional structure, and income distribution as necessary conditions, and low growth rates or low rates of return in the banks' home economy as sufficient ones. Only given these prerequisites does the question of expectations enter in, and it must be connected to the issue of competition.

Finally, this book contributes to the discussion of capital export by insisting on the necessity to pay serious attention to both supply and demand and to study the nature of their relationship. Although any economist will say that this is an obvious point, it is not always adhered to in the literature. Some authors have focused heavily on supply factors, while others have insisted that demand is sufficient to account for loan patterns. Hall suggests that part of the problem is that analysts taking the viewpoint of borrowing countries concentrate on demand, whereas those studying lending countries assume that supply is the crucial factor. A number of authors have tried to approach the supply/demand relationship by using multiple regression analysis, typically with rates of return as independent variables. Edelstein went further to construct a structural model.

This book follows a qualitative alternative of specifying two types of linkage between borrowers and lenders, namely, structural and process linkages. The former arises from the lack of a capital goods industry and mature capital market, which means that Latin American countries normally need foreign capital. The latter derives from Latin America's short-term economic links with the international economy and especially with the United States. A particularly severe need for foreign capital is brought about by trade problems arising from slow growth in the United States, which is then transmitted to Latin America via a fall or stagnation of export revenues. That same recession, however—given the necessary political, institutional, and distributional prerequisites—also triggers an increase in foreign lending that makes up for the export shortfall and also finances budget deficits.

To summarize, this book contributes to the theoretical discussion on capital export by discussing cycles, explanations for cycles, a model of cumulative causation, and the relationship between supply and demand. Not surprisingly, there are both similarities and differences between the conclusions here and those elsewhere in the literature. Since previous theories were based mainly on the experience of British capital export in the nineteenth century, the differences that emerge are partly the result of different historical circumstances. In addition, however, certain variables have been redefined, their relationships reconceptualized, and their importance reevaluated. These modifications are useful in reanalyzing the British case itself as well as in understanding other current and future lending experiences.

The Financial Crisis of the 1980s

The main part of this study ends in 1980. Since then, an international financial crisis—with Latin America at its center—has erupted. As noted in the introduction to the book, three questions have preoccupied analysts and policymakers concerned with the crisis. What will be the outcome of the current crisis? What *should* be the outcome? How can similar crises be avoided in the future? The discussion in the preceding chapters provides help in answering all three queries.

The main power to predict outcomes derives from the historical approach: if we can understand the difference between the 1920s and the 1970s, then we can understand the difference between the 1930s and the 1980s. A specific tool for projections derives from the analysis of Peru in Chapter 6. In 1980 U.S. lending to Latin America was no longer increasing rapidly but neither was it falling off. There was no indication of a 1930s-style phenomenon—massive defaults leading to a total cessation of lending for a lengthy period. In fact, extrapolating from the Peruvian experience of 1976–78, there was reason to predict that a 1930s situation was highly unlikely. Peru was not allowed to default on its loans; bankers and the International Monetary Fund worked with the Peruvian government (albeit in a fairly turbulent way) to restore the country's capacity to service its international debt, and then lending went forward again.

Furthermore, there were reasons to believe that the Peruvian case was not atypical of what the 1980s would bring. As has been repeatedly stressed in the book, 1970s lending took place in an institutional framework that was substantially different from U.S. lending in the 1920s or British lending in the nineteenth century. In earlier periods, defaults were possible because the banks ceased to be involved in the process once the bonds were sold to the public. Since the public at that time consisted mostly of individuals, there was no organized structure capable of exerting enough pressure to prevent defaults. Organizations of bondholders were formed in both Britain and the United States, and both governments helped to a limited extent to negotiate with debtors. These efforts, however, were merely attempts to salvage after the fact whatever was possible.

For a debt crisis resulting from the 1970s lending, the situation had changed in important ways, as the Peruvian case indicated. The banks refused to accept defaults because they themselves—large and powerful institutions rather than isolated individuals—would suffer the consequences. The banks still held the loans in their own portfolios and were owed interest and amortization. A default would have to be written off of profits, which would cause friction with stockholders as well as with bank examiners. The probable consequence (of primary concern to those who make decisions on lending) was that top executives identified as responsible would lose their jobs. Thus, efforts would have to be made to help borrowing countries recover rather than default. Furthermore, profits on foreign operations had become so important for the largest banks that their competitive position would not allow them to withdraw from international lending.

Extending the analysis a bit further, it did not seem unreasonable in 1980 to predict that the lending cycles that had characterized earlier periods might well disappear or at least become less pronounced. Rather than ending in defaults, followed by a cessation of lending, the new type of cycle would merely involve a decline in lending volume, while the banks in conjunction with governments and international agencies helped borrowers recover their repayment capacity.

How does this prediction hold up when we look at events after 1982 – a period when many experts began to talk of a repeat of the 1930s? On the surface, it holds up well during the crisis that began with Mexico's declaration in August 1982 that it could not meet its debt service obligations. Despite serious balance of payments problems in almost every Latin American country, no formal defaults have occurred. Governments of the major industrial nations have joined bankers and IMF officials in working out ways to deal with the queue of governments that have had to reschedule their debts. An international financial breakdown has thus far been averted, but what will happen from here on? Two outcomes are possible. On the one hand, the Peruvian situation might be repeated: the borrowers will get their economies in order and lending will go forward again. On the other hand, the pattern of the 1930s might be repeated: the banks will get out of Third World lending for the next several decades and turn their attention to the U.S. market with its technological advances and new developments in interstate banking. In my view, neither is possible as so stated.

It seems clear that the Peruvian scenario cannot be repeated insofar as it implies a return to lending at the same rate as in the 1970s. An annual increase of 25 to 30 percent is not feasible, for various reasons. The growth of the Euromarket has slowed substantially and does not seem likely in the near future to resume its earlier trend. The money-center banks have reached or exceeded their country-exposure limits for many Latin American borrowers. The smaller banks – and even some of the money-center institutions themselves – are no longer interested in participating in syndicated loans to Latin America. Moreover, new regulations may be imposed by Congress or the bank examiners that would limit the banks' possibilities to lend even if they desired to do so.

Nevertheless, saying that lending will not return to its previous rate of growth does not mean that it will end altogether. The institutional changes that have occurred in the past twenty years prevent this second outcome. Regardless of what the banks would like to do, it it impossible for them to pull out of international lending. To do so would bring on the very defaults they must avoid, given the percentage of their assets in Third World loans. Even the smaller regional banks, which could afford to withdraw and write off their losses, are being prevented from doing so at the present time. The persuasive powers of the larger banks, together with the Federal Reserve, have been sufficient to keep them involved in international lending. Consequently, net capital flow from the banks to Latin America (disbursements minus amortization) remained positive through 1984, although it dropped substantially as shown in Table 23. In 1985 U.S. banks pulled some money out of the region, although the outflow of long-term capital, the topic of this study, seems to have stopped in 1986. Thus, the transfer of resources from Latin America in the 1980s has resulted mainly from interest payments rather than a total cessation of lending—an important difference in comparison with the circumstances of the 1930s and the nineteenth century.

Another significant difference is the role of international agencies and the governments (however reluctant) of the advanced industrial world. In previous epochs of default, international agencies did not exist and governments generally refused to intervene. Now, the International Monetary Fund has taken a central role in persuading banks to stretch out payments and provide new money and in persuading debtor governments to

TABLE 23
Private Bank Loans to Latin America: 1980–86
(billions of dollars)

Year	All Banks		U.S. Banks	
	All Loans	Long-Term	All Loans	Long-Term
1980	$33.9	$11.6	$10.6	$0.9
1981	33.7	15.7	12.9	5.1
1982	17.6	7.9	8.4	5.3
1983	8.2	12.7	2.1	3.7
1984	3.7	15.3	2.0	9.2
1985	9.1[a]	8.6	−4.7	−4.4
1986[b]	−	−	−2.4	0.7

SOURCES: *Maturity Distribution of International Bank Lending* (various issues) for all banks; *Country Exposure Lending Survey* (various issues) for U.S. banks.

[a] Part of increase is due to wider coverage.
[b] First six months only.

modify their economic policies. The World Bank is also gradually providing complementary funds. After a period of not-very-benign neglect, the U.S. government has seen fit to undertake a major initiative in the form of the Baker Plan. Although criticized from all sides (and obviously insufficient to resolve the problems), this scheme indicates a commitment to deal with the debt issue as a necessary step in maintaining the solvency of the banks themselves.

Many economists and other observers claim that the bank loans made since 1982 are "involuntary" and should not be considered in the same light as "voluntary" lending. The crucial point, however, is that involuntary loans did not exist in the past, because no institution was there to bring them about. Furthermore, even involuntary loans provide capital that can have the consequence of improving the accounts of debtor countries sufficiently to permit voluntary lending to resume on a modest scale. The banks are not pleased with the current situation, but they have little choice other than to continue making loans. The main question is whether a case-by-case "muddle through" strategy will be followed or whether a more generalized mechanism will be devised.

Debtor governments are even less pleased with the current situation. Their growth rates have plunged, and their resulting social and political problems are enormous. Most balance of payments progress has been purchased at the expense of imports and therefore of growth. Nevertheless, these governments see themselves as forced to continue servicing their debts to some extent in order to maintain future access to the international capital markets. Latin American governments' options have also changed from the 1930s and the nineteenth century, since they are now charged with promoting growth and building modern economies, and foreign capital is seen as essential to these tasks. Although it is true that debtor governments might gain by joining together to force better terms on the banks—and, in some cases, even by defaulting—these governments do not seem to regard this step as feasible.

The combination of banks trying to protect their capital base and debtor governments trying to protect their future access to international finance has led to a situation in which all parties *perceive* their options as severely constrained. These perceptions point to continued negotiations, with multilateral agencies and industrial governments playing an important role. The argument presented in this book—that widespread default will not occur as it did in prior decades and centuries—is heavily based on the expectation of public participation. Such participation is now required because of the greater interdependence of the world economy in general and the involvement of the largest U.S. banks in particular.

Beyond the question of how the current crisis *will* be resolved is how it *should* be resolved. The basis for approaching the normative issue derives from the initial responsibility for the loans. On whose initiative were they made? This book provides an unequivocal answer: U.S. banks wanted to lend *and* Latin American governments wanted to borrow. The banks saw the opportunity to make substantial profits on Third World loans. In fact, while their industrial counterparts were immersed in the worst recession since the 1930s, the banks were earning record profits. Furthermore, the reason for lending was not just the opportunity for high profits on Third World loans; the banks could have been losing money had it not been for Third World lending. Accepting petrodollar deposits, which they perceived as necessary for competitive reasons, required them to locate borrowers who would pay higher interest rates than were being paid on the deposits.

If Third World borrowers were an answer to the banks' dilemma, the banks also provided a solution to the problems of Third World governments. The governments of oil-importing countries had to pay the inflated price of petroleum and maintain the high growth rates to which their citizens had become accustomed in the post–World War II period. High growth rates had become crucial to the governments' own legitimacy, especially in those cases where authoritarian regimes had largely justified their rule on their predecessors' inability to promote growth. Ironically, the situation was not dissimilar for oil exporters. Rising expectations led to expenditures that exceeded even the vastly increased revenues that petroleum provided. Thus, both groups of countries turned eagerly to the Euromarket for additional resources.

Another set of actors also bears significant responsibility. The governments of the advanced industrial countries did not want to get directly involved in the recycling of petrodollars in the 1970s, nor were they willing to provide funds to enable the multilateral agencies to do so. Rather, they encouraged the banks to take the lead in dealing with the enormous international disequilibria that resulted from the oil price increases. Later, these same governments followed economic policies that greatly exacerbated the debt crisis. Their financial "beggar thy neighbor" policies of monetary contraction, leading to high interest rates and slow growth, made servicing the debt much more difficult than anyone had foreseen a decade earlier.

Insofar as lending banks, borrowing governments, and the governments of the advanced industrial countries were all responsible for the debt crisis, then fairness dictates that all should share the sacrifices to resolve it. Moreover, it is in the self-interest of all three groups of actors for Latin American countries to regain their capacity for economic growth. The political, social, and economic benefits for the Latin Americans are obvious, but substantial advantages would also accrue to the banks (which would receive payment on past loans as well as be assured of future customers) and the industrial countries (which would acquire purchasers for their exports and greater political stability in the Third World).

These apparently uncontroversial conclusions, of course, stand in stark contrast to what is presently taking place in Latin America. Deepening recession is hitting many countries in the region as the debtors—and especially the poorest groups within those nations—are bearing the lion's share of the adjustment burden. Not only is this situation unjust, it is also at odds with historical solutions to debt crises, including that of the 1930s. Under earlier institutional arrangements, defaults on bond issues provided the time and resources needed for debtors to put their economies back in order. The question today is whether similar arrangements can be made without defaults, since the existing situation does not bode well for the future.

Concern for the future moves us to the final question: how

can recurrences of debt crisis be avoided? To do so, all actors already mentioned must play a role. For the borrowers, greater care must be taken in calculating manageable debt burdens and in matching loan maturities with uses of the money. For banks, a longer-term view is necessary if they want to participate in development finance. Likewise, they also need to pay more attention to the borrowers' ability to absorb and service the debt they are incurring. Those who have studied past financial crises would say that while this advice may be sound, it is not realistic. Both lenders and borrowers, by the very nature of the situations in which they are embedded, have a short-term outlook. The bankers who negotiate the loans will be promoted to other jobs before difficulties arise. The governments that receive them are more concerned about short-term political advantage than about what might happen to their successors. In fact, it is this very short-sightedness that makes loan manias possible.

This problem suggests that the governments of the banks' home countries and the multilateral agencies must take a more active role if future debt crises are to be avoided, just as their participation is essential if the present crisis is not to end in massive default. The model of cumulative causation suggested in this book is relevant to this process. The model's first necessary condition for a loan cycle to occur is that public agencies avoid regulating the banks and avoid cheap loans that would compete with the banks' more expensive money. While this condition fits the present laissez-faire attitude in the industrial countries, the absence of greater government participation – both in regulation and lending – virtually assures future crises.

The point is not to eliminate private lending but to prevent it from assuming the form of "mania, panic, and crash" that Kindleberger records for the past two-and-a-half centuries. Current institutional arrangements guarantee that public agencies will be involved once a crisis does erupt, since the large financial institutions cannot be allowed to go bankrupt; hence prudence would seem to dictate an earlier involvement to prevent crises from occurring in the first place. Many plans have been put forward for government participation. Which is chosen is less important than is reaching consensus that today's interdependent world economy requires an active public role in international finance. Failure to do so means that we will be doomed to continue repeating the mistakes of the past, ad infinitum.

Appendixes

Statistical Data, Sources, and
Methodology

APPENDIX I
CAPITAL FLOW SERIES

This section of the appendix displays the data series on capital export to all regions and separately to Latin America. All data are given in current prices, but the deflator is shown as well (Table II.C), so that the series can easily be converted into constant (1958) prices. In addition, the appendix provides definitions of terms and details on the sources employed, and, where necessary, it explains the methods used to modify the data from the original series. Some evaluative comments are also included with respect to the series that were newly constructed.

I.A. Net U.S. Capital Export to Latin America: 1899–1984

(1) PORTFOLIO INVESTMENT: 1899–1984

The basic data series that underlies the entire study is U.S. net long-term portfolio investment in Latin America. Net is defined as flows from the United States to Latin America minus repayments. Long-term means longer than one year. Latin America includes the twenty republics in existence throughout the period: Argentina, Bolivia, Brazil, Chile, Colombia, Costa Rica, Cuba (until 1959), Dominican Republic, Ecuador, El Salvador, Guatemala, Haiti, Honduras, Mexico, Nicaragua, Panama, Paraguay, Peru, Uruguay, and Venezuela. Portfolio investment consists of bonds issued in the U.S. market and international bonds floated by U.S. banks together with credits made by U.S. banks.

Dickens (1933, app. A) is the basic source for the period 1899–1914. He provides information on the gross amount of each bond issued in New York; net figures were obtained by estimating repayments based on his data on maturities. Net figures for 1915–35 are from Lewis (1938, app. E). Her data are net estimates of the gross data published by the U.S. Bureau of Foreign and Domestic Commerce (United States 1930a, app. A). Lewis's data, in turn, are corrected to include loans with maturities between two and five years that Lewis classifies as short term; data to make these corrections are taken from the same source (1930a, app. A). Net flows for 1936–45 come from *Treasury Bulletin* (March 1942, 63; June 1946, 103–6). From 1946 through 1959, information on portfolio investment comes from the *Survey of Current Business* supplement (United States 1963a, table 5e, lines 33–34, and table 68); the first table provides data on Latin American net securities transactions, while the second is net bank claims on Latin American borrowers. From 1960 through 1980, securities transactions and long-term bank claims are taken from *Survey of Current Business* (June issues, section on U.S. international transactions by region). The data for long-term bank claims had to be estimated for 1978–80, since the Commerce Department no longer provides a disaggregation of long- and short-term claims. For 1970–80, this total above is supplemented by U.S.-managed Euroloans to Latin America. This last data set comes from the data base described in Appendix V. Since Euroloans are reported in gross terms, net figures were estimated by the following procedure. The ratio of net to gross increase in Latin American debt from financial institutions, as reported in *World Debt Tables* (1978, 1981), was multiplied for each year by the total volume of Euroloans to Latin America managed by U.S. banks (from Appendix V). This number was then added to the figures on securities transactions and loans from U.S. bank home offices to get a total for U.S. portfolio investment in Latin America. Finally, for 1981–84, data are claims by U.S. banks of over one-year maturity as reported by the *Country Exposure Lending Survey*. These figures are added to bond issues from the *Survey of Current Business* (June issues).

Given the centrality of this series, a few comments are in order with respect to its reliability. First, in overall terms, confidence can be placed in the long-term trends as manifested in the five subperiods. Although slightly different dates might be used, there is no doubt that the 1920s and 1970s stand apart from the rest of the century as far as portfolio investment is concerned. The more problematic issue concerns short-term variation within periods. The nature of the data – identification of individual bond issues – in the 1900–30 period, plus sources for cross-checking (*NYSE Listings* and FBPC data on defaults), provide relative confidence about the general accuracy for the early years. Reliability during the period of net negative lending, however, is less certain, especially after the Lewis estimates end in 1935. The methods behind the *Treasury Bulletin* figures are unclear, and no cross-checking sources have been located. From 1946 the U.S. government has published balance of payments statistics separately by region. Although a thorough evaluation of these data would require examination of the individual components, and discussion with those who constructed the series, a degree of confidence derives from the fact that the U.S. series matches the general trends of the United Nations estimates from the Latin American side. (See United Nations 1965 and the annual *Economic Survey of Latin America*.) The remaining question, then, concerns the Euroloan estimates. Although some small issues are undoubtedly missing (the World Bank estimates that an additional 15 percent of loans were not made public), the large majority are captured. Again cross-checking with various sources (such as *Maturity Distribution of International Bank Lend-*

ing, *World Financial Markets*, *Country Exposure Lending Survey*, and individual country data) leads to a sufficient degree of confidence to make use of the data acceptable. It should be noted, however, that the Euroloan figures are for *U.S.-managed* loans. The assumption is that the amount of U.S. money lent was similar to the volume managed by U.S. banks.

(2) DIRECT INVESTMENT: 1900–84

Direct investment is defined according to the U.S. government definition: investment where U.S. firms own at least 10 percent of equity. Figures include only new capital flows from the United States to Latin America; reinvested earnings are *not* included. The main problem with direct investment data concerns the pre–World War II period. Some difficulties exist with the methodology described below for making year-to-year estimates before 1946, but this series is much less important to the study than is portfolio investment, so the consequence of error is less serious. Further, the totals for subperiods are more reliable than year-to-year data.

The basic data sources for 1900–35 are Lewis (1938, app. D) and United States (1930a, app. A). The latter supplies data on bond issues floated by U.S. corporations for the purpose of investment in Latin America, while the former provides estimates of U.S. foreign investment stock in Latin America at five-year intervals. To arrive at an annual flow estimate, the following procedure was used. For each five-year period, the volume of corporate bond issues was subtracted from the Lewis estimate of new investment flow. Half of the remaining amount was discarded as representing reinvested earnings; this figure comes from the post–World War II proportions and was adopted for lack of alternative information. The resultant sum was added to the amount of corporate securities and the total apportioned among the five years of the period according to the net increase in overall U.S. direct investment (United States 1976, U19). For 1931–39 an extrapolation was based on overall U.S. direct investment (ibid.). The 1940–45 estimates come from United States (1948, 132) figures for total U.S. long-term investment in Latin America minus figures for portfolio investment described above. From 1946 to 1959, data are from United States (1963a, table 5e, line 32) and for 1960–84 from *Survey of Current Business* (August issues, annual survey on direct foreign investment).

(3) SUPPLIERS' CREDITS: 1900–80

Suppliers' credits are loans with maturities over one year provided directly by producers. Before World War II, such credits were virtually nonexistent. Data for 1946–59 are calculated as a residual by subtracting portfolio investment from "other [that is, nondirect] long-term" investment provided in United States (1963a, table 5e, line 35). From 1960 to 1978, the source is the category long-term loans from "nonbanking concerns" in the *Survey of Current Business* (June issues). For 1979 and 1980, the figure had to be estimated, since the long-term/short-term division is not provided.

(4) PRIVATE INVESTMENT: 1900–80

Private investment is the sum of portfolio investment, direct investment, and suppliers' credits.

(5) GOVERNMENT LOANS: 1900–84

Government loans are defined to include loans and grants (the latter from the current account) – except grants of military goods and services. The assumed absence of government flows to Latin America prior to 1936 is based on the overall government accounts (United States 1976, U17–18), which indicate that almost all government loans between 1900 and 1935 were aid to the European combatants during World War I. A very small part of those funds may have gone to Latin America, but the sums were not significant enough to be reported in the government documents consulted. Government flows between 1936 and 1939 are Export-Import Bank loans whose net amounts were estimated from United States (1940) by taking disbursements minus estimated repayments. Between 1940 and 1945, government flows have two components; one is loans (United States 1948, 94) and the other is grants via the Latin American share of the lend-lease program (ibid., 140). The latter was apportioned by year according to total yearly allocation of lend-lease money. From 1946 to 1959, the figures are from United States (1963a, table 5e, lines 28, 38–39). The 1960–84 data are from *Survey of Current Business* (June issues).

(6) TOTAL CAPITAL EXPORT: 1900–80

Total capital export is the sum of private investment plus government loans and grants.

I.B. Net U.S. Capital Export to All Regions: 1900–80

(7) PORTFOLIO INVESTMENT: 1900–80

Definitions pertaining to total U.S. portfolio investment are the same as those for Latin America. The source for total portfolio investment for 1900–45 is "other [that is, nondirect] long-term" private capital flows from United States (1976, U20). After World War II, when suppliers' credits began to assume importance, the source is shifted to United States (1963a, table 1, lines 33–34, and table 68) and *Survey of Current Business* (June 1981, table 1, lines 51 and 54) to permit these credits to be excluded. That is, portfolio investment always consists of bank credits and bond issues. From 1970 the figures are supplemented by estimates of U.S.-managed Euroloans using a methodology similar to that for Latin America. In this case, the total amount of U.S.-

managed Euroloans for each year was taken from Appendix V data. The net/gross ratio was assumed to be the same as that for Latin America. This net amount for each year was then added to home office loans and securities transactions (from *Survey of Current Business,* June 1981, 38–39, lines 51 and 54) to obtain a figure for total portfolio investment. For 1978–80 the figure for home office loans is estimated, since the long-term/short-term distinction has been eliminated.

(8) DIRECT INVESTMENT: 1900–80

Direct investment is defined in the same way as for Latin America—that is, excluding reinvested earnings. From 1900 through 1965, the source is United States (1976, U19). From 1966 through 1980, data are from *Survey of Current Business* (June 1981, 38–39, line 49).

(9) SUPPLIERS' CREDITS: 1900–80

Suppliers' credits are defined as for Latin America. For 1946–59, they are calculated as a residual by subtracting portfolio investment from "other long-term" investment as reported in United States (1963a, table 1, line 35). For 1960–78, the source is long-term loans from "nonbanking concerns" from *Survey of Current Business* (June 1981, 38–39, line 52). For 1979–80 the data are estimated, since long- and short-term figures are no longer separated.

(10) PRIVATE INVESTMENT: 1900–80

Private investment is the sum of portfolio investment, direct investment, and suppliers' credits.

(11) GOVERNMENT LOANS: 1900–80

Government capital flows are again loans and grants, excluding grants in kind. The source from 1900 to 1918 is United States

(1976, U17–18). From 1919 to 1959, it is United States (1963a, table 1, lines 28 and 37). After 1959 data are from *Survey of Current Business* (June 1981, 38–39, lines 34, 44–45).

(12) TOTAL CAPITAL EXPORT: 1900–80

Total capital export is the sum of private investment plus government loans and grants.

TABLE I.A

Net U.S. Capital Export to Latin America: 1899–1984
(millions of dollars)

Year	(1) Portfolio Investment	(2) Direct Investment	(3) Suppliers' Credits	(4) Private Investment	(5) Government Loans	(6) Total Capital Export
1899	20	–	0	–	0	–
1900	1	13	0	14	0	14
1901	1	30	0	31	0	31
1902	1	46	0	47	0	47
1903	5	20	0	25	0	25
1904	24	28	0	52	0	52
1905	-1	23	0	22	0	22
1906	0	39	0	39	0	39
1907	9	19	0	28	0	28
1908	84	19	0	103	0	103
1909	30	50	0	80	0	80
1910	-1	-49	0	-50	0	-50
1911	18	55	0	73	0	73
1912	-13	146	0	133	0	133
1913	12	64	0	76	0	76
1914	6	25	0	31	0	31

TABLE I.A *(continued)*

Year	(1) Portfolio Investment	(2) Direct Investment	(3) Suppliers' Credits	(4) Private Investment	(5) Government Loans	(6) Total Capital Export
1915	−1	74	0	73	0	73
1916	6	146	0	152	0	152
1917	20	103	0	123	0	123
1918	3	52	0	55	0	55
1919	21	72	0	93	0	93
1920	−7	107	0	100	0	100
1921	198	70	0	268	0	268
1922	118	118	0	236	0	236
1923	16	105	0	121	0	121
1924	72	170	0	242	0	242
1925	107	73	0	180	0	180
1926	274	118	0	392	0	392
1927	296	90	0	386	0	386
1928	234	153	0	387	0	387
1929	38	184	0	222	0	222
1930	114	90	0	204	0	204
1931	−34	67	0	33	0	33

Year						
1932	-34	-5	0	-39	0	-39
1933	-33	-5	0	-38	0	-38
1934	-27	-5	0	-32	0	-32
1935	-32	-5	0	-37	0	-37
1936	-15	-5	0	-20	1	-19
1937	-162	-5	0	-167	0	-167
1938	3	-5	0	-2	14	12
1939	-24	-5	0	-29	13	-16
1940	-14	35	0	21	18	39
1941	-21	-25	0	-46	-2	-48
1942	-31	52	0	21	73	94
1943	-32	35	0	3	178	181
1944	-44	-48	0	-92	105	13
1945	-42	133	-4	87	60	147
1946	-44	71	-90	-63	73	10
1947	-9	457	-109	339	99	438
1948	-22	333	-26	285	56	341
1949	-19	332	1	314	69	383
1950	-18	40	-9	13	54	67
1951	-4	182	-26	152	110	262
1952	-17	302	-17	268	87	355
1953	-21	137	-7	109	372	481

TABLE I.A (*continued*)

Year	(1) Portfolio Investment	(2) Direct Investment	(3) Suppliers' Credits	(4) Private Investment	(5) Government Loans	(6) Total Capital Export
1954	100	70	3	173	73	246
1955	235	167	−25	377	96	473
1956	59	618	−5	672	74	746
1957	106	1,164	58	1,328	257	1,585
1958	66	299	−15	350	562	912
1959	118	218	26	362	337	699
1960	231	95	34	360	242	602
1961	77	173	94	344	790	1,134
1962	84	−44	86	126	624	750
1963	138	68	−147	59	565	624
1964	355	−21	138	472	436	908
1965	58	177	49	284	742	1,026
1966	97	194	−1	290	665	955
1967	309	110	113	532	724	1,256
1968	5	566	−79	492	955	1,447
1969	25	299	134	458	778	1,236
1970	165	316	187	668	774	1,442

1971	394	412	30	836	620	1,456
1972	1,260	44	16	1,320	683	2,003
1973	1,397	369	94	1,860	738	2,598
1974	2,414	25	299	2,738	994	3,732
1975	3,752	669	250	4,671	1,093	5,764
1976	4,987	-219	-117	4,651	795	5,446
1977	4,169	594	-111	4,652	798	5,450
1978	5,432	844	-169	6,107	683	6,790
1979	5,914	1,335	-89	7,160	649	7,809
1980	4,891	1,055	-230	5,716	827	6,543
1981	5,153	1,614	—	—	863	—
1982	5,302	1,410	—	—	2,000	—
1983	3,042	539	—	—	1,018	—
1984	7,010	324	—	—	2,487	—

NOTE: Dashes signify that data were not available.

TABLE I.B

Net U.S. Capital Export to All Regions: 1900–80
(millions of dollars)

Year	(7) Portfolio Investment	(8) Direct Investment	(9) Suppliers' Credits	(10) Private Investment	(11) Government Loans	(12) Total Capital Export
1900	87	56	0	143	0	143
1901	123	89	0	212	0	212
1902	40	65	0	105	0	105
1903	−40	81	0	41	0	41
1904	−11	80	0	69	0	69
1905	93	46	0	139	0	139
1906	−46	92	0	46	0	46
1907	−24	89	0	65	0	65
1908	87	48	0	135	0	135
1909	24	88	0	112	0	112
1910	−34	124	0	90	0	90
1911	28	95	0	123	0	123
1912	70	139	0	209	0	209
1913	27	138	0	165	0	165
1914	14	76	0	90	0	90
1915	790	0	0	790	0	790

1916	1,064	0	0	1,064	0	1,064
1917	594	0	0	594	3,656	4,250
1918	396	0	0	396	4,028	4,424
1919	75	94	0	169	2,367	2,536
1920	400	154	0	554	175	729
1921	477	111	0	588	-30	558
1922	669	153	0	822	-8	814
1923	235	148	0	383	-84	299
1924	703	182	0	885	-28	857
1925	603	268	0	871	-27	844
1926	470	351	0	821	-30	791
1927	636	351	0	987	-46	941
1928	752	558	0	1,310	-49	1,261
1929	34	602	0	636	-38	598
1930	70	294	0	364	-77	287
1931	-350	222	0	-128	-14	-142
1932	-267	16	0	-251	-26	-277
1933	80	-32	0	48	7	55
1934	-202	17	0	-185	5	-180
1935	-82	-34	0	-116	-1	-117
1936	-189	12	0	-177	-3	-180
1937	-241	-35	0	-276	-2	-278

TABLE I.B (continued)

Year	(7) Portfolio Investment	(8) Direct Investment	(9) Suppliers' Credits	(10) Private Investment	(11) Government Loans	(12) Total Capital Export
1938	-24	-16	0	-40	9	-31
1939	-104	-9	0	-113	14	-99
1940	-36	-32	0	-68	51	-17
1941	-19	-47	0	-66	1,323	1,257
1942	84	-19	0	65	6,525	6,590
1943	58	-98	0	-40	12,847	12,807
1944	62	-71	0	-9	14,079	14,070
1945	345	100	0	445	7,561	8,006
1946	-23	230	-104	103	5,293	5,396
1947	-136	749	185	798	6,121	6,919
1948	61	721	8	790	4,918	5,708
1949	117	660	-37	740	5,649	6,389
1950	189	621	306	1,116	3,640	4,756
1951	-33	508	470	945	3,191	4,136
1952	415	852	-201	1,066	2,380	3,446
1953	104	735	-289	550	2,055	2,605
1954	248	667	72	987	1,554	2,541

Year					
1955	171	823	70	1,064	2,211	3,275
1956	470	1,951	133	2,554	2,362	4,916
1957	728	2,442	131	3,301	2,574	5,875
1958	1,057	1,181	387	2,625	2,587	5,212
1959	710	1,372	216	2,298	1,986	4,284
1960	818	1,674	40	2,532	2,244	4,776
1961	898	1,598	127	2,623	2,504	5,127
1962	1,095	1,654	132	2,881	2,756	5,637
1963	1,880	1,976	-162	3,694	3,133	6,827
1964	1,658	2,328	485	4,471	3,550	8,021
1965	991	3,468	88	4,547	3,397	7,944
1966	403	3,625	112	4,140	3,189	7,329
1967	1,073	3,049	281	4,403	4,438	8,841
1968	1,231	2,855	220	4,306	4,045	8,351
1969	1,252	3,130	424	4,806	3,938	8,744
1970	1,793	4,413	586	6,792	3,308	10,100
1971	2,524	4,441	168	7,133	4,109	11,242
1972	4,060	3,214	243	7,517	3,906	11,423
1973	7,091	3,195	396	10,682	3,981	14,663
1974	9,512	1,275	474	11,261	5,757	17,018
1975	15,852	6,196	366	22,414	6,360	28,774

TABLE I.B *(continued)*

Year	(7) Portfolio Investment	(8) Direct Investment	(9) Suppliers' Credits	(10) Private Investment	(11) Government Loans	(12) Total Capital Export
1976	22,076	4,253	42	26,371	7,493	33,864
1977	16,567	5,494	99	22,160	6,513	28,673
1978	25,725	4,713	53	30,491	7,711	38,202
1979	20,835	4,984	74	25,893	7,319	33,212
1980	22,557	1,548	65	24,170	10,104	34,274

APPENDIX II
U.S. ECONOMIC SERIES

This appendix provides data on basic U.S. economic trends. All data are in current prices; the deflator is shown in Table II.C so that the data can be transformed into constant (1958) dollars.

II.A. U.S. Merchandise Trade: 1899–1980

(1–2) MERCHANDISE EXPORTS AND IMPORTS: 1899–1980

Merchandise trade data include exports and imports of all goods except those transferred under military grant programs. The source for the period 1899–1945 is United States (1976, U1 and U9). For 1946–59, data are from United States (1963a, table 1, lines 4 and 14). From 1960 through 1980, the source is the *Survey of Current Business* (June 1981, 38–39, lines 2 and 18).

(3) TRADE BALANCE: 1899–1980

The trade balance is equal to exports minus imports.

II.B. U.S. Economic Output Indicators: 1899–1980

(4) GROSS NATIONAL PRODUCT: 1899–1980

Gross national product is the sum before depreciation of goods and services produced by U.S. citizens, including those living abroad. The source for 1899–1946 is United States (1976, F1). From 1947 through 1978, data are from *Survey of Current Busi-*

ness (January 1980, 36). For 1979–80, the source is the same (March 1981, 7).

(5) INDUSTRIAL OUTPUT: 1899–1980

Industrial output is represented by an index calculated by the Federal Reserve Board. The total series is an aggregate of 235 individual sectoral studies with weights adjusted periodically. The main source for the series is the Federal Reserve Board (1977), which includes the years 1919–75. For 1976–80, data are calculated from the *Federal Reserve Bulletin* (various issues, Industrial Production News Release). For the years before the Federal Reserve index began (1899–1918), the index was extrapolated backward based on an index of manufacturing output created for the National Bureau of Economic Research (Kendrick 1961, 465–66). Although the published index measures real output, it is presented here reflated by the GNP deflator (see section (11) below) since all other series are in current prices. The reflated series is converted into an index with 1960 as the base year.

(6) INVESTMENT: 1899–1980

The investment data are gross nonresidential fixed investment, which consists of producers' durable equipment and nonresidential construction. Nonresidential fixed investment, plus residential construction and changes in business inventories, together constitute gross private domestic investment, the investment component of GNP. From 1929 the Commerce Department has published a series on nonresidential fixed investment, which is the main source used here. The data for 1929 to 1945 come from United States (1976, F54); for 1946–78, they are from *Survey of Current Business* (January 1980, 7). In December 1980 there was a change in definition of the variable so that the old series was extrapolated forward based on the percentage increase in the new series. Data are from *Survey of Current Business* (March 1981, 7). Before 1929 the estimate of nonresidential fixed investment is based on Kuznets (1961), combining his categories of gross producers' durables (his table R-33) and "other" construction (his table R-30). The latter is private nonresidential construction.

(7) MONEY SUPPLY

Money supply figures are the M2 series, which includes currency, demand deposits, and time deposits. The source for 1899–1970 is United States (1976, X415); for 1971–80, it is *Statistical Abstract of the United States* (various years).

II.C. U.S. Rates of Return and Price Deflator: 1899–1980

(8) RATE OF RETURN ON TOP-GRADE U.S. BONDS: 1900–80

Top-grade bonds represent the safest return to an investor within the private sector of the U.S. economy. The particular indicator chosen is the Moody AAA Corporate Bond Index, which began in 1919 and is published monthly in *Moody's Industrial Manual*. Figures are the annual average of the monthly data. Prior to 1919 an approximation to the Moody index was obtained by extrapolating backward based on the Homer/Durand index of corporate bond yield prepared for the National Bureau of Economic Research. It can be found in United States (1976, X487) and is available for the years from 1900.

(9) RATE OF RETURN ON AVERAGE U.S. BONDS: 1917–80

Average U.S. bonds represent a somewhat riskier investment than top-grade bonds. The indicator here is the Moody Composite Corporate Bond Index, which includes all bonds rated by the Moody Investor Service, from AAA to C. This index is also published in *Moody's Industrial Manual* and is used here from its inception in 1917. No earlier figures have been calculated.

(10) RATE OF RETURN ON SHORT-TERM U.S. BUSINESS LOANS: 1919–80

Short-term business loans are a major investment for U.S. commercial banks. The rate shown in this series is the actual rate paid by business in New York City, the location of most of the principal international banks. This rate is slightly higher than the prime rate – the benchmark rate for top corporate borrowers – but it is slightly lower than business loan rates in other U.S. cities. From 1919 to 1966, the source is United States (1976, X467), which gives the rates reported by member banks to the Federal Reserve. From 1967 the same statistics come from the *Federal Reserve Bulletin* (various issues, table 1.35).

(11) U.S. PRICE DEFLATOR: 1899–1980

The deflator used throughout this study is the implicit price deflator for gross national product as calculated by the Commerce Department. The base year is 1958. The index, with 1958 base year, is from United States (1976, F5) for the period 1899–1970. After 1970 the 1958-based series was extrapolated forward, using the 1972-based index from *Survey of Current Business* (January 1980, 40; March 1981, 14). There are problems with this deflator as there are with any other that is used over a long time period – that is, the weights of different components will change. The other way of normalizing the data series would be to divide them by some other series, say, portfolio investment as a percentage of GNP. The latter method has the problem of introducing a second source of variation (GNP itself) as well as increasing problems of interpretation. Note that in both the long- and short-term patterns of portfolio investment – the key data series – there is very little difference between normalizing via 1958 prices and using the portfolio investment/GNP ratio.

TABLE II.A
U.S. Merchandise Trade: 1899–1980
(millions of dollars)

Year	(1) Exports	(2) Imports	(3) Trade Balance
1899	1,363	735	628
1900	1,534	894	640
1901	1,585	912	673
1902	1,473	996	477
1903	1,575	1,019	556
1904	1,563	1,062	501
1905	1,751	1,215	536
1906	1,921	1,365	556
1907	2,051	1,469	582
1908	1,880	1,159	721
1909	1,857	1,522	335
1910	1,995	1,609	386
1911	2,228	1,576	652
1912	2,532	1,866	666
1913	2,600	1,829	771
1914	2,230	1,815	415
1915	3,686	1,813	1,873
1916	5,560	2,423	3,137
1917	6,398	3,006	3,392
1918	6,432	3,103	3,329
1919	8,891	3,995	4,896
1920	8,481	5,384	3,097
1921	4,586	2,572	2,014
1922	3,929	3,184	745
1923	4,266	3,866	400
1924	4,741	3,684	1,057
1925	5,011	4,291	720
1926	4,922	4,500	422
1927	4,982	4,240	742
1928	5,249	4,159	1,090

TABLE II.A *(continued)*

Year	(1) Exports	(2) Imports	(3) Trade Balance
1929	5,347	4,463	884
1930	3,929	3,104	825
1931	2,484	2,120	364
1932	1,667	1,343	324
1933	1,736	1,510	226
1934	2,238	1,763	475
1935	2,404	2,462	−58
1936	2,590	2,546	44
1937	3,451	3,181	270
1938	3,243	2,173	1,070
1939	3,347	2,409	938
1940	4,124	2,698	1,426
1941	5,343	3,416	1,927
1942	9,187	3,499	5,688
1943	15,115	4,599	10,516
1944	16,969	5,043	11,926
1945	12,473	5,245	7,228
1946	11,707	5,073	6,634
1947	16,015	5,979	10,036
1948	13,193	7,563	5,630
1949	12,149	6,879	5,270
1950	10,117	9,108	1,009
1951	14,123	11,202	2,921
1952	13,319	10,838	2,481
1953	12,281	10,990	1,291
1954	12,799	10,354	2,445
1955	14,280	11,527	2,753
1956	17,379	12,804	4,575
1957	19,390	13,291	6,099
1958	16,264	12,952	3,312
1959	16,282	15,310	972

TABLE II.A *(continued)*

Year	(1) Exports	(2) Imports	(3) Trade Balance
1960	19,650	14,758	4,892
1961	20,108	14,537	5,571
1962	20,781	16,260	4,521
1963	22,272	17,048	5,224
1964	25,501	18,700	6,801
1965	26,461	21,510	4,951
1966	29,310	25,493	3,817
1967	30,666	26,866	3,800
1968	33,626	32,991	635
1969	36,414	35,807	607
1970	42,469	39,866	2,603
1971	43,319	45,579	−2,260
1972	49,381	55,797	−6,416
1973	71,410	70,499	911
1974	98,306	103,649	−5,343
1975	107,088	98,041	9,047
1976	114,745	124,051	−9,306
1977	120,186	151,689	−31,503
1978	142,054	175,813	−33,759
1979	184,473	211,819	−27,346
1980	223,966	249,308	−25,342

TABLE II.B
U.S. Economic Output Indicators: 1899–1980

Year	(4) GNP ($ billions)	(5) Industry (1960=100)	(6) Investment ($ billions)	(7) Money Supply ($ billions)
1899	17.4	2.2	2.3	6.1
1900	18.7	2.2	2.6	6.6
1901	20.7	2.5	2.9	7.5
1902	21.6	2.9	3.1	8.2
1903	22.9	2.9	3.2	8.7
1904	22.9	2.9	3.4	9.2
1905	25.1	3.3	3.6	10.2
1906	28.7	3.6	3.7	11.1
1907	30.4	3.7	3.9	11.6
1908	27.7	3.0	4.2	11.4
1909	33.4	4.0	4.2	12.7
1910	35.3	4.3	4.2	13.3
1911	35.8	4.0	4.6	14.1
1912	39.4	5.0	4.6	15.1
1913	39.6	5.3	4.3	15.7
1914	38.6	5.2	4.6	16.4
1915	40.0	6.3	5.0	17.6
1916	48.3	8.5	5.7	20.9
1917	60.4	10.4	6.9	24.4
1918	76.4	11.6	8.3	26.7
1919	84.0	11.6	8.6	31.0
1920	91.5	13.9	8.6	34.8
1921	69.6	9.0	8.7	32.9
1922	74.1	10.5	8.8	33.7
1923	85.1	12.8	8.8	36.6
1924	84.7	11.9	9.8	38.6
1925	93.1	13.3	10.5	42.1
1926	97.0	13.9	10.8	43.7
1927	94.9	13.5	11.5	44.7
1928	97.0	14.4	11.4	46.4

TABLE II.B *(continued)*

Year	(4) GNP ($ billions)	(5) Industry (1960=100)	(6) Investment ($ billions)	(7) Money Supply ($ billions)
1929	103.1	15.9	10.6	46.6
1930	90.4	13.0	8.3	45.7
1931	75.8	9.8	5.0	42.7
1932	58.0	6.9	2.7	36.1
1933	55.6	7.9	2.4	32.2
1934	65.1	9.2	3.2	34.4
1935	72.2	10.8	4.1	39.1
1936	82.5	12.7	5.6	43.5
1937	90.4	14.5	7.3	45.7
1938	84.7	11.3	5.4	45.5
1939	90.5	13.8	5.9	49.3
1940	99.5	16.1	7.5	55.2
1941	124.5	21.8	9.5	62.5
1942	157.9	28.1	6.0	71.2
1943	191.6	36.6	5.0	89.9
1944	210.1	40.4	6.8	106.8
1945	211.9	35.6	10.1	126.6
1946	208.5	34.1	17.0	138.7
1947	232.8	43.0	22.9	146.0
1948	259.1	48.3	26.2	148.1
1949	258.0	44.9	24.3	147.5
1950	286.2	52.7	27.1	150.8
1951	330.2	61.1	31.1	156.5
1952	347.2	64.9	31.2	164.9
1953	366.1	70.9	34.3	171.2
1954	366.3	68.1	34.0	177.2
1955	399.3	77.9	38.3	183.7
1956	420.7	84.0	43.7	186.9
1957	442.8	88.4	46.7	191.8
1958	448.9	84.7	41.6	201.1
1959	486.5	96.2	45.3	210.1

TABLE II.B *(continued)*

Year	(4) GNP ($ billions)	(5) Industry (1960=100)	(6) Investment ($ billions)	(7) Money Supply ($ billions)
1960	506.0	100.0	47.7	210.7
1961	523.3	102.0	47.1	221.2
1962	563.8	111.6	41.2	233.9
1963	594.7	119.8	53.6	249.2
1964	635.7	129.9	59.7	264.7
1965	688.1	145.5	71.3	285.9
1966	753.0	162.7	81.4	308.0
1967	796.3	171.8	82.1	331.8
1968	868.5	189.9	89.3	361.6
1969	935.5	208.0	98.9	385.2
1970	982.4	212.8	100.5	401.3
1971	1,063.4	227.4	104.1	446.6
1972	1,171.1	258.5	116.8	496.6
1973	1,306.9	296.6	136.0	539.8
1974	1,412.9	324.2	150.6	578.7
1975	1,528.8	326.4	150.2	628.5
1976	1,702.2	378.3	164.9	700.1
1977	1,899.5	423.2	189.4	765.2
1978	2,127.6	480.4	221.1	827.9
1979	2,413.9	547.2	254.9	900.8
1980	2,626.1	576.5	269.7	988.2

TABLE II.C
U.S. Rates of Return and Price Deflator: 1899–1980

Year	(8) Top-Grade Bonds (%)	(9) Average Bonds (%)	(10) Business Loans (%)	(11) GNP Deflator (1958=100)
1899	–	–	–	23.2
1900	3.90	–	–	24.3
1901	3.19	–	–	24.1
1902	3.24	–	–	24.9
1903	3.39	–	–	25.2
1904	3.54	–	–	25.5
1905	3.44	–	–	26.1
1906	4.66	–	–	26.7
1907	4.78	–	–	27.8
1908	5.01	–	–	27.6
1909	3.96	–	–	28.6
1910	4.18	–	–	29.4
1911	4.02	–	–	29.1
1912	3.97	–	–	30.3
1913	4.66	–	–	30.1
1914	4.56	–	–	30.7
1915	4.39	–	–	32.1
1916	3.42	–	–	36.0
1917	3.98	4.55	–	44.7
1918	5.39	6.16	–	50.3
1919	5.49	6.27	5.5	57.4
1920	6.12	7.08	6.3	65.4
1921	5.97	7.04	6.3	54.5
1922	5.10	5.95	5.1	50.1
1923	5.12	6.04	5.2	51.3
1924	4.00	5.80	4.6	51.2
1925	4.88	5.47	4.5	51.9
1926	4.73	5.21	4.7	51.1
1927	4.57	4.97	4.5	50.0
1928	4.55	4.94	5.0	50.8

TABLE II.C *(continued)*

Year	(8) Top-Grade Bonds (%)	(9) Average Bonds (%)	(10) Business Loans (%)	(11) GNP Deflator (1958=100)
1929	4.83	5.21	5.8	50.6
1930	4.55	5.09	4.4	49.3
1931	4.58	5.81	3.8	44.8
1932	5.01	6.87	4.2	40.2
1933	4.49	5.89	3.4	39.3
1934	4.00	4.96	2.5	42.2
1935	3.60	4.46	1.8	42.6
1936	3.24	3.87	1.7	42.7
1937	3.26	3.94	1.7	44.5
1938	3.19	4.19	1.7	43.9
1939	3.01	3.77	1.8	43.2
1940	2.84	3.55	1.8	43.9
1941	2.77	3.34	1.8	47.2
1942	2.83	3.34	2.0	53.0
1943	2.73	3.16	2.2	56.8
1944	2.72	3.05	2.1	58.2
1945	2.62	2.87	2.0	59.7
1946	2.53	2.74	1.8	66.7
1947	2.61	2.86	1.8	74.6
1948	2.82	3.08	2.2	79.6
1949	2.66	2.96	2.4	79.1
1950	2.62	2.86	2.4	80.2
1951	2.86	3.08	2.8	85.6
1952	2.96	3.19	3.3	87.5
1953	3.20	3.43	3.5	88.3
1954	2.90	3.16	3.4	89.6
1955	3.06	3.25	3.5	90.9
1956	3.36	3.57	4.0	94.0
1957	3.89	4.21	4.5	97.5
1958	3.79	4.16	4.1	100.0
1959	4.38	4.65	4.8	101.6

TABLE II.C *(continued)*

Year	(8) Top-Grade Bonds (%)	(9) Average Bonds (%)	(10) Business Loans (%)	(11) GNP Deflator (1958=100)
1960	4.41	4.73	5.0	103.3
1961	4.35	4.66	4.8	104.6
1962	4.33	4.62	4.8	105.8
1963	4.26	4.50	4.8	107.2
1964	4.40	4.57	4.8	108.8
1965	4.49	4.64	4.8	110.9
1966	5.13	5.34	5.0	113.9
1967	5.51	5.82	5.8	117.6
1968	6.18	6.51	6.5	122.3
1969	7.03	7.36	8.0	128.2
1970	8.04	8.51	8.2	135.2
1971	7.39	7.94	6.0	142.1
1972	7.21	7.63	5.6	147.9
1973	7.44	7.80	8.1	156.5
1974	8.57	9.03	11.1	171.7
1975	8.83	9.57	8.4	188.0
1976	8.43	9.01	7.2	197.8
1977	8.02	8.43	7.2	209.5
1978	8.73	9.07	9.6	224.8
1979	9.63	10.12	13.4	244.6
1980	11.94	12.75	16.2	266.5

NOTE: Dashes signify that data were not available.

APPENDIX III
LATIN AMERICAN
REGIONAL ECONOMIC SERIES

This appendix displays the regional data series for Latin America. All are presented in current prices. Given the lack of Latin American inflation data for the entire period, the U.S. deflator (Table II.C) was used to convert the Latin American data into constant (1958) figures when this was necessary for the analysis.

III.A. Latin American Fiscal Data: 1900–80

(1–2) GOVERNMENT REVENUES AND EXPENDITURES: 1900–80

No data are available on government revenue and expenditure for Latin America as a region. Therefore, it was necessary to construct individual country series for the entire period, convert them to dollars, and aggregate them in order to obtain a regional total. The resulting series should be considered as no more than a rough approximation owing to difficulties with country data sources and the method of conversion into dollars. In both cases, the problems are most serious before World War II. The work of the International Monetary Fund (IMF) in assembling exchange rate information makes that variable somewhat less problematic after 1945; budget data also improve with the establishment of the various U.N. agencies. Only for the 1970s are detailed statistics being published for all countries in the

IMF's *Government Finance Statistics Yearbook*. In terms of coverage, the data series presented here generally include current revenue and current plus capital expenditure for the central government only. In many cases in the 1970s, these categories are expanded to include social security and "extrabudgetary accounts" or "decentralized agencies." In no case are government corporations included. The general principle was to take the broadest coverage possible without going to individual country sources.

For 1900–17 the main source is the Corporation of Foreign Bondholders Annual Report (various issues). Coverage varied from two countries in 1900 to twelve in 1917, but the largest countries are always included. From 1918 to 1930, data are from *Moody's Municipal and Government Manual* (various issues). The source for 1930–39 is the Foreign Bondholders' Protective Council Annual Report. Between 1940 and 1971, a combination of the *U.N. Statistical Yearbook* and *International Financial Statistics* was used. Cross-checking was also done with the various reports of the U.N. Economic Commission for Latin America. For 1972–80 the source is *Government Finance Statistics Yearbook* (1980, 1984). The one exception to these sources is the use of Bacr (1965, 288–89), which gives a 1900–60 series for Brazil.

Exchange rate information, for converting these figures into dollars, was obtained from the following sources. For 1900–29 United States (1930b) was used. Statistics for the 1930–38 period are already in dollars in the FBPC Annual Report. For 1939–49 *International Financial Statistics* (1950) was used. The 1978 and 1982 *International Financial Statistics Yearbooks* ("rf" series) provide the source for 1950–80. Note that a preferable method of conversion (used in obtaining regional GDP estimates below) would be to put all the country series into constant local currency and then convert them into dollars. This method has not proved feasible, however, owing to lack of deflators for each country for the entire period.

(3) FISCAL BALANCE: 1900–80

The fiscal balance is government revenue minus expenditure.

III.B. Latin American Merchandise Trade and Balance of Payments: 1910–80

(4–5) MERCHANDISE EXPORTS AND IMPORTS: 1910–80

Latin American trade data on a regional basis were in better shape than those on fiscal transactions. In particular, it was possible to obtain dollar estimates although no single source contained a very long series. In addition to piecing these series together, it was frequently necessary to make corrections for different reporting of imports CIF or FOB (exports were always reported FOB). The correction was based on the IMF estimate that CIF figures are generally about 10 percent higher than FOB. In Table III.B, all imports are reported CIF. No data have been located for 1899–1909, so these series begin in 1910. The initial source, for 1910–29, is Pan American Union (1931). From 1930 to 1938, data come from United States (1942). The years 1939–60 are taken from United Nations (1965, 24, 41, 55). *International Financial Statistics Yearbook* (1982) provides data for 1961–80.

(6) TRADE BALANCE: 1910–80

The trade balance consists of exports minus imports.

(7) CURRENT ACCOUNT: 1946–80

Current account information for the region is available only since the establishment of the U.N. Economic Commission for Latin America (ECLA) after World War II. The data were already available in dollars, so the main problem was bringing an entire series together from various ECLA publications. For 1946 to 1959, the source is United Nations (1965, 244–45). Data for 1960–66 are from ECLA's *Economic Survey of Latin America* (1965, 80; 1967, 85). The source for 1967–80 is another ECLA publication, the *Statistical Yearbook for Latin America* (1976, 60–61; 1981, 144). The last reference has been revised to include only the nineteen countries used in the study.

III.C. Indicators of Economic Growth in Latin America: 1939–80

(8) GROSS DOMESTIC PRODUCT: 1939–80

In the case of Latin America, the gross product series available is for gross domestic, rather than gross national, product. The former measure represents goods and services produced within a country's territorial boundaries, whether by citizens or foreigners. For most Latin American countries, the attempt to calculate total domestic output did not begin until after World War II. In a few cases (see Appendix IV), data are available from earlier in the century. The data source used for 1939–76 is a recent ECLA publication (United Nations 1978) that results from several decades of gathering and standardizing statistics. Individual country data were put into constant (1970) local currency and then converted into 1970 dollars. The constant price series is brought up to date through extrapolation based on figures in ECLA's *Economic Survey of Latin America* (1980, 11). In Table III.C, the entire series is reflated by the U.S. gross national product deflator to match the other series that are in current prices.

(9–10) INVESTMENT: 1950–80

Regional estimates on investment are available from 1950 in various U.N. sources and could be cross-checked from 1960 by information from the Interamerican Development Bank (1981). It was also possible to make a separate estimate of public investment for these same years. In all cases, the concept measured is gross domestic investment; it was not possible to separate fixed investment for the entire period, nor could residential and nonresidential investment be distinguished. Investment figures are based on the investment coefficient (gross domestic investment/ gross domestic product). The absolute amounts were then calculated, based on the GDP series described in Section (8) above. The investment coefficient for 1950–59 comes from the *Economic Survey of Latin America* (1963, 29). For 1960–80 it is from Interamerican Development Bank (1981).

Calculation of public investment was based on information on public investment as a percentage of gross domestic investment. Sources include the *Economic Survey of Latin America* (1963, 29) for 1950–59; the same source (1967, 5) for 1960–67; and the *Statistical Yearbook for Latin America* (1978, 106–7) for 1970–77. The periods 1968–69 and 1978–80 were extrapolated, assuming no change in public investment as a percentage of total investment.

III.D. Rates of Return and Terms of Trade in Latin America: 1899–1980

(ii) BOND YIELDS: 1899–1980

Although it was impossible to obtain data on domestic rates of return for Latin American countries, it was possible to assemble a series of yields on bonds floated in U.S. markets for those years when flotations were made. For 1931–54 no data are available because no bonds were issued. For those occasional years in the 1900–30 period when no bonds were issued, an extrapolation of yields was based on international yields; see Dickens (1933) and United States (1930a). The source for 1899–1914 is Dickens

(1933, app. A), which reports amounts, maturities, and yield for each bond issue. Similar statistics are available for the 1915–30 period from United States (1930a, app. A). For 1955–69, the source is World Bank (1972a, 1972b), which reports interest rate rather than yield, but the difference is not very significant since bonds in this period were generally issued at par so that yield and interest rate would be the same. Data on yield from 1970 to 1980 are from Appendix V. In all cases, the average annual yield, weighted by the dollar value of bonds, is used.

(12) INTEREST RATES ON BANK CREDITS: 1971–80

As with bond yields, the interest rates presented here are those paid on Latin America's international loans, not on domestic money markets. Even among international loans, interest rates are available only for one group of loans (Euroloans); no information could be obtained on interest rates from loans originating in home offices of U.S. banks. The source of this information, of relevance only during the 1970s when Euroloans were made, is the data bank described in Appendix V, which contains interest rate data on each publicized Euroloan. Again, the average weighted interest rate for each year is used.

(13) TERMS OF TRADE: 1916–80

Constructing a terms of trade series for the Latin American region required piecing together various partial series as well as changing to a single base year for the index. The year selected was 1963. The source for all the partial series is the U.N. Economic Commission for Latin America, which has paid particular attention to the terms of trade question; the earliest available data are for 1916. From 1916 to 1924, the source is ECLA's *Economic Survey of Latin America* (1949, 20, 25); in this period, a series was calculated that represents the average of Latin America's terms of trade with Britain and the United States. From 1925 to 1947, the same source is used (ibid., 17); but in this later period, a broader measure is available that includes all of Latin America's trade partners. Data for 1948–63 are from the *Economic Survey of Latin America* (1969, 269). For 1964–80 the source is ECLA's *Statistical Yearbook for Latin America* (1973, 54–55; 1979, 326–27; 1981, 504–5).

TABLE III.A
Latin American Fiscal Data: 1900–80
(millions of dollars)

Year	(1) Revenue	(2) Expenditure	(3) Balance
1900	122	151	−29
1901	169	181	−12
1902	183	189	−6
1903	216	201	15
1904	245	247	−2
1905	286	270	16
1906	331	318	13
1907	363	356	7
1908	366	381	−15
1909	379	444	−65
1910	424	501	−77
1911	451	528	−77
1912	499	577	−78
1913	518	572	−54
1914	371	551	−180
1915	323	475	−152
1916	364	465	−101
1917	406	526	−120
1918	637	744	−107
1919	726	810	−84
1920	876	942	−66
1921	640	764	−124
1922	686	814	−128
1923	764	806	−42
1924	838	845	−7
1925	1,007	1,051	−44
1926	1,132	1,239	−107
1927	1,242	1,401	−159
1928	1,304	1,470	−166
1929	1,323	1,439	−116

TABLE III.A *(continued)*

Year	(1) Revenue	(2) Expenditure	(3) Balance
1930	1,341	1,461	−120
1931	831	926	−95
1932	964	1,104	−140
1933	855	892	−37
1934	1,028	1,091	−63
1935	1,043	1,050	−7
1936	1,141	1,169	−28
1937	1,301	1,328	−27
1938	1,077	1,210	−133
1939	1,101	1,192	−91
1940	1,094	1,290	−196
1941	1,159	1,394	−235
1942	1,280	1,613	−333
1943	1,507	1,925	−418
1944	1,910	2,372	−462
1945	2,181	2,787	−606
1946	2,724	3,299	−575
1947	3,463	3,654	−191
1948	3,978	4,802	−824
1949	3,630	4,195	−565
1950	3,862	4,295	−433
1951	5,095	5,283	−188
1952	5,572	5,903	−331
1953	6,220	7,384	−1,164
1954	5,885	6,588	−703
1955	6,132	7,072	−940
1956	5,998	6,988	−990
1957	7,327	8,138	−811
1958	7,411	9,374	−1,963
1959	7,092	8,666	−1,574
1960	7,867	9,275	−1,408

TABLE III.A *(continued)*

Year	(1) Revenue	(2) Expenditure	(3) Balance
1961	8,662	10,316	−1,654
1962	7,694	9,609	−1,915
1963	8,539	10,364	−1,825
1964	9,219	11,310	−2,091
1965	10,083	11,827	−1,744
1966	11,831	13,776	−1,945
1967	11,590	13,119	−1,529
1968	13,081	14,588	−1,507
1969	14,482	16,294	−1,812
1970	19,613	21,541	−1,928
1971	22,951	25,830	−2,879
1972	30,476	35,140	−4,664
1973	37,975	43,006	−5,031
1974	56,935	61,573	−4,638
1975	59,674	69,275	−9,601
1976	68,886	79,259	−10,373
1977	81,970	90,737	−8,767
1978	96,804	108,104	−11,300
1979	119,763	128,474	−8,711
1980	151,392	170,050	−18,658

TABLE III.B

Latin American Merchandise Trade and Balance of Payments: 1910–80
(millions of dollars)

Year	(4) Exports	(5) Imports	(6) Balance	(7) Current Account
1910	1,309	1,120	189	–
1911	1,317	1,225	92	–
1912	1,589	1,326	263	–
1913	1,489	1,427	62	–
1914	1,331	974	357	–
1915	1,664	906	758	–
1916	1,890	1,232	658	–
1917	2,059	1,418	641	–
1918	2,413	1,648	765	–
1919	3,100	2,055	1,045	–
1920	3,491	2,942	549	–
1921	2,031	2,080	–49	–
1922	2,108	1,649	459	–
1923	2,451	2,052	399	–
1924	2,906	2,151	755	–
1925	2,802	2,461	341	–
1926	2,670	2,363	307	–
1927	2,888	2,358	530	–
1928	3,030	2,442	588	–
1929	2,954	2,500	454	–
1930	1,993	1,827	166	–
1931	1,490	1,045	445	–
1932	1,039	631	408	–
1933	1,145	797	348	–
1934	1,676	1,048	628	–
1935	1,739	1,158	581	–
1936	1,911	1,266	645	–
1937	2,420	1,690	730	–
1938	1,834	1,518	316	–
1939	1,719	1,370	349	–

TABLE III.B *(continued)*

Year	(4) Exports	(5) Imports	(6) Balance	(7) Current Account
1940	1,596	1,338	258	–
1941	1,930	1,447	483	–
1942	2,003	1,345	658	–
1943	2,558	1,520	1,038	–
1944	2,962	1,861	1,101	–
1945	3,153	2,236	917	–
1946	4,697	3,781	916	436
1947	6,046	6,364	−318	−965
1948	6,634	6,282	352	−359
1949	5,494	5,506	−12	−494
1950	6,656	5,623	1,033	322
1951	7,823	8,066	−243	−1,052
1952	7,075	7,859	−784	−1,311
1953	7,609	6,755	854	85
1954	7,921	7,617	304	−384
1955	8,065	7,748	317	−426
1956	8,767	8,202	565	−535
1957	9,132	9,685	−553	−1,861
1958	8,516	8,884	−368	−1,231
1959	8,414	8,279	135	−694
1960	8,077	8,079	−2	−1,132
1961	7,957	8,136	−179	−1,303
1962	8,447	8,281	166	−1,240
1963	8,893	8,030	863	−373
1964	9,569	8,783	786	−699
1965	10,058	9,028	1,030	−420
1966	10,630	10,011	619	−1,051
1967	10,594	10,323	271	−1,560
1968	11,204	11,365	−161	−2,355
1969	12,363	12,402	−39	−2,049
1970	13,855	14,242	−387	−2,726
1971	14,103	15,896	−1,793	−4,126

TABLE III.B *(continued)*

Year	(4) Exports	(5) Imports	(6) Balance	(7) Current Account
1972	16,236	17,720	−1,484	−4,049
1973	23,789	23,256	533	−3,338
1974	36,596	40,035	−3,439	−7,474
1975	33,406	43,368	−9,962	−13,791
1976	38,628	44,156	−5,528	−11,636
1977	46,049	50,012	−3,963	−11,528
1978	49,463	56,102	−6,639	−18,436
1979	68,126	74,272	−6,146	−20,069
1980	89,750	98,043	−8,293	−27,969

NOTE: Dashes signify that data were not available.

TABLE III.C

Indicators of Economic Growth in Latin America: 1939–80
(millions of dollars)

Year	(8) Gross Domestic Product	(9) Gross Domestic Investment	(10) Public Investment
1939	12,202	–	–
1940	12,411	–	–
1941	14,176	–	–
1942	16,211	–	–
1943	17,912	–	–
1944	19,671	–	–
1945	20,527	–	–
1946	24,749	–	–
1947	29,408	–	–
1948	32,866	–	–
1949	33,516	–	–
1950	35,629	5,380	1,689
1951	40,302	7,254	1,908
1952	42,431	8,062	2,201
1953	44,770	7,521	1,813
1954	48,286	9,174	2,780
1955	52,127	9,157	2,747
1956	56,151	10,107	3,305
1957	61,786	11,183	4,035
1958	66,437	11,361	3,954
1959	69,295	12,404	4,031
1960	75,428	14,633	4,639
1961	81,500	15,892	4,641
1962	85,955	16,246	4,825
1963	90,021	16,204	4,958
1964	98,206	19,052	6,497
1965	105,569	22,170	8,025
1966	113,157	23,876	8,404
1967	121,850	24,736	8,608

TABLE III.C *(continued)*

Year	(8) Gross Domestic Product	(9) Gross Domestic Investment	(10) Public Investment
1968	135,504	28,456	10,159
1969	152,234	33,796	12,369
1970	171,682	38,285	14,319
1971	192,499	43,890	16,810
1972	214,208	47,340	22,297
1973	245,888	57,538	25,662
1974	288,923	78,009	36,196
1975	326,671	79,054	36,681
1976	358,976	86,154	39,975
1977	397,422	95,779	44,441
1978	445,990	108,822	50,493
1979	515,969	125,896	58,416
1980	591,917	149,755	69,486

NOTE: Dashes signify that data were not available.

TABLE III.D

Rates of Return and Terms of Trade in Latin America: 1899–1980

Year	(11) Bond Yield (%)	(12) Bank Interest Rate (%)	(13) Terms of Trade (1963=100)
1899	5.0	–	–
1900	6.0	–	–
1901	5.7	–	–
1902	5.0	–	–
1903	4.5	–	–
1904	4.6	–	–
1905	4.5	–	–
1906	5.5	–	–
1907	5.0	–	–
1908	4.8	–	–
1909	4.7	–	–
1910	4.5	–	–
1911	4.5	–	–
1912	4.4	–	–
1913	6.0	–	–
1914	5.5	–	–
1915	6.3	–	–
1916	6.3	–	153.2
1917	6.5	–	162.6
1918	8.2	–	135.6
1919	6.4	–	112.1
1920	7.3	–	104.7
1921	7.9	–	77.5
1922	7.4	–	88.3
1923	5.9	–	99.7
1924	6.7	–	106.1
1925	6.7	–	106.8
1926	6.9	–	100.2
1927	6.7	–	106.8
1928	6.6	–	108.8

TABLE III.D *(continued)*

Year	(11) Bond Yield (%)	(12) Bank Interest Rate (%)	(13) Terms of Trade (1963=100)
1929	6.8	–	101.8
1930	7.4	–	84.0
1931	–	–	68.2
1932	–	–	74.0
1933	–	–	76.1
1934	–	–	94.3
1935	–	–	88.8
1936	–	–	98.1
1937	–	–	105.3
1938	–	–	88.7
1939	–	–	86.7
1940	–	–	82.6
1941	–	–	84.0
1942	–	–	85.1
1943	–	–	85.2
1944	–	–	81.4
1945	–	–	84.3
1946	–	–	110.7
1947	–	–	119.9
1948	–	–	120.0
1949	–	–	112.0
1950	–	–	135.0
1951	–	–	134.0
1952	–	–	123.0
1953	–	–	132.0
1954	–	–	135.0
1955	4.0	–	125.0
1956	5.0	–	123.0
1957	5.9	–	124.0
1958	4.8	–	115.0
1959	5.7	–	107.0

TABLE III.D *(continued)*

Year	(11) Bond Yield (%)	(12) Bank Interest Rate (%)	(13) Terms of Trade (1963=100)
1960	5.8	–	106.0
1961	6.7	–	105.0
1962	7.0	–	99.0
1963	6.9	–	100.0
1964	6.4	–	102.0
1965	6.5	–	98.0
1966	7.3	–	100.0
1967	7.1	–	97.0
1968	7.5	–	98.0
1969	7.9	–	101.0
1970	9.1	–	103.0
1971	8.5	7.8	100.2
1972	8.1	7.0	103.3
1973	8.3	10.5	116.2
1974	9.6	12.1	136.1
1975	10.0	8.7	119.6
1976	9.7	7.2	123.8
1977	8.5	7.6	131.0
1978	9.3	10.1	117.5
1979	10.0	12.8	122.7
1980	12.6	15.3	128.5

NOTE: Dashes signify that data were not available.

APPENDIX IV
LATIN AMERICAN
COUNTRY ECONOMIC SERIES

Owing to lack of space, tables on individual country data are not presented. This appendix, then, contains only notes on the sources used. Five statistical series – volume of portfolio investment, fiscal balance, trade balance and current account, economic growth indicators, and yield – were constructed for the three largest countries: Argentina, Brazil, and Mexico. The series on fiscal and trade data are also available for the others; see Chapter 4. Data sources for Peru are discussed in Chapter 6.

IV.A. Portfolio Investment by Country: 1899–1980

Portfolio investment series for the three countries are from the same sources used in Appendix I. They include Dickens (1933) for 1899–1914; United States (1930a) for 1915–30; World Bank (1972a, 1972b) for 1946–69; and Appendix V data for 1970–80. Only in certain periods were sufficient loans given to any one country for a series to be complete enough to make calculations with it. These periods were 1899–1913 (Mexico), 1920–30 (Argentina and Brazil), 1961–69 (Mexico), and 1970–80 (Brazil and Mexico).

IV.B. Fiscal Balance by Country: 1900–80

The construction of fiscal data series, as well as the sources used, are described in Appendix II.

IV.C. Merchandise Trade and Balance of Payments by Country: 1900–80

ARGENTINA: 1910–80

Dollar figures for Argentine merchandise exports and imports are from the following sources: Pan American Union (1931) for 1910–29; United States (1942) for 1930–38; Diaz-Alejandro (1970a, 464, 479, 485) for 1939–49; and *International Financial Statistics Yearbook* (1979 and 1982) for 1950–80. For the current account of the balance of payments, sources are *International Financial Statistics* (1958) for 1951–55, Diaz-Alejandro (1970a, 487) for 1956–64, and *International Financial Statistics Yearbook* (1978 and 1982) for 1965–80.

BRAZIL: 1910–80

Sources for Brazilian merchandise trade are the same as those for Argentina except that 1939–49 data come from *International Financial Statistics* (1950). For the current account, sources include Baer (1965, 47) for 1939–47, Baer (1965, 273) for 1948–60, and *International Financial Statistics Yearbook* (1978) for 1961–64. Thereafter, sources are as for Argentina.

MEXICO: 1900–80

Mexican trade data for 1900–76 are from Nacional Financiera (1977a, 385). Nacional Financiera is the state-owned development bank in Mexico. From 1977 to 1980, trade figures are from *International Financial Statistics Yearbook* (1979) and the ECLA *Economic Survey of Latin America* (1981, 210). Current account figures for 1939–64 are from Reynolds (1970, 366). From 1965 to 1980, the sources are the same as for Argentina and Brazil.

IV.D. Indicators of Economic Output by Country: 1900–80

ARGENTINA: 1900–80

Argentina is the only country in Latin America where data on gross domestic product are available for the entire twentieth century. The source for 1900–75 is the ECLA study mentioned in Appendix III.C (United Nations 1978). From 1976 to 1980, this series is extrapolated forward based on the ECLA *Economic Survey of Latin America* (1980, 44). Gross domestic investment for Argentina has been calculated from 1935. Sources include Diaz-Alejandro (1970a, 410) for 1935–50, Diaz-Alejandro (1970a, 407–8, 410) for 1951–60, and Interamerican Development Bank (1981) for 1961–80.

BRAZIL: 1920–80

For Brazil the same GDP sources are used, but the Brazil series is only available from 1920. Investment figures begin in 1947. From that date until 1960, they are from Baer (1965, 226–27) and from the Interamerican Development Bank (1981) for 1961–80.

MEXICO: 1900–80

Mexico also has GDP statistics available for the first decade of the century, but no 1911–19 data exist because of the disruption of the 1910–17 Mexican Revolution. Data for 1900–10 are from Nacional Financiera (1977a, 23). From 1920 the sources are the same as for the other two countries. For investment the source from 1939 to 1960 is Reynolds (1970, 350–52, estimate 1); these estimates are for fixed investment only. The Interamerican Development Bank (1981) data are used from 1961 to 1980.

IV.E. Rates of Return by Country: 1900–80

For all three countries, rates of return on both bonds and loans are taken from the sources listed in Section IV.A. Average annual yields and interest rates, weighted by the dollar value of bonds and loans, are used.

APPENDIX V
DATA BANK ON
INTERNATIONAL LOANS

Like Appendix IV, this appendix does not provide actual data series. Rather it describes a computerized data bank that I constructed and used in the preparation of the book. It consists of 11,542 entries representing individual private loans (bonds and bank credits) to all countries during the periods 1920–30 and 1970–80. These entries are subdivided as follows:

Type of Loan	Latin America	Other Regions
1920s		
Bonds by U.S. banks	180	282
1970s		
Credits by U.S. banks	631	1,445
Credits by non-U.S. banks	812	2,630
Bonds by U.S. banks	70	996
Bonds by non-U.S. banks	181	4,315

Each entry records the following items of information: (1) identification number, (2) name of the bank(s) managing the loan, (3) country of origin of the bank(s), (4) borrowing country, (5) borrowing institution, (6) date of the transaction, (7) amount of the loan, (8) maturity, (9) interest rate, (10) purpose, and (11) guarantor (if any). For bond issues, the banks' purchasing price, banks' selling price, yield, and collateral (if any) are also provided. For credits, additional information concerns management fees. Some of the important data for Latin America are summarized in tables in Chapter 3. In addition, information from the data bank was used to help construct some of the series described in the other appendixes.

Sources for the 1920s

Three major sources were used to construct the 1920s portion of the data bank. The first (United States 1930a) is a U.S. Commerce Department publication that records all bond issues floated in the U.S. market for foreign governments or U.S. corporations for foreign investment purposes between 1920 and 1929. For 1930 it was updated with the Commerce Department's *Trade Information Bulletin* 746 (1931). Information is provided on borrowing country, amount of bond issue, interest, maturity, price, and yield. The second major source is the U.S. Senate hearings (United States 1932) called in 1931–32 to investigate the 1920s foreign loans. The major banks were ordered to bring their records on all issues in which they had participated; these were then published in the hearing documents. This source enabled me to verify the Commerce Department records and to add information on banks managing the loans and often on the loans' purpose. The third major source is the *New York Stock Exchange Listings,* which summarize the prospectuses for each issue floated on the NYSE. (The vast majority of bond issues, both by number and value, are included in this source.) The listings were especially useful in identifying purpose and collateral. Other sources were also consulted for cross-checking and finding missing information. The two most important were the annual report of the Foreign Bondholders' Protective Council and Record Group 151 (Bureau of Foreign and Domestic Commerce) of the U.S. National Archives in Washington, D.C.

Sources for the 1970s

For the 1970s the main source used was the World Bank archive. The Financial Studies Division of the Programming and Budgeting Department gave me access to their computer data bank and their files on publicly disclosed loans – that is, I used data from the bank's Capital Market System (CMS), not the confidential Debtor Reporting System (DRS). For both bonds and Euroloans (that is, loans made via the banks' foreign offices), the World Bank has a computer data bank covering 1972–80. It includes information on borrower, bank(s), date, amount, interest rate, and maturity. For bonds, offering price and yield are given; for credits, fees (when available) are listed. I was able to supplement these data by using the World Bank's files of prospectuses for bond issues and their clipping files for Euroloans. In this way, I could usually determine the lead manager(s) and obtain some information on the purpose of the loan. For the 1970–71 period, I obtained a list of bonds from the World Bank (1972a, 1972b) and used their collection of prospectuses to fill in additional information. For Euroloans I was able to use the Morgan Guaranty Trust archive connected with their publication *World Financial Markets*. Both the World Bank (CMS) and Morgan Guaranty sources on Euroloans provide information only on publicly announced loans. Since the World Bank also has confidential information from the borrowing countries (the DRS), they were able to estimate for me that about 85 percent of all international loans (that is, from home *and* foreign offices) were included in the publicized Euroloan data.

Evaluation

There are clearly problems with the data described above – including incomplete coverage and incomplete information on loans that are identified. The data for the 1920s are of better quality since all capital transfers in that period were via bond issues and more data have to be made public for bonds. For Euroloans in the 1970s, the data should be taken as only a rough approximation of trends. Much more work needs to be done. Nevertheless, for both decades, I believe the data bank to include the most complete information available to a researcher without access to confidential (government and bank) sources.

BIBLIOGRAPHY

Books, Articles, and Chapters

Abrahams, P.
1969   "American Bankers and the Economic Tactics of Peace: 1919." *Journal of American History* 56 (3):572–83.
1976   *The Foreign Expansion of American Finance and Its Relationship to the Foreign Economic Policies of the United States, 1907–1921.* New York: Arno Press.

Abramovitz, M.
1959   "Historical and Comparative Rates of Production." In U.S. Congress, *Hearings Before the Joint Economic Committee of the United States,* 86th Cong., 1st sess., pt. 2.

Adams, C. A.
1968   "The Export-Import Bank and American Foreign Policy, 1934–39." Ph.D. dissertation, Cornell University.

Aldcroft, D.
1977   *From Versailles to Wall Street, 1919–1929.* Berkeley: University of California Press.

Angell, J.
1933   *Financial Foreign Policy of the United States.* New York: Council on Foreign Relations.

Asheshov, N.
1977   "Peru's Flirtation with Disaster." *Institutional Investor, International Edition* (October):37–41.

Atkinson, A. B.
1975   *The Economics of Inequality.* Oxford: Clarendon Press.

Bacha, E., and C. Diaz-Alejandro
1981   *Financial Markets: A View from the Semi-Periphery.* Discussion Paper 367. New Haven: Yale University, Economic Growth Center.

Bacha, E., and P. Malan
1987   "Brazil's Debt: From the Miracle to the Fund." In A. Stepan, ed., *Democratizing Brazil?* New York: Oxford University Press.

Baer, W.
1965   *Industrialization and Economic Development in Brazil.* Homewood, Ill.: Richard D. Irwin.
1983   *The Brazilian Economy.* 2nd ed. New York: Praeger.

Ballesteros, M., and T. Davis
1963   "The Growth of Output and Employment in Basic Sectors of the Chilean Economy, 1908–57." *Economic Development and Cultural Change* 11 (2), pt. I:152–76.

Barbour, V.
1950   *Capitalism and Amsterdam in the 17th Century.* Ann Arbor: University of Michigan Press.

Basadre, J.
1964   *Historia de la República del Perú*. 14 vols. Lima: Ediciones Historia.

Basch, A., and M. Kybal
1970   *Capital Markets in Latin America*. New York: Praeger.

Baster, A.S.J.
1935   *The International Banks*. London: P. S. King and Son.

Beckel, J., and S. Lluch
1982   "Capital Goods: Size of Markets, Sectoral Structure and Demand Prospects in Latin America." *CEPAL Review* 17:111–20.

Bell, G.
1974   *The Eurodollar Market and the International Financial System*. London: Macmillan.

Belliveau, N.
1976   "What the Peruvian Experiment Means." *Institutional Investor, International Edition* (October):31–36.

Bench, R.
1977   "How the U.S. Comptroller of the Currency Analyzes Country Risk." *Euromoney* (August):47–51.

Bergsten, C. F., et al.
1985   *Bank Lending to Developing Countries: The Policy Alternatives*. Washington, D.C.: Institute for International Economics.

Bertram, I. G.
1974   "Development Problems in an Export Economy: A Study of Domestic Capitalists, Foreign Firms and Government in Peru, 1919–30." D. Phil. dissertation, Oxford University.

Block, F.
1977   *The Origins of International Economic Disorder.* Berkeley: University of California Press.

Bloomfield, A.
1968   *Patterns of Fluctuation in International Investment Before 1914.* Princeton Studies in International Finance, no. 21. Princeton: International Finance Section, Department of Economics, Princeton University.

Bollinger, W.
1971   "The Rise of United States Influence in the Peruvian Economy, 1869–1921." M.A. thesis, UCLA.

Bonilla, H.
1974   *Guano y burguesía en el Perú.* Lima: Instituto de Estudios Peruanos.
1977   *Gran Bretaña y el Perú: los mecanismos de un control económico.* Vol. 5. Lima: Instituto de Estudios Peruanos.
1980   *Un siglo a la deriva.* Lima: Instituto de Estudios Peruanos.

Brimmer, A.
1973   "International Capital Markets and the Financing of Economic Development." Speech presented at Atlanta University, Atlanta.

Brown, W. A.
1940 *The International Gold Standard Reinterpreted, 1914–1934*. New York: National Bureau of Economic Research.

Brownlee, W. E.
1979 *Dynamics of Ascent: A History of the American Economy*. 2nd ed. New York: Knopf.

Burga, M., and A. Flores-Galindo
1979 *Apogeo y crisis de la República Aristocrática*. Lima: Ediciones Rikchay Perú.

Burns, A.
1977 "The Need for Order in International Finance." Speech presented at annual dinner of the Columbia University Graduate School of Business, New York.

Cairncross, A. K.
1953 *Home and Foreign Investment, 1870–1913*. Cambridge: Cambridge University Press.
1958 "The English Capital Market Before 1914." *Economica* 25(98):142–46.

Caravedo, B.
1977 *Clases, lucha política y gobierno en el Perú, 1919–1933*. Lima: Retama Editorial.

Carey, J.
1964 *Peru and the United States, 1900–62*. Notre Dame: University of Notre Dame Press.

Carosso, V.
1970   *Investment Banking in America: A History*. Cambridge: Harvard University Press.

Cavarozzi, M.
1976   "The Government and the Industrial Bourgeoisie in Chile, 1938–64." Ph.D. dissertation, University of California, Berkeley.

Chandler, L.
1970   *America's Greatest Depression, 1929–1941*. New York: Harper & Row.

Chenery, H., and A. Strout
1966   "Foreign Assistance and Economic Development." *American Economic Review* 56(4):679–733.

Clapham, J. H.
1966   *The Bank of England*. Cambridge: Cambridge University Press.

Cleveland, H., and T. Huertas
1985   *Citibank, 1812–1970*. Cambridge: Harvard University Press.

Cline, W.
1984   *International Debt: Systemic Risk and Policy Response*. Washington, D.C.: Institute for International Economics.

Corey, L.
1930   *The House of Morgan*. New York: Grosset & Dunlap.

Corti, E. C.
1928 *The Rise of the House of Rothschild.* New York: Cosmopolitan Books.

Cotler, J.
1978 *Clases, estado y nación en el Perú.* Lima: Instituto de Estudios Peruanos.

Cottrell, P. L.
1975 *British Overseas Investment in the Nineteenth Century.* London: Macmillan.

Cumberland, W.
1921 W. W. Cumberland to State Department. SD 823.51/196, 10/31/21. Record Group 59. National Archives, Washington, D.C.
1922 F. A. Sterling to U.S. Secretary of State. SD 823.51/269, 9/12/22. Record Group 59. National Archives, Washington, D.C.

Darity, W.
1985 *Loan Pushing: Doctrine and Theory.* International Finance Discussion Paper 253. Washington, D.C.: Federal Reserve Board.

Davis, L. E.
1966 "The Capital Markets and Industrial Concentration: The U.S. and the U.K., a Comparative Study." *Economic History Review* 19(2):255–72.

de Cecco, M.
1974 *Money and Empire.* London: Basil Blackwell.

1985 "The International Debt Problem in the Interwar Period." *Banca Nazionale del Lavoro Quarterly Review* 152:45–64.

de la Melena, G.
1973 *La reforma financiera.* Lima: Ministerio de Economía y Finanzas.
1976 "Aspectos financieros del Plan del Gobierno Revolucionario de la Fuerza Armada y acciones previstas en el Plan de Desarrollo 75–78." In E. Kerbusch, ed., *Cambios estructurales en el Perú 1968–75.* Lima: Fundación Friedrich Ebert.

de Roover, R.
1963 *The Rise and Decline of the Medici Bank, 1397–1494.* Cambridge: Harvard University Press.

Deane, P., and W. A. Cole
1967 *British Economic Growth, 1688–1959: Trends and Structure.* 2nd ed. Cambridge: Cambridge University Press.

Delamaide, D.
1984 *Debt Shock.* New York: Anchor Books.

Devlin, R.
1980 *Los bancos transnacionales y el financiamiento externo de América Latina: la experiencia del Perú 1965–76.* Santiago: Naciones Unidas.
1987 *The Structure and Performance of International Banking During the 1970s and Its Impact on the Crisis in Latin America.* Helen Kellogg Institute, Working Paper 90. Notre Dame: University of Notre Dame.

Diaz-Alejandro, C.
1965 "On the Import Intensity of Import Substitution." *Kyklos* 18(3):495–509.
1970a *Essays on the Economic History of the Argentine Republic.* New Haven: Yale University Press.
1970b "Direct Foreign Investment in Latin America." In C. Kindleberger, ed., *The International Corporation.* Cambridge: MIT Press.
1976 "The Post-1971 International Financial System and the Less Developed Countries." In G. K. Helleiner, ed., *A World Divided.* Cambridge: Cambridge University Press.
1983 "Stories of the 1930s for the 1980s." In P. Armella et al., eds., *Financial Policies and the World Capital Market.* Chicago: University of Chicago Press.

Dice, C. A., and W. J. Eiteman
1926 *The Stock Market.* New York: McGraw-Hill.

Dickens, P.
1933 "The Transition Period in American International Financing, 1897–1914." Ph.D. dissertation, George Washington University.

Dornbusch, R.
1985 "External Debt, Budget Deficits, and Disequilibrium Exchange Rates." In G. Smith and J. Cuddington, eds., *International Debt and the Developing Countries.* Washington, D.C.: World Bank.

Drake, P.
1986 "The Money Doctor in the Andes: U.S. Expansion in Latin America from World War I to the Great Depres-

sion." San Diego: University of California, San Diego. Mimeo.

Eaton, J., et al.
1986   "The Pure Theory of Country Risk." *European Economic Review* 30(3):481–514.

Edelstein, M.
1971   "Rigidity and Bias in the British Capital Market, 1870–1913." In D. N. McCloskey, ed., *Essays on a Mature Economy: Britain After 1840*. Princeton: Princeton University Press.
1981   "Foreign Investment and Empire: 1860–1914." In R. Floud and D. N. McCloskey, eds., *The Economic History of Britain Since 1700*. Vol. 2. Cambridge: Cambridge University Press.
1982   *Overseas Investment in the Age of High Imperialism: The United Kingdom, 1850–1914*. New York: Columbia University Press.

Ehrenberg, R.
1928   *Capital and Finance in the Age of the Renaissance: A Study of the Fuggers and Their Connections*. Reprint. New York: Augustus M. Kelley, 1963.

Einhorn, J. P.
1974   *Expropriation Politics*. Lexington, Mass.: Heath.
1978   "International Bank Lending: Expanding the Dialogue." *Columbia Journal of World Business* 13(3): 123–34.

Elsasser, E.
1954   "The Export-Import Bank and Latin America, 1934–45." Ph.D. dissertation, University of Chicago.

Enders, T., and R. Mattione

1984   *Latin America: The Crisis of Debt and Growth*. Washington, D.C.: Brookings Institution.

Federal Reserve Board

1943   *Banking and Monetary Statistics, 1914–41*. Washington, D.C.: FRB.

1976   *Banking and Monetary Statistics, 1941–70*. Washington, D.C.: FRB.

1977   *Industrial Production*. Rev. ed. Washington, D.C.: FRB.

Feinberg, R.

1980   "U.S. Human Rights Policy: Latin America." *International Policy Report* 6(1):1–13.

Feinstein, C. H.

1972   *National Income Expenditure and Output of the United Kingdom, 1855–1970*. Cambridge: Cambridge University Press.

Feis, H.

1930   *Europe: The World's Banker, 1870–1914*. Reprint. New York: Augustus M. Kelley, 1961.

1950   *The Diplomacy of the Dollar: 1919–1932*. New York: Norton.

Felix, D.

1987   "Alternative Outcomes of the Latin American Debt Crisis: Lessons from the Past." *Latin American Research Review* 22(2).

Ferrer, A.

1985   "From Debt Crisis to Financial Viability." *Journal of Development Planning* 16:121–32.

Fishlow, A.

1984   "The Debt Crisis: Round Two Ahead?" In R. Feinberg and V. Kallab, eds., *Adjustment Crisis in the Third World*. New Brunswick: Transaction Books.

1985   "Lessons from the Past: Capital Markets During the 19th Century and the Interwar Period." *International Organization* 39(3):383–439.

FitzGerald, E.V.K.

1977   *Pattern of Saving and Investment in Mexico, 1939–76*. Center for Latin American Studies, Working Paper 30. Cambridge: University of Cambridge.

1978   "The Fiscal Crisis of the Latin American State." In J. Toye, ed., *Taxation and Economic Development*. London: Frank Cass.

1979   *The Political Economy of Peru: 1956–78*. Cambridge: Cambridge University Press.

Fleisig, H.

1972   "The United States and the World Periphery During the Early Years of the Great Depression." In H. Van der Wee, ed., *The Great Depression Revisited*. The Hague: Nijhoff.

Fleming, A.

1981   *Private Capital Flows to Developing Countries and Their Determination*. Staff Working Paper 484. Washington, D.C.: World Bank.

Fleming, A., and S. Howson

1980   "Conditions in the Syndicated Medium-Term Euro-Credit Market." *Bank of England Quarterly Bulletin* 20(3):311–18.

Ford, A. G.
1965   "Overseas Lending and Internal Fluctuations, 1870–1914." *Yorkshire Bulletin of Economic and Social Research* 17(1):19–31.
1971   "British Investment in Argentina and Long Swings, 1880–1914." *Journal of Economic History* 31(3):650–63.

Foxley, A.
1983   *Latin American Experiments in Neo-Conservative Economics.* Berkeley: University of California Press.

Frieden, J.
1985   "Studies in International Finance: Private Interests and Public Policy in the International Political Economy." Ph.D. dissertation, Columbia University.

Friedman, I.
1977   *The Emerging Role of Private Banks in the Developing World.* New York: Citicorp.

Furtado, C.
1976   *Economic Development in Latin America.* 2nd ed. Cambridge: Cambridge University Press.

García, A.
1985   "President García Delivers Inaugural Address." *Foreign Broadcast Information Service* (July 29):J3–J24.

Gisselquist, D.
1981   *The Political Economics of International Bank Lending.* New York: Praeger.

Goff, F.
1976   "Chase's Rocky Road." *NACLA's Latin America and Empire Report* 10(4):1–40.

Goldsmith, R.
1958   *Financial Intermediaries in the American Economy Since 1900.* Princeton: Princeton University Press.
1968   *Financial Institutions.* New York: Random House.

González-Casanova, P., ed.
1977   *América Latina en los años treinta.* Mexico: UNAM.

Goodhart, C.A.E.
1969   *The New York Money Market and the Finance of Trade, 1900–1913.* Cambridge: Harvard University Press.
1984   *Monetary Theory and Practice: The U.K. Experience.* London: Macmillan.

Griffin, K.
1970   "The Role of Foreign Capital." In K. Griffin, ed., *Financing Development in Latin America.* London: Macmillan.

Gwynne, S. C.
1983   "Adventures in the Loan Trade." *Harpers* (September):22–26.

Hagerman, G.
1977   "Citicorp in Brazil–Decades of Growth." In *Diversification in International Banking.* New York: Citicorp.

Hall, A. R.
1957 "A Note on the English Capital Market as a Source of Funds for Home Investment Before 1914." *Economica* 24(93):59–66.
1958 "The English Capital Market Before 1914–A Reply." *Economica* 25(100):339–43.
1963 *The London Capital Market and Australia, 1870–1914.* Canberra: Australian National University.

Hanley, T.
1976 *United States Multinational Banking: Current and Prospective Strategies.* New York: Salomon Brothers.

Hawley, J.
1977 "U.S. Restriction of the Export of Capital, 1961–71: State Policy and Long-Term Economic Perspectives." Ph.D. dissertation, McGill University.
1984 "Protecting Capital from Itself: U.S. Attempts to Regulate the Eurocurrency System." *International Organization* 38(1):131–65.

Heimann, J.
1977 "We Don't Blacklist Countries: We Just Evaluate Risk." *Euromoney* (December):88–91.

Heraud-Solari, C., ed.
1974 *Ley de bancos.* Lima: Mosca Azul.

Hidy, R. W.
1949 *The House of Baring in American Trade and Finance.* Cambridge: Harvard University Press.

Hirschman, A. O.
1968   "The Political Economy of Import-Substituting Industrialization in Latin America." In C. Nisbet, ed., *Latin America: Problems in Economic Development*. New York: Free Press.

Hobsbawm, E. J.
1968   *Industry and Empire*. Harmondsworth: Penguin Books.

Hobson, J. A.
1894   *The Evolution of Modern Capitalism*. Reprint. London: Allen & Unwin, 1954.
1902   *Imperialism*. Reprint. London: Allen & Unwin, 1938.

Hunt, S.
1973   *Growth and Guano in Nineteenth-Century Peru*. Discussion Paper 34. Princeton: Princeton University, Woodrow Wilson School.
1975   "Direct Foreign Investment in Peru: New Rules for an Old Game." In A. Lowenthal, ed., *The Peruvian Experiment*. Princeton: Princeton University Press.

Interamerican Development Bank (IDB)
1980   *External Financing of Latin American Countries*. Washington, D.C.: IDB.
1981   Unpublished data series on Latin American economies, 1960–80.

International Finance Corporation
1981   "Implications of Alternative Financial Systems for Securities Market Development." Paper presented at conference on Latin American Experiences in Developing Capital Markets, Quito.

Jenks, L. H.
1927   *The Migration of British Capital to 1875.* New York: Knopf.
1928   *Our Cuban Colony: A Study in Sugar.* Reprint. New York: Arno Press, 1970.

Johnston, R. B.
1982   *The Economics of the Euro-Market.* New York: St. Martin's Press.

Jones, C.
1977   "Commercial Banks and Mortgage Companies." In D.C.M. Platt, ed., *British Imperialism, 1840–1930.* Oxford: Clarendon Press.

Jones, G.
1924   G. Jones to J. Klein. Set 612, Latin America General, 1/19/24. Record Group 151. National Archives, Washington, D.C.

Joslin, D.
1963   *A Century of Banking in Latin America.* London: Oxford University Press.

Kahler, M.
1985   "Politics and International Debt: Explaining the Crisis." *International Organization* 39(3):357–82.

Karl, T.
1982   "The Political Economy of Petrodollars: Oil and Democracy in Venezuela." Ph.D. dissertation, Stanford University.

1983   "The Paradox of the Rich Debtor: The Foreign Borrowing of Oil-Exporting Countries." Paper presented at APSA annual meeting, Chicago.

Kaufman, R.
1985   "Democratic and Authoritarian Responses to the Debt Issue: Argentina, Brazil, Mexico." *International Organization* 39(3):473–504.

Kemmerer, E.
1931   *Informe sobre el crédito público del Perú.* Lima: Banco Central de Reserva.

Kendrick, J.
1961   *Productivity Trends in the United States.* Princeton: Princeton University Press.
1973   *Postwar Productivity Trends in the United States, 1948–69.* New York: National Bureau of Economic Research.

Kenen, P.
1983   "A Bailout Plan for the Banks." *New York Times* (March 6):Section 3, p. 3.

Keynes, J. M.
1937   "Alternative Theories of the Rate of Interest." *Economic Journal* 47:241–52.

Kindleberger, C. P.
1964   *Economic Growth in France and Britain, 1851–1950.* Cambridge: Harvard University Press.
1973   *The World in Depression, 1929–1939.* Berkeley: University of California Press.

1978   *Manias, Panics, and Crashes.* New York: Basic Books.
1984   *A Financial History of Western Europe.* London: Allen & Unwin.
1985   *Keynesianism vs. Monetarism and Other Essays in Financial History.* London: Allen & Unwin.

Kindleberger, C. P., and J.-P. Laffargue, eds.
1982   *Financial Crisis: Theory, History, and Policy.* Cambridge: Cambridge University Press.

Klare, M., and C. Arnson
1979   "Exporting Repression: U.S. Support for Authoritarianism in Latin America." In R. Fagen, ed., *Capitalism and the State in U.S.–Latin American Relations.* Stanford: Stanford University Press.

Kolko, G.
1963   *The Triumph of Conservatism: A Reinterpretation of American History, 1900–1916.* New York: Macmillan.

Kotz, D. M.
1978   *Bank Control of Large Corporations in the United States.* Berkeley: University of California Press.

Kraft, J.
1984   *The Mexican Rescue.* New York: Group of Thirty.

Kuczynski, M.
1976   "Semi-Developed Countries and the International Business Cycle." *BOLSA Review* (January):2–14.

Kuczynski, P.-P.

1977 *Peruvian Democracy Under Economic Stress.* Princeton: Princeton University Press.

1981 "The Peruvian External Debt: Problem and Prospect." *Journal of Interamerican Studies and World Affairs* 23(1): 3–28.

1982 "Latin American Debt." *Foreign Affairs* 61(2):344–64.

Kuznets, S.

1952 *Long-Term Changes in National Income of the United States Since 1869.* Income and Wealth, Series II. Cambridge: Bowes & Bowes.

1953 *Shares of Upper Income Groups in Income and Saving.* New York: National Bureau of Economic Research.

1961 *Capital in the American Economy: Its Formation and Financing.* Princeton: Princeton University Press.

LaFeber, W.

1963 *The New Empire: An Interpretation of American Expansion, 1860–1898.* Ithaca: Cornell University Press.

Landes, D. S.

1969 *The Unbound Prometheus.* Cambridge: Cambridge University Press.

Lary, H. B.

1943 *The United States in the World Economy.* U.S. Department of Commerce, Bureau of Foreign and Domestic Commerce, Economic Series no. 23. Washington, D.C.: GPO.

Lavington, F.

1921 *The English Capital Market.* London: Methuen.

Leff, N.
1968   *The Capital Goods Sector in Brazilian Economic Growth.*
       Cambridge: Harvard University Press.

Lenin, V. I.
1917   *Imperialism: The Highest Stage of Capitalism.* Reprint.
       New York: International Publishers, 1939.

Lessard, D., and J. Williamson, eds.
1987   *Capital Flight and Third World Debt.* Washington, D.C.:
       Institute for International Economics.

Letelier, I., and M. Moffitt
1978   *Human Rights, Economic Aid and Private Banks: The Case
       of Chile.* Washington, D.C.: Transnational Institute.

Lever, H., and C. Huhne
1986   *Debt and Danger: The World Financial Crisis.* Boston:
       Atlantic Monthly Press.

Levinson, J., and J. de Onis
1970   *The Alliance That Lost Its Way.* Chicago: Quadrangle
       Books.

Lewis, C.
1938   *America's Stake in International Investments.* Washington,
       D.C.: Brookings Institution.

Lewis, W. A.
1978   *Growth and Fluctuations, 1870–1914.* London: Allen &
       Unwin.
1980   "The Slowing Down of the Engine of Growth." *American Economic Review* 70(4):556–64.

List, F.

1856 *The National System of Political Economy.* Reprint. New York: Augustus M. Kelley, 1966.

Lowenthal, A.

1974 "'Liberal,' 'Radical,' and 'Bureaucratic' Perspectives on U.S. Foreign Policy: The Alliance for Progress in Retrospect." In J. Cotler and R. Fagen, eds., *Latin America and the United States.* Stanford: Stanford University Press.

McClam, W.

1982 "Financial Fragility and Instability: Monetary Authorities as Borrowers and Lenders of Last Resort." In C. Kindleberger and J.-P. Laffargue, eds., *Financial Crises: Theory, History and Policy.* Cambridge: Cambridge University Press.

McCloskey, D. N.

1970 "Did Victorian Britain Fail?" *Economic History Review* 23(3):446–59.

———, ed.

1971 *Essays on a Mature Economy: Britain After 1840.* Princeton: Princeton University Press.

MacKaman, F. H.

1977 "United States Loan Policy, 1920–1930: Diplomatic Assumptions, Governmental Policies, and Conditions in Peru and Mexico." Ph.D. dissertation, University of Missouri.

McKinnon, R. I.

1984 "Pacific Growth and Financial Interdependence: An Overview of Bank Regulation and Monetary Control."

Pacific Economic Papers 117. Canberra: Australian National University, Australia-Japan Research Center.

McQueen, C. A.
1926   *Peruvian Public Finance.* U.S. Department of Commerce, Trade Promotion Series no. 30. Washington, D.C.: GPO.

Madden, J., et al.
1937   *America's Experience as a Creditor Nation.* New York: Prentice-Hall.

Magdoff, H.
1977   "How to Make a Molehill Out of a Mountain: Reply to Szymanski." *Insurgent Sociologist* 7(2):106–12.

Maizels, A.
1965   *Industrial Growth and World Trade.* Cambridge: Cambridge University Press.

Makin, J.
1984   *The Global Debt Crisis.* New York: Basic Books.

Malan, P.
1985   "Debt, Trade and Development: The Crucial Years Ahead." *Journal of Development Planning* 16:133–42.

Malthus, T. R.
1820   *Principles of Political Economy.* Reprint. New York: Augustus M. Kelley, 1951.

Mamalakis, M. J.
1976   *The Growth and Structure of the Chilean Economy: From Independence to Allende.* New Haven: Yale University Press.

Marsh, M.
1928   *Bankers in Bolivia.* New York: Vanguard Press.

Martel, J.
1978   "Domination by Debt: Finance Capital in Argentina." *NACLA Report on the Americas* 12(4):20–32.

Marx, K.
1894   *Capital.* Vol. 3. Reprint. New York: International Publishers, 1967.

Massad, C.
1983   "The External Debt and the Financial Problems of Latin America." *CEPAL Review* 20:142–63.

Mathew, W. M.
1977   "Anthony Gibbs and Sons, the Guano Trade and the Peruvian Government, 1842–1861." In D.C.M. Platt, ed., *Business Imperialism 1840–1930.* Oxford: Clarendon Press.

Mathis, F. J., ed.
1975   *Offshore Lending by U.S. Commercial Banks.* New York: Bankers Association for Foreign Trade.

Maxfield, S., and L. Armijo
1986   "The Political Economy of Development Finance: Mexico and Brazil Compared." Paper presented at Latin American Studies Association Congress, Boston.

Mayer, R. S.
1968 "The Influence of Frank A. Vanderlip and the National City Bank on American Commerce and Foreign Policy, 1910–1920." Ph.D. dissertation, Rutgers University.

Meier, G. M.
1953 "Economic Development and the Transfer Mechanism: Canada, 1895–1913." *Canadian Journal of Economics and Political Science* 19(1):1–19.

Mendelsohn, M. S.
1980 *Money on the Move: The Modern International Capital Market*. New York: McGraw-Hill.

Mentre, P.
1984 *The Fund, Commercial Banks, and Member Countries*. Occasional Paper 26. Washington, D.C.: International Monetary Fund.

Merrill Lynch White Weld
1979 "Canadian and Foreign Investments of Major Life Insurance Companies." New York: Merrill Lynch White Weld. Mimeo.

Mikesell, R.
1962a "Classification and Functional Analysis of Public Foreign Investment." In R. Mikesell, ed., *U.S. Private and Government Investment Abroad*. Eugene: University of Oregon Books.
1962b "The Export-Import Bank of Washington." In R. Mikesell, ed., *U.S. Private and Government Investment Abroad*. Eugene: University of Oregon Books.

1962c   "U.S. Postwar Investment Abroad: A Statistical Analysis." In R. Mikesell, ed., *U.S. Private and Government Investment Abroad*. Eugene: University of Oregon Books.

Minsky, H.

1964   "Longer Waves in Financial Relations: Financial Factors in the More Severe Depressions." *American Economic Review* 54(3):324–35.

1982   "The Financial Instability Hypothesis: Capitalist Processes and the Behavior of the Economy." In C. Kindleberger and J.-P. Laffargue, eds., *Financial Crises: Theory, History, and Policy*. Cambridge: Cambridge University Press.

1986   *Stabilizing an Unstable Economy*. New Haven: Yale University Press.

Mintz, I.

1951   *Deterioration in the Quality of Foreign Bonds Issued in the United States, 1920–30*. New York: National Bureau of Economic Research.

Mitchell, B., and P. Deane

1962   *Abstract of British Historical Statistics*. Cambridge: Cambridge University Press.

Mitra, J. D.

1979   *The Capital Goods Sector in LDCs: A Case for State Intervention?* Staff Working Paper 343. Washington, D.C.: World Bank.

Moffitt, M.
1983   *The World's Money: International Banking from Bretton Woods to the Brink of Insolvency.* New York: Simon & Schuster.

Moggridge, D.
1982   "Policy in the Crises of 1920 and 1929." In C. Kindleberger and J.-P. Laffargue, eds., *Financial Crises: Theory, History, and Policy.* Cambridge: Cambridge University Press.

Moore, G. H.
1980   *Business Cycles, Inflation and Forecasting.* Cambridge: Ballinger.

Morgan, E. V., and W. A. Thomas
1962   *The Stock Exchange.* London: Elek Books.

Morrow, D.
1927   "Who Buys Foreign Bonds?" *Foreign Affairs* 5(2): 219–32.

Munro, D.
1964   *Intervention and Dollar Diplomacy in the Caribbean, 1900–1921.* Princeton: Princeton University Press.

Nacional Financiera
1977a   *Statistics on the Mexican Economy.* Mexico: NAFINSA.
1977b   *Una estrategia para desarrollar la industria de bienes de capital.* Mexico: NAFINSA.

Nearing, S., and J. Freeman
1925   *Dollar Diplomacy.* New York: B. W. Huebsch.

Nelson, J.
1984   "The Politics of Stabilization." In R. Feinberg and V. Kalab, eds., *Adjustment Crisis in the Third World.* New Brunswick: Transaction Books.

Ness, W.
1974   "Financial Markets as a Development Strategy: Initial Results from the Brazilian Experience." *Economic Development and Cultural Change* 22(3):453–72.

North, D. C.
1962   "International Capital Movements in Historical Perspective." In R. Mikesell, ed., *U.S. Private and Government Investment Abroad.* Eugene: University of Oregon Books.

Odjagov, M.
1977   "Transnational Banking." New York: U.N. Centre on Transnational Corporations. Mimeo.

Organization for Economic Cooperation and Development (OECD)
1985   *External Debt of Developing Countries in 1984.* Paris: OECD.

Organization of American States (OAS)
1973   *The Capital Markets of the United States in Relation to the Financing of Latin American Industry.* Washington, D.C.: OAS.

1976 "Evaluación de los resultados de la política de fomento de los mercados de capitales en América Latina." In *Memoria de la XIIa Reunión de Técnicos de Bancos Centrales del Continente Americano*. Vol. 4. Montevideo: Banco Central del Uruguay.

Ortiz de Zevallos, F.
1980 "Peru: Prepared for the '80s." *Institutional Investor, International Edition*, Special Section (July):1–24.

Pan American Union (PAU)
1931 *Foreign Trade of Latin America 1910–1929*. Washington, D.C.: GPO.
1952 *The Foreign Trade of Latin America Since 1913*. Washington, D.C.: PAU

Parrini, C. P.
1969 *Heir to Empire: United States Economic Diplomacy, 1916–1923*. Pittsburgh: University of Pittsburgh Press.

Peru
1935 *Extracto estadístico del Perú*. Ministerio de Hacienda y Comercio, Dirección Nacional de Estadística.
1947 *Debates*. Senado. 2a Legislatura Extraordinaria de 1946.
1971 *Plan nacional de desarrollo para 1971–75*. Presidencia de la República.
1981a *Cuentas nacionales del Perú, 1950–1980*. Presidencia de la República. Instituto Nacional de Estadística.
1981b "Política de endeudamiento externo." Banco Central de Reserva. *Reseña económica* (Julio).
1981c *Desarrollo de la deuda externa peruana 1968–79*. Banco Central de Reserva.

Petras, J., and M. Morley
1975   *The United States and Chile: Imperialism and the Over-throw of the Allende Government.* New York: Monthly Review Press.

Phelps, C. W.
1927   *Foreign Expansion of American Banks.* New York: Ronald Press.

Philip, G.D.E.
1978   *The Rise and Fall of the Peruvian Military Radicals, 1968–1976.* London: Athlone Press.

Pike, F. B.
1967   *The Modern History of Peru.* London: Weidenfeld & Nicolson.

Platt, D.C.M.
1968   *Finance, Trade and Politics in British Foreign Policy, 1815–1914.* London: Oxford University Press.
1980   "British Portfolio Investment Before 1870: Some Doubts." *Economic History Review* 33(1):1–16.
1985   *Foreign Finance in Continental Europe and the United States, 1815–1870.* London: Allen & Unwin.

Portocarrero Maisch, G.
1981   "Del monetarismo al keynesianismo: la política económica durante la crisis del 30." *Economía* (Lima) 7: 65–98.

Prest, A. R.
1948   "National Income in the United Kingdom, 1870–1946." *Economic Journal* 58:31–62.

Price, H. B.
1955 *The Marshall Plan and Its Meaning.* Ithaca: Cornell University Press.

Quijano, A.
1973 *Imperialismo, clases sociales y estado en el Perú, 1890–1930.* Lima: Mosca Azul.

Quiroz, A.
1986 "Financial Institutions in Peruvian Export and Society, 1884–1930." Ph.D. dissertation, Columbia University.

Reich, C.
1977 "Why the IMF Shuns a 'Super' Role." *Institutional Investor, International Edition* (September):35–41.

Reynolds, C. W.
1970 *The Mexican Economy: Twentieth Century Structure and Growth.* New Haven: Yale University Press.

Reynolds, G.
1914 "The Effect of the European War on American Credits." *Journal of Political Economy* 22(10):925–36.

Ricardo, D.
1817 *The Principles of Political Economy and Taxation.* Reprint. London: J. M. Dent and Sons, 1973.

Riley, J.
1980 *International Government Finance and the Amsterdam Capital Market, 1740–1815.* Cambridge: Cambridge University Press.

Riner, D.
1983   "Market Imperfections and International Debt: Why Banks Overlend." Paper presented at APSA annual meeting, Chicago.

Rippy, J. F.
1959   *British Investments in Latin America, 1822–1949.* Hamden, Conn.: Archon Books.

Rohatyn, F.
1982   "The State of the Banks." *New York Review of Books* (November 4):3–6.

Royal Institute of International Affairs (RIIA)
1937   *The Problem of International Investment.* London: Oxford University Press.

Sachs, J.
1982   "LDC Debt in the 1980s: Risk and Reforms." In P. Wachtel, ed., *Crises in the Economic and Financial Structure.* Lexington, Mass.: Lexington Books.
1984   *Theoretical Issues in International Borrowing.* Princeton Studies in International Finance, no. 34. Princeton: International Finance Section, Department of Economics, Princeton University.

Sampson, A.
1982   *The Money Lenders.* New York: Viking Press.

Saville, J.
1961   "Some Retarding Factors in the British Economy Before 1914." *Yorkshire Bulletin of Economic and Social Research* 13(1):51–60.

Schumpeter, J.
1939   *Business Cycles.* New York: McGraw-Hill.

Schydlowsky, D. M., and J. Wicht
1979   *Anatomía de un fracaso económico: Perú 1968–1978.*
Lima: Universidad del Pacífico.

Silva Ruete, J.
1981   *Yo asumo el activo y el pasivo de la revolución.* Lima: Centro
de Documentación e Información Andina.

Simon, M.
1967   "The Pattern of New British Portfolio Investment,
1865–1914." In J. H. Adler, ed., *Capital Movements
and Economic Development.* London: Macmillan.

Singh, A.
1977   "U.K. Industry and the World Economy: A Case of De-
Industrialization?" *Cambridge Journal of Economics* 1(2):
113–36.

Skidmore, T.
1967   *Politics in Brazil.* London: Oxford University Press.

Smart, W.
1911   *Economic Annals of the Nineteenth Century.* Vols. 1–2.
Reprint. New York: Augustus M. Kelley, 1964.

Smiley, G.
1983   "Did Incomes for Most of the Population Fall from
1923 to 1929?" *Journal of Economic History* 43(1):
209–16.

Smith, A.
1776 *The Wealth of Nations.* Reprint. New York: Random House, 1937.

Smith, R. F.
1960 *The United States and Cuba: Business and Diplomacy, 1917–1960.* New Haven: College and University Press.
1972 *The United States and the Revolutionary Nationalism in Mexico, 1916–1932.* Chicago: University of Chicago Press.

Solis, L.
1979 *La realidad económica mexicana: retrovisión y perspectivas.* 2nd ed. Mexico City: Siglo XXI.

Spero, J. E.
1979 *The Failure of Franklin National Bank.* New York: Columbia University Press.

Spray, D., ed.
1964 *The Principal Stock Exchanges of the World.* Washington, D.C.: International Economics Publishers.

Stallings, B.
1978 *Class Conflict and Economic Development in Chile, 1958–73.* Stanford: Stanford University Press.
1979 "Peru and the U.S. Banks: The Privatization of Financial Relations." In R. Fagen, ed., *Capitalism and the State in U.S.–Latin American Relations.* Stanford: Stanford University Press.
1982 "Euromarkets, Third World Countries, and the International Political Economy." In H. Makler and N. Smelser, eds., *The New International Economy.* London: Sage Publications.

1983a "International Capitalism and the Peruvian Military Government, 1968–78." In C. McClintock and A. Lowenthal, eds., *The Peruvian Experiment Reconsidered.* Princeton: Princeton University Press.

1983b "Latin American Debt: What Kind of Crisis?" *SAIS Review* 3(2):27–40.

Stepan, A.

1978 *The State and Society: Peru in Comparative Perspective.* Princeton: Princeton University Press.

Stone, I.

1968 "British Long-Term Investment in Latin America, 1865–1913." *Business History Review* 42(3):311–39.

1977 "British Direct and Portfolio Investment in Latin America Before 1914." *Journal of Economic History* 37(3):690–722.

Stone, J. M.

1971 "Financial Panics: Their Implications for the Mix of Domestic and Foreign Investments of Great Britain: 1880–1913." *Quarterly Journal of Economics* 85(2): 304–26.

Szymanski, A.

1977 "Capital Accumulation on a World Scale and the Necessity of Imperialism." *Insurgent Sociologist* 7(2):35–53.

Taylor, L.

1985 "The Theory and Practice of Developing Country Debt: An Informal Guide for the Perplexed." *Journal of Development Planning* 16:195–228.

Thomas, B.
1958   "Migration and International Investment." In B. Thomas, ed., *The Economics of International Migration.* London: Macmillan.
1973   *Migration and Economic Growth.* 2nd ed. Cambridge: Cambridge University Press.

Thorp, R., ed.
1984   *Latin America in the 1930s.* London: Macmillan.

Thorp, R., and G. Bertram
1976   "Industrialization in an Open Economy: The Case of Peru, 1890–1970." In R. Miller et al., eds., *Social and Economic Change in Modern Peru.* Liverpool: University of Liverpool, Latin American Studies Centre.
1978   *Peru 1890–1977: Growth and Policy in an Open Economy.* London: Macmillan.

Tugwell, F.
1975   *The Politics of Oil in Venezuela.* Stanford: Stanford University Press.

Tulchin, J.
1971   *The Aftermath of War: World War I and U.S. Policy Toward Latin America.* New York: New York University Press.

Turlington, E.
1930   *Mexico and Her Foreign Creditors.* New York: Columbia University Press.

UCLA Center for Medieval and Renaissance Studies (UCLA)
1979   *The Dawn of Modern Banking.* New Haven: Yale University Press.

Ugarteche, O.
1980   *Teoría y práctica de la deuda externa en el Perú.* Lima: Instituto de Estudios Peruanos.
1986   *El estado deudor, economía política de la deuda: Perú y Bolivia 1968–84.* Lima: Instituto de Estudios Peruanos.

United Nations
1953   *A Study of Trade Between Latin America and Europe.* Department of Economic Affairs.
1955   *Foreign Capital in Latin America.* Department of Economic and Social Affairs.
1965   *External Financing in Latin America.* Economic Commission for Latin America.
1970   "Mobilization of Domestic Resources." *Economic Bulletin for Latin America* 15(2):94–147.
1971   "Financial Intermediation in Latin America." *Economic Bulletin for Latin America* 16(2):1–56.
1978   *Series históricas del crecimiento de América Latina.* Economic Commission for Latin America.
1985a   *Preliminary Overview of the Latin American Economy 1985.* Economic Commission for Latin America.
1985b   *External Debt in Latin America: Adjustment Policies and Renegotiation.* Economic Commission for Latin America.

United States
1921   *Report of the Secretary of the Treasury to the President on the Second Pan American Financial Conference at Washington, January 19–24, 1920.*
1927   *Foreign Loans.* Hearings before Committee on Foreign Relations, U.S. House of Representatives. 69th Cong., 2nd sess.

1930a   *Handbook on American Underwriting of Foreign Securities.*
        Department of Commerce, Trade Promotion Series,
        no. 104.

1930b   *Handbook of Foreign Currency and Exchange.* Department
        of Commerce, Trade Promotion Series, no. 102.

1932   *Sale of Foreign Bonds or Securities in the United States.* Parts
        1–4. Hearings before Committee on Finance, U.S.
        Senate. 72nd Cong., 1st sess.

1933   *Stock Exchange Practices.* Part 6. Hearings before Com-
        mittee on Banking and Currency, U.S. Senate. 72nd
        Cong., 2nd sess.

1934   *Stock Exchange Practices.* Report of the Committee on
        Banking and Currency, U.S. Senate. Senate Report no.
        1455. 73rd Cong., 1st sess.

1940   *Hearings on S4204, a Bill to Provide for Increasing the
        Lending Authority of the Export-Import Bank of Wash-
        ington and for Other Purposes.* Committee on Banking
        and Currency, U.S. Senate. 76th Cong., 3rd sess.

1942   *The Foreign Trade of Latin America.* Tariff Commission.
        Report no. 146, 2nd series.

1947   *Census of American-Owned Assets in Foreign Countries.*
        Treasury Department.

1948   *International Transactions of the United States During the
        War, 1940–1945.* Department of Commerce. Eco-
        nomic Series no. 65.

1963a   *Balance of Payments, Statistical Supplement.* Rev. ed. De-
        partment of Commerce.

1963b   *Raw Materials in the U.S. Economy, 1900–61.* Depart-
        ment of Commerce, Bureau of the Census. Working
        Paper no. 6.

1976   *Historical Statistics of the United States, Colonial Times to
        1970.* Department of Commerce, Bureau of the
        Census.

1981   *Money Income of Families and Persons in the United States: 1979.* Bureau of the Census. Current Population Reports, P-60, no. 129.

1983a   *International Financial Markets and Related Problems.* Hearings before Committee on Banking, Finance and Urban Affairs, U.S. House of Representatives. 98th Cong., 1st sess.

1983b   *Global Economic Outlook.* Hearings before Subcommittee on International Economic Policy and Committee on Foreign Relations, U.S. Senate. 98th Cong., 1st sess.

Van der Wee, H.

1963   *The Growth of the Antwerp Market and the European Economy.* 3 vols. The Hague: Martinus Nijhoff.

Vanderlip, F.

1935   *From Farm Boy to Financier.* New York: D. Appleton Century.

Vanek, J.

1967   *Estimating Foreign Resource Needs for Economic Development.* New York: McGraw-Hill.

Villanueva, V.

1973   *Ejército peruano: del caudillaje anárquico al militarismo reformista.* Lima: Juan Mejía Baca.

Villela, A., and W. Suzigan

1977   *Government Policy and the Economic Growth of Brazil, 1889–1945.* Brazilian Economic Studies, no. 3. Rio de Janeiro: IPEA.

Wai, U. T.
1976   "Criteria for Judging the Results of Policies to Promote Capital Markets." In *Memoria de la XIIa Reunión de Técnicos de Bancos Centrales del Continente Americano.* Vol. 4. Montevideo: Banco Central del Uruguay.

Wai, U. T., and H. Patrick
1973   "Stock and Bond Issues and Capital Markets in Less-Developed Countries." *IMF Staff Papers* 20(2): 253–317.

Weaver, F.
1980   *Class, State, and Industrial Structure: The Historical Process of South American Growth.* Westport, Conn.: Greenwood Press.

Weinert, R.
1978   "Why the Banks Did It." *Foreign Policy* 30:143–48.
1983   "International Finance: Banks and Bankruptcy." *Foreign Policy* 50:138–49.

Weisskopf, T.
1972   "The Impact of Foreign Capital Inflow on Domestic Savings in Underdeveloped Countries." *Journal of International Economics* 2(1):25–38.

Wellons, P.
1974   *Borrowing by Developing Countries on the Eurocurrency Market.* Paris: OECD.

West, R. C.
1977   *Banking Reform and the Federal Reserve, 1863–1923.* Ithaca: Cornell University Press.

Wilkins, M.

1970 *The Emergence of Multinational Enterprise: American Business Abroad from the Colonial Era to 1914.* Cambridge: Harvard University Press.

——, ed.

1977 *British Overseas Investments, 1907–1948.* New York: Arno Press.

Williams, B.

1929 *Economic Foreign Policy of the United States.* New York: McGraw-Hill.

Williams, W. A.

1959 *The Tragedy of American Diplomacy.* New York: Delta Books.

Williamson, J. G.

1964 *American Growth and the Balance of Payments, 1820–1913.* Chapel Hill: University of North Carolina Press.

1985 *Did British Capitalism Breed Inequality?* London: Allen & Unwin.

Williamson, J. G., and P. Lindert

1980 *American Inequality: A Macroeconomic History.* New York: Academic Press.

Wilson, C.

1941 *Anglo-Dutch Commerce and Finance in the Eighteenth Century.* Cambridge: Cambridge University Press.

Wilson, J. H.
1971   *American Business and Foreign Policy: 1920–1933.* Boston: Beacon Press.

Winch, D.
1969   *Economics and Policy: A Historical Study.* London: Hodder & Stoughton.

Winkler, M.
1933   *Foreign Bonds: An Autopsy.* Philadelphia: Ronald Swain Co.

Winningham, J.
1978   "Liability Management Banking." Ph.D. dissertation, University of Wisconsin, Madison.

World Bank
1972a   "Chronological List of Privately-Placed Foreign and International Bonds in Major Capital Markets, 1952–69." Washington, D.C.: Work Bank. Mimeo.
1972b   "Chronological List of Publicly-Issued Foreign and International Bonds in Major Capital Markets: 1946–69." Washington, D.C.: World Bank. Mimeo.

Wynne, W. H.
1951   *State Insolvency and Foreign Bondholders.* Vol. 2. New Haven: Yale University Press.

Periodical Publications

Andean Report (Lima)
Banco Central de Reserva del Perú, *Memoria Anual* (Lima)

Bank for International Settlements, *Annual Report* (Basle)

Bank of America, *Annual Report* (San Francisco)

Bankers' Almanac and Yearbook (London)

Business Week (New York)

Caretas (Lima)

Chase Manhattan Bank, *Annual Report* (New York)

Citicorp, *Annual Report* (New York)

Corporation of Foreign Bondholders, *Annual Report* (London)

Country Exposure Lending Survey (Washington, D.C.: Federal Financial Institutions Examination Council)

Economic Survey of Latin America (Santiago: U.N. Economic Commission for Latin America)

Federal Reserve Bulletin (Washington, D.C.: Federal Reserve Board)

Financial Times (London)

Foreign Bondholders' Protective Council (FBPC), *Annual Report* (New York)

Government Finance Statistics Yearbook (Washington, D.C.: International Monetary Fund)

IMF Survey (Washington, D.C.: International Monetary Fund)

Interamerican Development Bank (IDB), *Annual Report* (Washington, D.C.)

International Financial Statistics (Washington, D.C.: International Monetary Fund)

International Monetary Fund (IMF), *Annual Report* (Washington, D.C.)

Latin America (London)

Latin America Economic Report (London)

Maturity Distribution of International Bank Lending (Basle: Bank for International Settlements)

Memorandum on the Balance of Payments (Geneva: League of Nations)

Monthly Bulletin of Statistics (Geneva: League of Nations)

Moody's Industrial Manual (New York: Moody's Investors Service)

Moody's Municipal and Government Manual (New York: Moody's Investors Service)

New York Stock Exchange Listings (NYSE) (New York: New York Stock Exchange)

The New York Times (New York)

Peruvian Times (Lima)

La Prensa (Lima)

Statistical Abstract of the United States (Washington, D.C.: Bureau of the Census)

Statistical Yearbook for Latin America (Santiago: U.N. Economic Commission for Latin America)

Survey of Current Business (Washington, D.C.: Department of Commerce)

Trade Information Bulletin (Washington, D.C.: Department of Commerce)

Treasury Bulletin (Washington, D.C.: Treasury Department)

United Nations Statistical Yearbook (New York: United Nations)

U.S. Overseas Loans and Grants and Assistance from International Organizations (Washington, D.C.: Agency for International Development)

Wall Street Journal (New York)

Washington Post (Washington, D.C.)

West Coast Leader (Lima)

World Bank, *Annual Report* (Washington, D.C.)

World Debt Tables (Washington, D.C.: World Bank)

World Economic Outlook (Washington, D.C.: International Monetary Fund)

World Financial Markets (New York: Morgan Guaranty Trust)

Interviews

Approximately fifty interviews were conducted between January 1978 and April 1984 with bankers, government and ex-government officials, officials of international organizations, and economists in New York, Washington, London, Lima, Mexico City, Caracas, Santiago, and Buenos Aires. Since interviewees were promised that their names and institutions would not be revealed, the interviews are identified by a four-digit code. The first number identifies the person as (1) a banker, (2) a government or ex-government official, (3) an international agency official, or (4) a university-based economist. The second digit refers to the interviewee's country: (1) United States, (2) Peru, (3) Mexico, (4) Venezuela, (5) Chile, (6) Argentina, (7) Brazil, or (8) Great Britain. The final two digits identify the individual.

INDEX